Wendy Carlos

OXFORD CULTURAL BIOGRAPHIES

Gary Giddins, Series Editor

A Generous Vision: The Creative Life of Elaine de Kooning
Cathy Curtis

Wendy Carlos: A Biography
Amanda Sewell

Wendy Carlos

A Biography

AMANDA SEWELL

OXFORD
UNIVERSITY PRESS

Oxford University Press is a department of the University of Oxford. It furthers
the University's objective of excellence in research, scholarship, and education
by publishing worldwide. Oxford is a registered trade mark of Oxford University
Press in the UK and certain other countries.

Published in the United States of America by Oxford University Press
198 Madison Avenue, New York, NY 10016, United States of America.

© Oxford University Press 2020

All rights reserved. No part of this publication may be reproduced, stored in
a retrieval system, or transmitted, in any form or by any means, without the
prior permission in writing of Oxford University Press, or as expressly permitted
by law, by license, or under terms agreed with the appropriate reproduction
rights organization. Inquiries concerning reproduction outside the scope of the
above should be sent to the Rights Department, Oxford University Press, at the
address above.

You must not circulate this work in any other form
and you must impose this same condition on any acquirer.

CIP data is on file at the Library of Congress
ISBN 978–0–19–005346–8

1 3 5 7 9 8 6 4 2

Printed by Sheridan Books, Inc., United States of America

For my father

Contents

Series Editor's Foreword

Edison tamed electricity in the late 1870s. He made it record sound, photograph moving images, and lighten the night. In the ninety years that followed, several musicians and inventors attempted to use electricity not only to build machines that capture and preserve musical performance or amplify instruments already in existence, but to produce the thing itself: the notes and chords and dynamics of music, borne out of that invisible source of energy to create an entirely new palette of sounds and options. Yet the Wilbur-and-Orville of electronic music was a reclusive 29-year-old composer, recording engineer, and lifelong inventor who, working with a Moog modular synthesizer that she custom designed in partnership with its creator Robert Moog, electrified none other than Johann Sebastian Bach.

Today, it may be difficult to imagine the fireworks set-off in the fall of 1968, when Columbia Records released *Switched-On Bach*. The bestselling classical record of all time, it topped the classical charts for an astonishing three years, ultimately earning Platinum certification, even reaching No. 10 on the pop charts. No mere novelty or dormitory diversion, it was welcomed by no less a Bach-expert than Glenn Gould, who praised its "unflagging musicality." Electronic music had arrived, serious excursions as well as shoddy imitations. It was everywhere, in jazz as well as rock, in synthesized transformations of old swing bands as well as the classics.

Still, the guiding force behind *Switched-On Bach* was nowhere unidentified on the front of the famous album jacket, which credited the work to Trans-Electronic Music Productions, Inc. You had to read the small print on the back to read of her "dazzling display of virtuosity," "artistry," and "genius." Moreover, she was identified as a man, Walter Carlos. For at the very moment she was igniting a musical revolution, she was also in the vanguard of a movement she considered relatively insignificant, gender reassignment. As Amanda Sewell makes rivetingly clear in this brave, important biography, the bias against transgender people was so thick that for over a decade, Carlos hid her identity, fearful of physical as well as critical attacks, on occasion even pasting on false sideburns to impersonate Walter in photo ops. The tragedy and irony of Wendy Carlos's career is that while she wished to speak of music (and solar eclipses, for which she traveled the world as an expert photographer), most of the media was more interested in a personal area that she considered invasive and beside the point.

The biographer can have no more difficult a challenge than to choose a living subject. Some subjects are happy to help, but their memories are no longer trustworthy; some offer help as a lever to try and assert control; others do everything they can to obstruct the biographer; and others maintain a zone of silence. Wendy Carlos appears to belong to the last category, and one can only hope that she will appreciate the industry, fairness, and eloquence of Amanda Sewell in tracking down every conceivable document to create this dramatic and convincing portrait of an artist whose story deserves to be told. If Carlos's music is unknown to later generations, as it appears to be, it is largely because she removed all of it from the marketplace in 2009; it is almost impossible to find copies of *Beauty in the Beast*, her score to *A Clockwork Orange*, and even her Bach recordings. It will be a fine thing if this book encourages her to give her music and us a second chance.

Gary Giddins
Series Editor

Acknowledgments

I am so grateful to Katie Chapman, Seth Cluett, Jeannette Di Bernardo Jones, Kerry O'Brien, Christine Wisch, Reba Wissner, and others for sending me invaluable primary and secondary sources. Archives staff members at the New York Public Library, the Kinsey Institute Library (Indiana University), the Library of Congress, and the Carl A. Kroch Library (Cornell University) facilitated my access to remarkable collections of materials. Thanks also go to Brian Carey at the Woodmere Branch of the Traverse Area District Library and to the staff of the Bonisteel Library at Interlochen Center for the Arts for wrangling my frequent interlibrary loan requests.

Dana Baitz offered invaluable suggestions for framing the manuscript. Des Harmon provided crucial feedback on several aspects of the text. Trevor Pinch generously sent me copies of unpublished materials. I owe Allan Kozinn special acknowledgment for sharing a massive file of resources with me. The information contained in these documents was priceless in shaping the content of this book.

The people whose friendship and mentorship have sustained me throughout this process are innumerable. Dan Melamed provided spiritual and intellectual guidance throughout the process. Lauron Kehrer is my friend, my work wife, and my first go-to for all of my scholarly writing. Norm Hirschy, Oxford University Press editor extraordinaire, has been enthusiastic about this project since its inception. His support at every stage has kept me energized and hopeful, even during some very challenging times.

The research in this book was supported in part by the Judith Tick Fellowship, awarded by the Society for American Music. I also received support from the Paul Charosh Fellowship, awarded by the Society for American Music. My deepest gratitude to my colleagues at Interlochen Public Radio and Interlochen Center for the Arts for their enthusiasm and support.

My husband, Trenton Bruce, is my chef, my teammate, my provider of a constant stream of animal GIFs, and the person who reminds me to step away from the computer at regular intervals and take a break. My parents, Dennis and Leeandra, have supported my professional life unconditionally ever since I first uttered the word "musicology" to them as an undergraduate student. My father's terminal illness kept him from being able to understand anything about this book, but there is no doubt in my mind that had he been able, he would have launched a one-man marketing campaign to promote it. I dedicate this book to him.

Introduction

The Phenomenon of Wendy Carlos

The year 1968 was an unforgettable year for many reasons. The films *2001: A Space Odyssey, Bullitt, Planet of the Apes,* and *Funny Girl*premiered. Apollo 8 took William Anders, Frank Borman, and Jim Lovell to the far side of the moon. Martin Luther King Jr. was assassinated. The musical *Hair* opened on Broadway. Shirley Chisholm became the first African American woman elected to Congress. Mattel introduced Hot Wheels cars. The Beatles released *The White Album*. The television program *Mister Rogers' Neighborhood* made its national debut. Yale University announced it would begin to admit women students. Three different albums by the Jimi Hendrix Experience ruled the charts. Robert F. Kennedy was assassinated. President Lyndon B. Johnson signed the Civil Rights Act. NBC cut off the final minute of a football game between the Oakland Raiders and the New York Jets to go to a broadcast of the film *Heidi* (with a score by a then-unknown John Williams).

In such a remarkable year, full of unprecedented global events and pop culture phenomena, Columbia Records released an unassuming album called *Switched-On Bach*. It was released in conjunction with Terry Riley's *In C* and J. Marks and Shipen Lebzelter's *Rock and Other Four Letter Words* as part of Columbia's Bach to Rock campaign. *Switched-On Bach* featured familiar music of Johann Sebastian Bach rendered on the Moog modular synthesizer. The synthesizer, an analog electronic music instrument, had largely been relegated to academic music laboratories until this point, and it had yet to gain much attention or interest from the broader public.

The album *Switched-On Bach* was a smash hit in a way that nobody had anticipated. It settled in at the number-one spot on the *Billboard* classical charts for more than three years. It spent a good amount of time on the *Billboard* Top 200 Albums chart, holding its own alongside albums from the Beatles, the Rolling Stones, Sly and the Family Stone, and Aretha Franklin. Practically overnight, *Switched-On Bach* made household names out of

Robert Moog, the creator of the modular synthesizer, and Walter Carlos, the musician who used the synthesizer to render Bach's music so skillfully.

Everyone from Hugh Downs to Leonard Bernstein wanted to meet Walter Carlos and have him demonstrate what he could do with the Moog synthesizer. Apart from a few interviews given soon after *Switched-On Bach* was released, though, Walter Carlos was nowhere to be found. Every couple of years during the 1970s, a new album would be released under his name. The albums included the soundtrack to the Stanley Kubrick film *A Clockwork Orange*, an album called *Sonic Seasonings* whose style anticipated what would later be called ambient music, and several more albums of Moog synthesizer renditions of classical music in the mold of *Switched-On Bach*. A few letters to the editors of various publications were signed with Walter Carlos's name during this time. But the man himself didn't seem to exist.

In 1979, *Playboy* magazine published an interview with a woman named Wendy Carlos. She explained that at birth she had been assigned male and given the name Walter, but she had transitioned to female in the late 1960s, just as her first album *Switched-On Bach* was released.[1] She never expected the album to have the success it did, and she chose not to reveal her transition at the time because she was trying to protect both herself and her career. After more than a decade in hiding, though, she was ready to share her story and start releasing her music under her own name.

Although plenty of people made jokes at her expense once she revealed her transition, others were thrilled that one of their favorite musicians was not only alive but also still creating music. Within a couple of months, *Keyboard* magazine had published a massive interview with her (the longest it had ever published) and installed her on its advisory board. She was interviewed for the *New York Times*. She began working on new projects, including the soundtracks for Stanley Kubrick's *The Shining* and Disney's *TRON*, and she collaborated with the Kronos Quartet, the Berkeley Symphony Orchestra, and the London Philharmonic Orchestra. Carlos also began using computers and digital synthesis in the 1980s, creating original sounds and tuning systems.

By the 1990s, though, Carlos seemed to retreat from the public eye again. She gave far fewer interviews than she had in the past several years, and her "new albums" were primarily look-backs at material she had created in the 1960s and early 1970s; for example, *Switched-On Bach 2000*, released in 1992, included the exact same music that had appeared on the original 1968 *Switched-On Bach*, only rendered with state-of-the-art digital synthesizer technology. She remastered and re-released her entire catalogue on a new label, but when the label dissolved and all of the music reverted to her ownership, she didn't make it available online or in any digital distribution formats. In the twenty-first century, she's not heard from much unless a person posts her music on YouTube and is sent a Digital Millennium Copyright Act (DMCA) takedown notice from Serendip LLC, which Carlos owns with her partner, Annemarie Franklin.

Throughout her life, Wendy Carlos has articulated very specific ideas about how people should make and hear electronic music. In the 1960s and 1970s, for example, she expressed disappointment that other musicians used the Moog synthesizer as a kind of fancy keyboard instrument. In the 1970s, she asked Columbia to withdraw the quadraphonic version of *Switched-On Bach* because she was displeased with how it sounded. In the 1980s, she wanted musicians to push electronic music composition and production into new realms, exploring new timbres and tuning systems. By the 1990s, as she was remastering her catalogue, she was removing everything from the masters that she had always heard as an error or a glitch; she seemed genuinely puzzled when listeners told her they had always loved those parts and were disappointed that they had been removed. She has expressed criticism of compressed audio formats such as LPs and MP3s.

Carlos has said she operates according to what she calls her First Law: "For every parameter that you can control, you must control."[2] This desire for control is detectable not only in how she wanted to produce her music but also how she wanted others to listen to her music and produce their own music. For example, she has written several impassioned editorials over the years imploring musicians to use every tool at their disposal to push the boundaries of music. Carlos has also attempted to control how she has been portrayed by journalists, scholars, and others who have written or who want to write about her. As early as 1979, following her interview with *Playboy*, she wrote to journalist Arthur Bell, expressing dismay at the fact that he and the magazine's editorial staff had chosen to print almost everything she had said about her gender identity and transition and very little about anything else she had said. By the late 1990s, most of the interviews she gave to journalists were more than ten thousand words in length and made no mention of her gender.

Carlos's gender identity has shaped many aspects of her life, her career, how she relates to the public, and how the public has received her and her music. This is not to say that she wrote music in a specific way or used particular

kinds of instruments because of her gender; rather, cultural factors surrounding the treatment of transgender people affected many of the decisions
that Carlos has made over the decades. For example, she has said that she
retreated into the solitary world of the electronic music studio because there
she was relatively safe; she was afraid of physical and verbal harassment and
of losing the love and respect of the people in her life, so she pulled away and
channeled her loneliness and isolation into her work. Additionally, cultural
reception and perception of transgender people has colored how journalists,
scholars, and fans have written about Carlos and her music. In many, many
articles and reviews, authors write about Carlos's gender at equal or even at
greater length than they write about her music. Carlos has written that she
felt the media has treated her like a talking dog.

This book is the first full-length biography to be written about Wendy
Carlos. Her story is not only one of a person who blazed new trails in electronic music for decades but is also the story of a person who intersected
in many ways with American popular culture, medicine, and social trends
during the second half of the twentieth century and well into the 21st. She has
worked with an eclectic cast of remarkable artists, including Milton Babbitt,
Stanley Kubrick, Kent Nagano, "Weird Al" Yankovic, and Gloria Cheng. She
brought the sound of the Moog synthesizer to a generation of listeners and
musicians, helping to effect arguably one of the most substantial changes in
popular music's sound since musicians began using amplifiers. The fact that
she is transgender is one dimension of her story. There is much more to tell
about her life and about the ways in which her life reflects many dimensions
of American culture.

Wendy Carlos did not respond to repeated requests for interviews for this
book. She has given very few interviews since the late 1990s and has not
updated her website since 2009. Dozens of people who have worked with
Carlos over the past sixty years also declined or did not respond to requests to
be interviewed. Not one person in any of Carlos's past or present personal or
professional circles agreed to speak on the record about her for this project.

Although Carlos did not agree to participate in this biography, every ef-
fort has been made to use her words to construct the narrative of her life.
This biography relies heavily on published interviews Carlos has given since
the late 1960s. Archival collections at the New York Public Library, Indiana
University, Cornell University, and the Library of Congress held letters,
unpublished interviews, and other documents in Carlos's own hand and

voice. Allan Kozinn, Trevor Pinch, and Frank Trocco generously shared their unpublished interview notes and transcripts. Archival collections of the late Arthur Bell, Lucy Kroll, and Harry Benjamin contained additional documents that shed light on Carlos's life and art. Her website and album liner notes are also rich sources of information about her artistic process, her studio, her equipment, and her music's sound.

Carlos's music is not currently available through any online streaming sources such as Spotify or YouTube, nor is any of it available to download from commercial sources such as iTunes or Amazon Prime Music. She reissued her entire recorded catalogue on CD in the late 1990s and early 2000s on the label East Side Digital. Her catalogue reverted to her ownership in 2008, when East Side Digital stopped distributing CDs. Those who want to listen to her music are encouraged to check used music shops, online resellers such as eBay, and their local public and university libraries.

Notes

1. Readers who are interested in learning more about terminology and concepts related to transgender identity and experience are encouraged to consult the glossary at the end of this book.
2. One of the earliest appearances in print of this statement can be found in her June 1984 interview with John Diliberto of *Polyphony*, p. 12. In this interview with Diliberto, she refers to it as her "old rule," suggesting that she had been abiding by it well before 1984. For other instances, see, for example, Wendy Carlos, liner notes to *Switched-On Bach 2000* (Telarc: 1992), 5, note 2. In some places, she has written "can" and "must" in all capital letters, and in other places she italicizes them.

1

Origins (1939–1962)

Wendy Carlos has said that her background is eclectic: her mother's parents were from two different areas of Poland, and her father's ancestry was English and Portuguese (the "Carlos" family name is Portuguese).[1] Clarence and Mary met while working at the same movie theater.[2] On November 14, 1939, Clarence and Mary Carlos had their first child, who was assigned the male sex at birth and given the name Walter. Mary would give eventually birth to four children, only two of whom survived into adulthood; the other two each died within a couple of weeks of their births.[3]

In the early 1940s, Clarence helped his father start a textile factory called the Globe Narrow Fabrics Company. As an adult, Wendy Carlos recalled that her father's factory was loud and dirty, requiring a lot of blood, sweat, and tears from its employees.[4] Clarence ascended through the ranks at the Globe Narrow Fabrics Company, becoming an overseer by the early 1940s and a vice president of the company by the middle of the 1940s.

Mary's family enjoyed music and dance immensely.[5] Nearly every member of her extended family sang or played an instrument, including accordion, clarinet, trumpet, trombone, piano, and drums. Those who didn't play or sing danced while other family members played music. Carlos recalled fondly that almost every family wedding, party, or other get-together included live music.

Every member of her mother's family was expected to be literate in music, and Carlos was no exception. She started piano lessons at the age of six, when she was in the first grade. The family didn't have much money during her early childhood, so Clarence drew a keyboard on a piece of paper for Wendy to practice on.[6] Her parents pushed her hard to practice, using corporal punishment when they thought it was necessary. In more than one interview, Carlos has said her parents would slap her hands or hit her over the knuckles with a ruler to "motivate" her to practice.[7] She also took organ lessons for a couple of years but didn't progress very far because she didn't have an organ to practice on.[8]

The Carlos family scraped the money together to buy a Lester spinet after a few years, and Carlos continued to take piano lessons until she was 14 or 15 years old.[9] At times, she would accompany her mother, whom she has said was a gifted amateur lyric soprano.[10] According to Carlos, her early musical training was relatively limited. Most of the music she learned in her lessons was composed by Frederic Chopin and Franz Liszt, but she didn't study much music by German and Austrian composers such as Ludwig van Beethoven or Johann Sebastian Bach—likely because Rhode Island, like much of the United States during the postwar period of the 1940s and 1950s, was prickly toward anything German.[11] Mary played a few old classical recordings at home, but most of the classical music the young Carlos heard came over the radio.[12] It was cost-prohibitive for the family to be able to attend much live music, although they did get to the occasional ballet, concert, or opera.[13]

At the urging of her parents, Carlos took some pop music piano lessons in addition to her classical lessons, although she recalled that the lessons were with "a very old guy" whom, she recalled, had a dated perspective of pop music.[14] Despite her teacher's antiquated view of popular music, Carlos later expressed her gratitude for these lessons because they taught her about chord changes and other dimensions of pop music.[15] She began composing at a very early age.

From the time she was a child, Carlos was very resourceful. She has attributed her work ethic and creativity to the fact that her family was very poor in the early years of life: if she wanted something, she had to find a way to get it on a shoestring budget.[16] Much like her father had hand-drawn a piano keyboard for her to practice on until the family could afford a real piano, Carlos built things from scratch or otherwise improvised when her family couldn't afford them. For example, the hi-fi system that her family listened to music on was something Carlos had put together herself. She cut the wood to make the loudspeaker enclosure and used a soldering iron to wire a kit. She also designed some components herself when she wasn't able to get a kit.[17] When word of her aptitude got around, she began helping older people repair their older equipment or install newer equipment.[18] She has said she was a "smart-ass" and a "nerdy" child who learned skills quickly and enjoyed applying what she had learned.[19] She was similarly scrappy with music, checking out academic books from the library so that she could teach herself about harmony, counterpoint, and tuning and temperament.[20]

As a child, Carlos was confused about why her parents insisted on treating her like a boy when it was so clear to her that she was a girl.[21] Carlos's parents tried to pass off her behavior by suggesting that, for example, sleeping in her mother's clothes was just their child's way of expressing love for her mother.[22] As Carlos got older and continued wearing her mother's clothes, her parents would brush off the behavior by claiming that their child was simply getting ready for Halloween.[23] Carlos has said she knew from a very early age that if she continued to act like a girl, she was afraid she would lose her parents' love, so she started to hide her behavior and identity from them.[24] She was wracked with guilt about what she considered her secret.[25] Although she has not said her parents ever hurt her physically because of her gender identity or expression, one imagines that if her parents would crack her over the knuckles with a ruler when she didn't practice the piano enough, they might also have reacted with physical force in response to how she dressed or behaved as a child.

There was simply no cultural awareness or point of reference for understanding the identity of transgender people during the 1940s and 1950s. The concept was beginning to gain some attention in Europe but was largely absent from any discourse in the United States. As Joanne Meyerowitz has shown, if transgender people were mentioned in popular press accounts at all, they were pathologized or cast as freaks. In 1939, the same year Carlos was born, the men's magazine *True* ran a feature suggesting that women with masculine characteristics, female impersonators, people who enjoyed cross-dressing, and those who identified as transgender were probably all suffering from tumors that changed their behavior.[26] The experiences of transgender women such as Barbara Ann Richards, who petitioned the state of California in 1941 to change her legal name and gender from Edward and male to Barbara and female, were presented in media accounts as instances of "hermaphrodites whose female characteristics had come to the fore."[27] By and large, transgender people were depicted as victims of some type of physical pathology such as a tumor or hermaphroditism.

Even physicians in this period seemed to support the point of view that transgender people were sick, either physically or mentally. Writing in the early 1950s, the sexologist David Cauldwell coined the term "trans-sexual" to refer to those who wanted to change their sex. But even though Cauldwell understood the concept, he still thought transgender people were insane, wanted to destroy their sexuality, and wanted to mutilate their bodies. Anyone who didn't have a tumor or glandular disorder was probably just mentally ill, as far as Cauldwell was concerned. He saw transgender people as products of unhappy childhoods or, alternately, of overindulgent families (most likely mothers).[28] If physicians who specialized in sex viewed trans-gender people so disdainfully at mid-century, it seems likely that an average Rhode Island working-class family would struggle to accept having a trans-gender child in their home.

Carlos has said that she made contrived attempts throughout her child-hood to fit in and "act like a boy" by playing sports and participating in other rough play, but she really preferred art and music.[29] She also preferred the company of girls to boys, which resulted in taunts from boys—and worse.[30] Carlos recalled older boys taunting her as early as elementary school with homophobic epithets such as "fairy," "pansy," and "sissy."[31] Although she said didn't know exactly what those words meant when she was a child, she knew what they implied: freak.[32] She tried to change her behavior to protect her-self, such as carrying her books on her hip (like boys were supposed to do) in-stead of cradling them in her arms (like girls did).[33] As a child, Carlos wasn't just called names: other kids threw rocks at her, punched her, and sexually assaulted her.[34] She regularly endured this kind of cruelty and abuse until she graduated from high school; she would continue to fear for her safety for many years.

Carlos dealt with her anxiety by working, throwing herself into projects so that she could escape the difficulties brought on by how other people treated her or how she feared other people would treat her.[35] Her creativity, innova-tiveness, and ability to build things from scratch, coupled with her relent-less drive, led to some pretty remarkable creations. She has said she coped with being a "misfit" child by writing plays and creating comedy routines to entertain the other children.[36] Her first known music composition was a trio for clarinet, accordion, and piano, the instrumentation of which reflects her mother's family's music-making as much as it does the classical and popular piano lessons that she had been taking.[37]At age 14, Carlos won a Westinghouse Science contest with a computer that she had built.[38]

She also created a small studio in the basement of her parents' house (in what she called the family's "rumpus room") where she began creating ru-dimentary electronic music.[39] Her years of fixing, building, and tinkering with electronics had equipped her with the knowledge of how audio equip-ment worked. By the time she was a teenager, she knew what an oscillator was and how to create a gating envelope out of photocells and light bulbs.[40] She created her own stereo tape machine, likely by converting an inexpensive mono reel-to-reel tape recorder to stereo, and she manufactured her own machine that could produce quadraphonic sound—that is, four-channel or surround sound.[41] This anxious, bullied teenager, working alone for hours and hours in her parents' Rhode Island basement laboratory, was independently developing many machines that would become the leading commercial audio trends during the 1960s.

The impetus for her experiments with electronic music was her exposure to a piece of electronic music composed by Pierre Henry (sometimes also spelled Henri). Henry composed *The Veil of Orpheus* in 1953, so Carlos could have heard a recording of it as early as age 14. *The Veil of Orpheus* is an example of what is called musique concrète, a primarily French genre of postwar electronic music in which composers manipulated existing recorded (concrete) sounds. Composers of musique concrète instead recorded sounds from the environment or used recordings of music or other sounds and tweaked them electronically, often rendering them unrecognizable from their source materials. Carlos recalled that a former high school classmate, who was now studying physics at Brown University, had come across a recording of the Henry piece and played it for her because he thought it was a joke.[42] She found *The Veil of Orpheus* to be anything but a joke, and hearing it transformed the way she approached music.

Years later, she told an interviewer that Henry was the greatest influence on her electronic music compositions.[43] She was moved by the drama of Henry's telling of the Greek tragic myth of Orpheus, and she was stunned by the kinds of sounds she heard in that piece. She recalled hearing extremely modern effects such as a prepared piano, an echo chamber, and tape echo effects.[44] At the same time, it sounded to her like Henry was replicating the sounds of ancient instruments by using boxes and metal containers as improvised percussion instruments.[45] She was completely fascinated by Henry's ability to manipulate existing sounds to the point that they were nearly unrecognizable, making them sound as if they had been generated anew instead of recorded from any sound that had ever existed in the real world.

Carlos was so inspired by *The Veil of Orpheus* that she immediately set out to create her own musique concrète piece.[46] Her concrete sounds came from what she could record around the house. She created reverb by putting a loudspeaker in the shower stall with a microphone.[47] Since she didn't have her own oscillator, she played test tone recordings on a variable record player.[48] She recalled "howling into a microphone" and also recording pitches, chords, and echoes on her parents' piano.[49] By the late 1950s, a teenaged Carlos was creating the same kinds of music in her rudimentary Rhode Island basement laboratory that composers in New York, Darmstadt, and Paris were making using the latest and most expensive equipment available on the market.

Inspired in part by Henry's music and in part by her own curious ear, Carlos also became interested in tuning and temperament when she was in high school. This passion would remain with her throughout her life, dominating much of her work during the 1980s. She checked out books on the subject of intonation from the public library and then tuned her parents' piano into the various systems she was reading about.[50] She bought a piano tuning hammer and wedges specifically so that she could create the sounds she had read about; she couldn't hear any examples of these tuning systems on any recordings at the time, so she had to render them herself if she wanted to experience them.[51] Carlos would painstakingly retune the piano in mean tone temperament, just intonation, and other scales and tuning systems that she had invented herself.[52] She would leave the piano in its new tuning system for a few days, play some music using that system, get tired of it, and retune the piano into an entirely different system.[53]

Carlos also began experimenting with electronic renditions of Johann Sebastian Bach's music while she was still in high school. She wrote a computer algorithm that composed four-part inventions in the style of Bach. Having programmed the computer with the basic rules of harmony and counterpoint, Carlos could generate her own Bach-style inventions that sounded, she claimed wryly, like something a student had written after just a few weeks of modal counterpoint lessons.[54] She grumbled decades later that contemporary algorithmic composition had not improved at all since her early "bleak" experiments with her homemade Bach program.[55]

When she graduated from high school, Carlos thought she would study science in college.[56] She liked computers, numbers, math, and technology, so she chose physics as her major when she entered Brown University in the late 1950s. From the start, she couldn't keep up with her classes. Her grammar school and high school training had left her utterly unprepared for a college major in physics. She hadn't taken geometry or trigonometry in high school, for example, and these gaps left her far behind her classmates in the physics department. Her grades were suffering as she struggled in vain to keep up with the academic work. Carlos has said that this period was extremely difficult for her because she went from being the student who was always at the top of the class in high school to barely being able to pass her college courses.

One of Carlos's physics professors at Brown was Wesley Nyborg, whose research on biophysical acoustics would revolutionize the use of ultrasound technology. Carlos has said that she and most of the Brown community regarded Nyborg as a bit of a maverick in the late 1950s because he was breaking a lot of ground with his pioneering research in biophysics. Nyborg told Carlos repeatedly that she should combine the studies of music and physics.[57] She didn't believe such a thing was possible at first, but repeated conversations with Nyborg about the topic began to change her mind. Nyborg advocated for her by contacting the music department directly and asking what they could do for his student who wanted to combine music and physics into a degree program.

The chair of Brown University's music department at the time was Arlan Coolidge, who jumped to help Carlos with a combined music and physics degree. He worked with her to develop a plan with the special projects program, which at the time consisted of classes that Brown offered without a syllabus or any particular restrictions or guidelines. Coolidge and Carlos went through the classes she had already taken and determined what remaining classes she could take in order to complete a bachelor's degree. She ended up taking as few science classes and as many music classes as possible to fulfill these improvised degree requirements.

Carlos has recalled this time of her life fondly, noting that Brown's general atmosphere at the time encouraged this kind of strange and unprecedented innovation. Her work with professors to find an academic niche was welcomed; she has said that people at Brown certainly thought she was "weird" and "a crackpot," but they accepted her and welcomed her new approach. The university may also have embraced her new degree program because she succeeded so admirably in the coursework that she and Coolidge had designed. She went from nearly failing out of the physics program to resuming her familiar and comfortable place at the top of the class; she has said that she earned multiple grades of A-plus and made the dean's list.

As a music student, Carlos took classes in music theory, counterpoint, and composition. One of her composition teachers was the celebrated American composer Ron Nelson. She has said that Nelson gave her some of the most valuable advice she ever received about music composition, which is that she should always be mindful about how her music would sound during a performance.[58] Nelson told her to imagine herself at the center of the performance hall and to envision the conductor preparing to start the performance of the piece: at that very moment, what sounds did she want to hear?[59]

Brown also had some resources for Carlos to continue creating electronic music. She had heard rumors that Brown had a secret audio research laboratory, but that information turned out to be false.[60] Brown's facilities did have a few audio oscillators, top-of-the-line equipment that would have cost several thousand dollars in the late 1950s.[61] These oscillators allowed Carlos to continue experimenting with various tuning systems. Carlos recalled that she and her classmates would tune one of the oscillators to a 440-Hz reference signal that was broadcast by the short-wave radio station WWV.[62] They tuned two against each other while watching an oscilloscope to ensure that they had created the desired ratio between sounds; once achieved, they would tape the sound, add it to their library, and start the process over again.[63] Carlos and her colleagues created a library of approximately one hundred different pitches, all of which fell within the same octave.[64] These various pitches could be used to create a variety of different scales in various tuning systems.

Although Carlos had found an academic niche at Brown with generous support from her professors and an opportunity to express herself intellectually, she still felt incredibly isolated socially. She has said that she felt paranoid during this period of her life, terrified that someone would learn about her gender identity and label her as deviant. [65] She almost never dated; she felt alienated and set apart from everyone around her. She has said that she hated herself and was convinced that her life was some kind of cruel mistake, so she threw herself into work in an attempt to quiet those thoughts and fears.[66]

Carlos's youth set a number of precedents for the rest of her life. She was extremely self-sufficient, building her own equipment, doing her own maintenance, and teaching herself information out of books. She was interested in many different types of music and sound, from (relatively) old-fashioned pop tunes to the Romantic piano music of Frederic Chopin and Franz Liszt to the strict counterpoint of Johann Sebastian Bach to many different systems of tuning and temperament to the electronic sounds of Pierre Henry. She was more technologically savvy at seventeen than most people would be in their entire lives. Plus, she was often an outsider. Academically and musically, she never quite fit into existing structures and ended up designing her own degree program at Brown. Her gender identity often made her feel different, wrong, and out of place, and she was frequently scared for her safety. Her parents seem to have ignored her attempts to express herself. Her peers taunted her and assaulted her. She had very few friends and thought that nobody would love her if they knew the truth about her gender. She has said that she hated herself during this time.[67] She did her best to combat her sense of isolation by working longer and harder than anyone around her.

In 1962, Carlos graduated from Brown University, having completed her unique music and physics curriculum. She decided to pursue a graduate degree in electronic music. At the time, she recalled, there were two options: the University of Toronto and Columbia University. Carlos picked Columbia because she thought New York seemed like it would be an "interesting town."[68] She has lived in New York ever since.

Notes

1. Andy Blinx, "Wendy Carlos: From Bach to the Future," *Grand Royal* 3 (1994): 60.
2. Frank Oteri, "Wendy's World: Wendy Carlos in Conversation with Frank J. Oteri," *NewMusicBox* (January 18, 2007): 6. http://www.newmusicbox.org/articles/wendys-world./.
3. Arthur Bell, "Wendy/Walter Carlos: A candid conversation with the 'Switched-On Bach' composer who, for the first time, reveals her sex-change operation and her secret life as a woman," *Playboy* 26, no. 5 (May 1979): 103 (hereafter "*Playboy* interview").
4. All information about Clarence Carlos's career is drawn from Wendy Carlos, "A Farewell to My Father," available at http://www.wendycarlos.com/parents/index.html.
5. All information about Mary Carlos's musical family is drawn from Blinx, "From Bach to the Future," 60.
6. Dominic Milano, "Wendy Carlos," *Contemporary Keyboard* (December 1979): 68 (hereafter Milano, "Wendy Carlos" (1979).
7. See, for example, Blinx, "From Bach to the Future," 60, and Milano, "Wendy Carlos" (1979), 68.
8. Milano, "Wendy Carlos" (1979), 68.
9. Milano, "Wendy Carlos" (1979), 68.
10. Carlos, "A Farewell to My Father."
11. Milano, "Wendy Carlos" (1979), 68.
12. Milano, "Wendy Carlos" (1979), 68.
13. Alan Baker, "An Interview with Wendy Carlos," *American Public Media* (January 2003), n.p. http://musicmavericks.publicradio.org/features/interview_carlos.html.
14. Milano, "Wendy Carlos" (1979), 68.
15. Milano, "Wendy Carlos" (1979), 68.
16. Baker, "Wendy Carlos," n.p.
17. Baker, "Wendy Carlos," n.p.
18. Baker, "Wendy Carlos," n.p.
19. Baker, "Wendy Carlos," n.p.
20. John Diliberto, "An Interview with Wendy Carlos," *Polyphony* (June 1984), 11.

21. Bell, "*Playboy* interview," 75.
22. Bell, "*Playboy* interview," 82.
23. Bell, "*Playboy* interview," 82.
24. Bell, "*Playboy* interview," 82.
25. Bell, "*Playboy* interview," 82.
26. Joanne Meyerowitz, *How Sex Changed: A History of Transsexuality in the United States* (Cambridge, MA: Harvard University Press, 2002), 32–33.
27. Meyerowitz, *How Sex Changed*, 40–41.
28. For more information about Cauldwell and his writings, see Meyerowitz, *How Sex Changed*, 44–46.
29. Bell, unpublished interview notes.
30. Bell, "*Playboy* interview," 82.
31. Bell, "*Playboy* interview," 82.
32. Bell, "*Playboy* interview," 82.
33. Bell, "*Playboy* interview," 82.
34. Bell, "*Playboy* interview," 82.
35. Bell, "*Playboy* interview," 83.
36. Bell, "*Playboy* interview," 82.
37. Robert Jacobson, "The End that Belies the Means: Interview with Walter Carlos" (1975): 1. Arthur Bell papers, Billy Rose Theatre Division, New York Public Library.
38. Bell, "*Playboy* interview," 82.
39. Doerschuk, "Wendy Carlos: The Magic in the Machine: Reflections from the First Great Modern Synthesist," *Keyboard* (August 1995): 53.
40. Baker, "Wendy Carlos," n.p.
41. Diliberto, "Wendy Carlos," 10.
42. Baker, "Wendy Carlos," n.p.
43. Milano, "Wendy Carlos" (1979), 72.
44. Baker, "Wendy Carlos," n.p.
45. Baker, "Wendy Carlos," n.p.
46. Doerschuk, "Wendy Carlos," 52.
47. Blinx, "From Bach to the Future," 60.
48. Blinx, "From Bach to the Future," 60.
49. Doerschuk, "Wendy Carlos," 52.
50. Jim Aiken, "Wendy Carlos: A Visionary Composer Wrestles her Computers into Submission," *Music and Computers* (November/December 1997): 58.
51. Freff (Connor Freff Cochran), "Tuning in to Wendy Carlos," *Electronic Musician* 2, no. 11 (November 1986). Reprinted without page numbers at http://www.wendycarlos.com/cochran.html.
52. Aiken, "Wendy Carlos," 58.
53. Aiken, "Wendy Carlos," 58.
54. Doerschuk, "Wendy Carlos," 56.
55. Doerschuk, "Wendy Carlos," 56.
56. Unless otherwise noted, all information about Carlos's time at Brown is drawn from Baker, "Wendy Carlos," n.p.

57. Blinx, "From Bach to the Future," 60.
58. Milano, "Wendy Carlos" (1979), 71.
59. Milano, "Wendy Carlos" (1979), 71.
60. Freff, "Wendy Carlos," n.p.
61. Freff, "Wendy Carlos," n.p.
62. Freff, "Wendy Carlos," n.p.
63. Freff, "Wendy Carlos," n.p.
64. Freff, "Wendy Carlos," n.p.
65. Bell, "*Playboy* interview," 83.
66. Bell, "*Playboy* interview," 83.
67. Bell, "*Playboy* interview," 83.
68. Milano, "Wendy Carlos" (1979), 69.

2

Foundations (1962–1967)

As a graduate student at Columbia University, Wendy Carlos studied and worked in the Columbia-Princeton Electronic Music Center, which is the oldest center for the study and production of electronic music in the United States.[1] In 1951, Vladimir Ussachevsky, a new professor of music at Columbia University, began making electronic music and recording his creations on tape recorders. Columbia's music department had recently purchased an Ampex 400 tape recorder, which, at that time, was the only commercially available tape machine that could create professional-quality reproductions of sound. During the early part of the 1950s, Ussachevsky and his colleagues, including engineer Peter Mauzey and fellow music professor Otto Luening, created music with instruments that could electronically generate sounds. They captured and recorded these electronically generated sounds on their magnetic tape recorder. They also created music directly on pieces of magnetic tape. Composers who created so-called tape music did so by literally manipulating the physical structure of the magnetic tape. A sound was recorded onto a strip of magnetic tape, and then the tape itself was cut into pieces. The composer could rearrange sections, repeat sections, reverse and invert sounds, and speed up and slow down sounds, all through physically manipulating a piece of tape.

At nearly the same time, a teenaged Wendy Carlos was also generating electronic sounds and splicing magnetic tape in a rudimentary electronic music studio in her parents' basement. Most of her equipment was homemade and created on a shoestring budget. In 1958, Ussachevsky and Luening formally co-founded the Electronic Music Center, having secured funding from a five-year $175,000 Rockefeller Foundation grant. Milton Babbitt, a professor of music at Princeton University, joined the center soon after, thereby creating the "Columbia-Princeton" name and association. The center was still in its infancy when Carlos began studying there in the fall of 1962. Its main equipment included three tape studios and the RCA Mark II Synthesizer.

The Mark II is a massive instrument that fills an entire room (see Figure 2.1). It uses rolls of punched paper (not unlike a player piano roll)

Figure 2.1 Left to right: Milton Babbitt, Peter Mauzey, and Vladimir Ussachevsky in front of RCA Mark II synthesizer, Prentis Hall, Columbia University, New York. Columbia-Princeton Electronic Music Center Archives, Rare Book & Manuscript Library, Columbia University Libraries. Used by permission.

to program the synthesizer using binary code. The composer punches holes into the paper that the machine then reads and turns into sounds. Each sound parameter (envelope, frequency, octave, timbre, and volume) has four columns of dots that the composer punches out to create a specific sound. The paper is about fifteen inches wide and can be fed through the synthesizer at about four inches per second. As the paper is fed through the machine, the resulting sounds are engraved on a shellac record. In addition, composers can produce high and low pass filtering, white noise, tremolo, glissando, and resonance, all of which add variety to the types of sounds.

Working with the Mark II requires equally large amounts of knowledge and patience. Each individual sound has to be punched out using a specific combination of holes. Any changes have to be re-punched and resubmitted through the machine. Babbitt recalled that he was able to generate one minute of music per workday, if he knew exactly what sounds he wanted and if the machine was working properly.

Babbitt and others have claimed that RCA initially built its first Mark II Synthesizer to be used in commercial recordings. According to Babbitt, "RCA made some very slick arrangements on that machine—sort of Mantovani pop."[2] The Mark II's career as an instrument for commercial recordings never took off, and RCA approached the center about building a second Mark II specifically for them to use. The catch was that RCA would build another Mark II only if Columbia was willing to foot the $500,000 bill of doing so. The five-year Rockefeller Foundation grant for the entire center was only $175,000, which would barely cover a third of the cost of the synthesizer. There was no way the center would have been able to afford its own Mark II under those terms. Eventually, RCA and the center came to an agreement: RCA would build the machine and rent it to the center, on the condition that RCA would maintain the synthesizer as well. Milton Babbitt recalled paying a nominal monthly rental fee for the first two years of the center's existence, after which RCA agreed to sell them the Mark II for a small symbolic amount, most likely one dollar.

Carlos was familiar with the Mark II and how it worked, as were all her fellow students and professors. She has said she found the Mark II was an "indirect, clumsy way" to make music and resulted in "rigid, un-felt, simulated" music.[3] Further, she noted, the machine required a pint of blood from anyone who wished to use it.[4] Most of her compositions during her time at Columbia, however, were created with tape. In addition to the Mark II, the center had three studios for producing tape-based electronic music using Ampex tape recorders. She recorded electronic sound sources, generated using standard laboratory audio oscillators and generators, onto magnetic tape, after which she physically manipulated the tape to achieve the desired sound. She recalled that every single note she created required her to splice 1/16" pieces of tape together in a process that was incredibly tedious.[5] She created each individual sound on its own piece of tape and then spliced those pieces of tape together in the order in which she wanted them to be heard, thereby creating a sequence of sounds that would become the piece of music.

During graduate school, Carlos worked most closely with Ussachevsky, whom she has called "a pioneer in the field of electronic music in the United States."[6] Because resources were scarce and time in the tape studio was at a premium, Carlos took the midnight to 6 a.m. shift in the studio and then slept during the day.[7] Working through the night, she had large uninter-rupted blocks of time to create music. Her friend and fellow graduate student Phillip Ramey, who also took the overnight studio shifts, recalled how they would stagger out of the building every morning at dawn and stumble across the street to the Chock Full o' Nuts to get some coffee.[8] Ramey also has said he and Carlos were the bane of night custodians in the building who were constantly interrupting them and claiming that they weren't allowed to be in the studio so late; it seems that Ussachevsky neglected to tell the custodial staff that some of his graduate students would be working through the night.[9]

Carlos's graduate thesis project was a two-hour long opera called *Noah*. It was the longest and most complicated piece of music than any other student in the lab had created. Carlos recalled that the piece got a big laugh out of her student colleagues, perhaps because it was so much larger than anything else anyone else had put together.[10] *Noah* was not the only piece Carlos cre-ated during graduate school. She also wrote music for electronics that would be accompanied by live instruments (or vice versa). Carlos explained years later that performing a strictly electronic composition for an audience in the early 1960s was problematic because the people in the audience didn't know how or where to focus their attention.[11] In early performances, she and her colleagues would dim the house lights, leave a small light on the stage, an-nounce the title of the piece, and press play on the tape machine. She recalled it being a "horrible" experience—the audience's discomfort became palpable after only a couple of minutes. Carlos and her colleagues realized that a live performance commanded the audience's attention immediately, so they de-cided to combine live music-making with electronics.[12]

One of the best-known pieces for live and synthesized music that came out of Columbia-Princeton during this period was *Philomel*, a work by Milton Babbitt. The piece is based on Ovid's tale in which Tereus, the King of Thrace, rapes Philomela, who is his wife Procne's sister. Tereus cuts out Philomela's tongue so that she can't tell Procne what happened, but Philomela weaves a tapestry to tell her sister instead. As an act of revenge, Procne kills her son and feeds him to Tereus. Tereus pursues the two sisters in a murderous rage, but the gods transform Procne into a swallow and Philomela into a nightin-gale. Philomela regains her voice when she becomes a nightingale. Poet John Hollander created an English-language text based on Ovid's tale specifically for Babbitt's musical setting.

The Ford Foundation commissioned *Philomel* in 1964. Babbitt wrote the piece for magnetic tape, synthesized sounds, and live soprano. He used the

RCA Mark II to create the synthesizer sounds. Soprano Bethany Beardslee provided the raw sounds for the tape music and also performed the live portion in concert. The taped music featured distorted versions of Beardslee's recorded voice that would sound in echo with her voice as she performed live. The work received its premiere in the Chapel at Amherst College, with a second performance soon after at the Metropolitan Museum of Art.[13] Carlos ran the tape machine for these performances of Babbitt's *Philomel*.[14]

Babbitt recalled that the first performance of the piece were well-received, not because of the music that he had written but because Beardslee was so excellent. According to him, when Beardslee was the performer, "It doesn't make any difference what the hell you write . . . Bethany goes out there and sings the way she can sing, and it didn't make much difference."[15] Babbitt's comment reflects what Carlos and her colleagues had learned the hard way: audiences seemed to respond far better to electronic music when it was paired with a compelling live component.

Carlos herself wrote at least two pieces for electronic and acoustic instruments while she was a graduate student: *Music for Flute and Magnetic Tape* and *Dialogue for Piano and Two Loudspeakers*. The piece for flute and tape was a set of variations: the flute stated an eleven-measure theme at the beginning, which was followed by six variations on that theme.[16] (Both of these pieces would eventually be released commercially about a decade later on her album *By Request*.) Carlos has said she also scored short student films while she was a student at Columbia, although it is not clear whether she wrote electronic or acoustic music, or both, for these films.[17] She has said scoring these films taught her the basics of synchronizing music and film, a skill that would serve her well later in her career.[18]

As incredibly technically complex as the composition of electronic music was at the time, the faculty and students at the center seem to have viewed themselves as artists and musicians as opposed to technicians. Carlos has said that her professors Babbitt, Luening, and Ussachevsky instilled in her and her graduate school colleagues an appreciation of the artistry that underpinned the composition and performance of music.[19] According to Carlos, her instructors at the center did not teach her how to compose; rather, they taught her specific techniques and skills such as orchestration, counterpoint, and sound production, and these skills then enabled her to compose music.[20] As she explained, electronic music was first and foremost a production of a musical event.[21] To her, creating electronic music was no different than creating any other kind of music because the experience was about expressing ideas musically using one's preferred tools for that mode of expression, whether they were a string quartet, a solo clarinet, the Mark II synthesizer, or pieces of magnetic tape that had been spliced together.[22]

Electronic music composition differed from other kinds of music composition in one key way, however: electronic music gave the composer the ultimate control over how the final product would sound. If Milton Babbitt punched a particular set of holes in a sheet of paper that was fed through the Mark II synthesizer, he knew exactly what sounds would come out of the machine. He could change those sounds simply by punching a different set of holes. If Carlos wanted a particular effect in a magnetic tape piece, she would rearrange the order of her tape splices.

Unlike other kinds of music composition, in which a human musician plays notes that the composer has written down on the page, the composer of electronic music generates, with a machine, the exact notes a listener is to hear. A live clarinet might be out of tune in one passage, or a performer's violin string could break during the performance, or a pianist might take far too slow a tempo in one particular phrase. A composer of electronic music did not have any kind of mediation in the form of a human performer and their instrument. Instead, an electronic composition sounded exactly the way the composer wanted it to every single time it was played back. The time spent producing electronic music at Columbia gave Carlos the ability to control every dimension of sound she created. This level of control in music was a topic that Carlos would return to again and again over the next several decades of her career. In the 1980s, she would coin what she called her First Law: "For every parameter that you can control, you must control."[23]

Carlos also acquired many skills during her years at Columbia that would benefit her in the following years and decades. That mind-numbing tedium of creating tiny tape splices, in particular, would serve Carlos well. She was accustomed to spending hours physically manipulating a medium in order to create sound. But not all of her experiences in graduate school were purely about composing music. She recalled that although she did spend plenty of time in the lab working on intricate multitrack sounds and music scores, Ussachevsky suggested that she support herself by learning how to work on the technical and engineering aspects of music as well as on the artistic.[24] Ussachevsky was well aware that a full-time career composing electronic music might not be possible for most of his graduate students, so he encouraged them to hone skills that could serve them in a variety of professional contexts. Electronic music was new, and it was expensive, so the odds of a

Columbia or Princeton graduate becoming a professor of electronic music at another university was pretty unlikely, at least in the early and mid-1960s. Ussachevsky encouraged his students to think beyond the academic context, and Carlos directly benefited from this advice. Carlos has said learning to splice tape as she had was a great learning experience, and that she was so proficient at it that her skills at tape editing helped her get her first job after graduate school.[25]

In 1965, Carlos graduated from Columbia University with a master's degree in music composition. Her first job out of graduate school was working as a recording engineer at Gotham Studios, a studio in New York that produced audio spots for radio shows and for the U.S. government, particularly the Department of Defense. She recalled years later that it was a "lovely" experience working there, and she worked very carefully and attentively to keep all the equipment tuned.[26] These skills would serve her well as she began building her own home electronic music studio and experimenting with synthesizers and other recording equipment to produce her own music.

In addition to her full-time work at Gotham, Carlos freelanced for various companies and produced music and sound effects for TV commercials. Her music was heard in commercials for Schaefer beer, frozen food, the *Yellow Pages*, and toothpaste in the mid-1960s.[27] She recalled that these freelance jobs paid extremely well, anywhere from $100 to $1,000 per gig.[28] Indeed, she has said she took all these side jobs composing for commercials because that was the money she used to purchase her own synthesizer modules and other recording equipment.[29]

Those analog synthesizer modules had been invented and manufactured by Robert A. Moog, and the relationship between Moog and Carlos would change both of their lives. Bob Moog was an engineer, physicist, inventor, and manufacturer of electronic musical instruments. In the early 1950s, he founded his own company and began manufacturing Theremin kits. The Theremin, invented in the 1920s by the Soviet physicist Léon Theremin, was an electronic musical instrument with two antennas. The performer did not even have to touch the instrument to produce sounds. Each antenna detected the position of the performer's hands and adjusted the sounds for both frequency (pitch) and amplitude (volume).

The Theremin was heard in films such as *Spellbound* (1945) and *The Day the Earth Stood Still* (1951). Its sound came to be associated with the otherworldly, and it was popular with composers of soundtracks for science fiction films in the 1950s. It also appeared prominently in the 1966 single "Good Vibrations" by the Beach Boys. Bob Moog recognized the demand for Theremins, so he designed his own kits, advertised them in hobbyist magazines, and started his factory to fill the orders that came in. By 1961, he had sold more than a thousand Theremin kits at about $50 per kit.[30]

Moog had been a student at Columbia University in the late 1950s, studying electrical engineering.[31] One of his instructors at Columbia was Ussachevsky's technical advisor. Decades later, Moog would claim that he had only heard "vague mention of this weird musician Ussachevsky who was doing something in the basement somewhere on campus."[32] This turns out to have been a bit of a fib: Moog actually wrote to Ussachevsky in 1959 when he learned about the formation of the Columbia-Princeton Electronic Music Center and its financial support from the Rockefeller Foundation.[33] He introduced himself as a Columbia alumnus and asked many questions about the center's goals, activities, publications, and employment opportunities. Moog explained in his letter to Ussachevsky that his own company, R. A. Moog Co., was researching and developing electronic musical instruments but thus far was only offering Theremins for sale—and he included a Theremin brochure with his letter. Moog seems to have gotten Ussachevksy's attention, because Moog would go on to build an envelope generator with a push button trigger for Ussachevsky in 1965.[34]

Other musicians outside of Columbia, including Walter Sear and Herbert Deutsch, would bring Moog in contact with the synthesizer. Sear, himself a manufacturer of tubas as well as a Theremin enthusiast, took Moog and his Theremin kits with him to trade shows; the sounds of the Theremin would lure customers in, and Sear would then try to sell them a tuba in addition to a Theremin kit. At one convention, the two met Herb Deutsch, a composer of experimental music who was interested in electronic music. Deutsch was seeking a way to make electronic music with equipment that was compact and portable, and he has said he thought that Moog might be just the person to help design that equipment.

Throughout the summer of 1964, Moog worked on inventing components of the device that would eventually become his modular synthesizer. Deutsch visited him frequently to offer feedback and insight. These collaborations would yield an analog electronic musical instrument that employed the technique of voltage control. Voltage control means that the output signal is modified by applying a small amount of current to the control input of a specific component.

With Deutsch, Moog developed voltage-controlled oscillators (VCOs) and voltage-controlled amplifiers (VCAs). The VCO is a circuit that generates a periodic waveform (usually sine, sawtooth, triangle, or pulse). The VCA allows for the control of a signal amplitude over a variable scale. Moog also created an envelope generator, which allows for adjusting the amplitude of a sound to create various effects, such as attack, decay, sustain, and release. Composers would use the envelope generator to create effects like the rapid sound decay of a harpsichord or the long-sustained sound of a pipe organ. Yet another breakthrough was Moog's creation of the voltage-controlled filter (VCF), which allows for filtering the audio spectrum to remove frequencies from a waveform or change the overtones.

These voltage-controlled components were triggered by a piano-looking keyboard: pressing a key on the synthesizer keyboard sent a voltage signal to a sound-generating oscillator, which then produced a specific pitch. The pitch could now be changed by simply increasing the voltage. Changing the control input by one volt would then produce a change of one octave in the output pitch. These keyboards were approximately five octaves in size, and the keyboard keys themselves were not touch-sensitive.

Moog had created the first modular synthesizer, also sometimes called the "patchable" synthesizer because all modules had to be connected with patch cords. Each of his inventions became a discrete module: VCAs, VCOs, envelope generators, VCFs, a sequencer, and a keyboard for triggering all of the various voltage control signals. (One also had the option of purchasing a ribbon controller to use as the triggering device instead of the keyboard.) There were also a number of accessories available for purchase, such as a ring modulator, frequency shifters, and a vocoder. One could purchase various modules and wire them together with patch cords, which were also available for purchase from Moog. Each module's output voltage as well as how the modules were connected controlled what sounds one created. The Moog modular synthesizer could not produce any sounds unless the components were patched together, plugged in, and connected to an amplifier and speaker.

Moog has said his synthesizers were not designed to synthesize music or sounds but rather to synthesize a complete musical instrument out of available components. As he explained, "All synthesizer music is made by musicians." Synthesizers can make sound patterns; only human beings make music!"[35] He was quick to note that the synthesizer functioned just as an acoustic instrument does in that most parts of the instrument, such as a fingerboard or hollow body, are not in the sound path but rather provide a means for the musician to control the sound.

Unlike the massive RCA Mark II synthesizer at Columbia, Moog's modular synthesizers—or least their individual modules—were relatively small and portable. Since the independent modules could be purchased separately and assembled to the purchaser's specifications, the size of the final synthesizer was largely up to the user. Many modular synthesizer assemblages could fit on a tabletop with various modules affixed to the wall above in racks, cases, or cabinets (see Figure 2.2). Moog manufactured cabinets in which one could house the various modules and accommodate all their connections and cords logically and neatly.

Moog first demonstrated prototypes of these synthesizer modules at the 1964 convention of the Audio Engineering Society (AES), where he was

Figure 2.2 Robert Moog in front of a Moog modular synthesizer, November 1968. Photograph by Sol Goldberg, Cornell University Office of Public Information. Division of Rare and Manuscript Collections, Cornell University Library. Used by permission.

offered a free exhibit booth because another presenter had cancelled at the last minute. Moog recalled setting up a card table and putting four of his modules on it, all the while wondering what on earth he was doing there. He ended up, to his own surprise, selling two or three synthesizer modules to the choreographer Alwin Nikolais. This 1964 AES convention is also where Moog and Carlos first encountered each other; she later claimed she had met him at the convention in 1963 but likely misremembered the date by one year because Moog didn't show any of his synthesizer modules until 1964.[36] She remembered that she had to wake him up to meet him because he was napping on a banquette on the mezzanine where the convention was held.[37] At the time, she was still in graduate school at Columbia and had no disposable income with which to purchase any of Moog's modules.[38]

They met again the next year at the same convention, soon after Carlos had graduated from Columbia and when Moog rolled out the first commercially available Moog modular synthesizers. By the 1966 AES convention, Carlos had been working at Gotham for just over a year and making some extra money on the side by producing TV commercial jingles and sound effects. That year, she was finally able to purchase one of Moog's first 900-series modules.[39] Bob Moog delivered the synthesizer modules personally to Carlos's apartment and ended up staying for the entire weekend to set up the equipment and show her how it worked.[40]

Moog's hands-on approach with Carlos was not unique. He was extremely attentive to the needs and wants of his customers and spent a lot of time seeking their opinions and integrating those opinions into his designs. He was acutely aware of the fact that his success as a manufacturer of these synthesizers would be directly related to the field of electronic music as a whole, and therefore it was important for him to be closely in touch with those who were using his products. He visited his customers at their homes and in their studios, as he had with Carlos when she first purchased some modules. He also created a short-lived trade magazine called *Electronic Music Review* that catered to creators and consumers of electronic music; most of the articles and reviews were written by Moog's staff, customers, and friends. He invited people to visit his factory in Trumansburg, New York, as he had with Deutsch and later would with Carlos. He included his home phone number in much of his correspondence with customers, encouraging them to call if they had questions or difficulties. By the time Carlos had purchased her first Moog modules in 1966, Moog had already worked closely with musicians including Alwin Nikolais, Lejaren Hillar, and Eric Siday. All three of these musicians had made suggestions for their personal setups that Moog would ultimately include in the standard features.

Carlos suggested many different features and modifications that would improve the capabilities of Moog's synthesizers and their constituent components. Moog recalled that every time he visited Carlos she had "not one but a whole handful of ideas."[41] Moog has said his 1967 catalog included many modules with features that originated as suggestions from Carlos.[42] Carlos has been credited with the concepts of portamento and a fixed filter bank, for example, and she has said Moog greatly improved their functionality based on her suggestions.[43] They also developed a polyphonic generator bank together, a custom item that had forty-nine oscillators and that allowed her to create chords and arpeggios. Moog later adapted this custom item he had created for Carlos into a more commercial version, in which the synthesizer contained a bank of fixed oscillators that Carlos would claim was good for "pop-style 'vamping'" and not much else.[44]

Moog and others have said Carlos was extremely demanding of him and his synthesizer modules. Indeed, nearly everything Moog manufactured for Carlos during that period was custom and was built to much higher specifications than any of the standard Moog modules being manufactured at the time. Raynold Weidenaar, a former employee at Moog's Trumansburg factory and the editor of the Moog-sponsored magazine *Electronic Music Review*, recalled that Carlos "was really holding Moog's feet to the fire in terms of the way things had to be, and the quality that [she] needed. [She] was a very demanding musician who's also very knowledgeable technically."[45] Moog's notes from this period include a lengthy list of modules Carlos that wanted, including, among others, a 49-note keyboard, a 440-hertz oscillator, a 911-A dual trigger delay and a panel to hold it, a 901-A oscillator controller, a dial-controlled voltage source, and an octal socket for the keyboard; she also needed four short patch cords and an extra 15-inch trigger cable.[46]

A letter from Carlos to Moog, likely written in 1967, offers a glimpse of what she was asking of him.[47] She was returning a defective enveloper to him and asked him to bring its replacement to her in New York that coming weekend. She also listed the following items that she had on order with him, instructing him to bring any or all of them that were ready: a 902 voltage-controlled amplifier (she already had two, and this would be her third), two new 911 envelope generators (or one new envelope generator and a replacement part for hers that was currently malfunctioning), an envelope delay unit, a 440-hertz standard oscillator on a standard panel, and a keyboard control with glissando capabilities. In the letter, she started to ask for a polyphonic generator, but then she scratched it out and told him she'd wait. Her decision to wait is likely because she knew that Moog probably wouldn't get everything on her list during his coming trip.

Carlos not only required custom individual modules, but she also asked Moog to rebuild her system in terms of its power supply. Most Moog modular setups at the time had a single power supply, but Carlos required two to accommodate all of her modules. Notes in Moog's hand about this custom design explain that one power supply would feed the various 901-series oscillators, the keyboards, and the linear controller, while a second power supply would feed all of the remaining modules.[48] Carlos didn't stop with custom designs for the modules and their power supply: she even made a number of suggestions for how Moog should build the cabinet that housed all of her modules. A pencil sketch in her hand lays out her desired setup, complete with exact measurements for each cabinet unit. Among her specifications are a music stand, a rounded front edge on the mixer housing, and a walnut enclosure with aluminum panels.[49]

Although Carlos and Moog worked together closely for many years and had a mutually beneficial professional relationship, she was, according to Moog, "always criticizing—constructively criticizing."[50] In fact, several of the first modules that she purchased from Moog were not factory models and instead had to be designed and built according to her specifications.[51] Carlos was always trying to improve Moog's synthesizer to fit her own needs; she seems to have had very specific ideas about what sounds she wanted to create and how Moog's modular synthesizer could help her create them. She greatly admired Moog, but she was frustrated with what she perceived as his slowness to respond to her requests as well as how few of her suggestions he ultimately incorporated into his latest models.[52]

Above just about anything else, Carlos wanted a touch-sensitive keyboard. Like a pipe organ, the Moog's keyboard produced notes that sounded the same no matter how heavily or lightly a key was pressed. Moog built a few prototypes for her in the late 1960s, but she was unhappy with them; she wrote that these early touch-sensitive keyboards were "far from good" but that they did adjust to the amount of pressure and speed, allowing for some vague sense of expression or phrasing.[53] More than three decades later, she would still be expressing dismay that early Moog synthesizers did not come out of the box with touch-sensitive keyboards and that it took until the late 1970s for Moog to make them standard.[54]

In the summer of 1967, Carlos and Moog collaborated on a demo record for the R. A. Moog Company 900-series modular synthesizer.⁵⁵ Carlos traveled to Moog's factory headquarters in Trumansburg, where they developed a narrative and a plan for the demo album. Carlos then returned to her studio and produced the album. This collaboration worked well for both parties: Moog was delighted to have the record to be able to give away to prospective customers, and Carlos was glad to be paid in trade, receiving discounted Moog modules in exchange for her production of the album.⁵⁶

Carlos had to work quickly because Moog wanted copies of the demo available for the AES convention that was to take place in the fall of 1967. Luckily, she had created and recorded all kinds of what she called "learning pieces" as she was teaching herself to use the instrument, and she incorporated several of these on the demo.⁵⁷ Narrated by Ed Stokes, the Moog demo record first explained what kinds of sounds synthesizers in the "classical studio" (i.e., academic laboratories such as the one at the Columbia-Princeton Center) could make, and Carlos provided sterile electronic bloops and bleeps in an effective parody of what she and her graduate student colleagues had been making in the lab just a few years earlier. The narrator critiqued these laboratories and their sounds for lacking "versatility and efficiency." The solution to this artistic problem was, of course, only available on the R. A. Moog 900-series modular synthesizer. For approximately the next six minutes, Stokes's voice takes the listener through various features of the Moog modular synthesizers, each feature of which is accompanied by brief sound clips that Carlos created using her Moog modular.

By 1968, Carlos had created a state-of-the-art home studio in her studio apartment. She had a number of Moog custom modules, a mixing board, an eight-track recorder, and several miscellaneous pieces of professional studio equipment. She had three of Moog's 904 voltage-controlled filters, two keyboards, and a number of custom foot buttons and toe pistons that Moog had built for her.⁵⁸ Moog recalled being impressed that Carlos's studio was so professional, efficient, and musically oriented, particularly because it "could easily have developed into a cranky, haywire assemblage."⁵⁹ She paid for all of her equipment by bartering with Moog as well as with the money she earned in her side gigs producing music and sound effects for TV commercials.⁶⁰ This studio would be where Carlos would produce her first full-length album, *Switched-On Bach*.

Moog took advantage of Carlos's expertise not only in the realm of the designs of his synthesizers but also in terms of his short-lived magazine,

Electronic Music Review.[61] Moog had realized that as interest in electronic music was growing, that community of practitioners needed its own magazine to serve as a sort of gathering place or focal point, and he published a total of eight issues of *EMR* between January 1967 and July 1968. The focus was intended to be practical, with reviews of equipment, how-to articles on various types of equipment, reviews of albums of electronic music, and lists of relevant events, publications, and recordings for people interested in electronic music. In fact, issues 2 and 3 were a comprehensive listing of every electronic music studio and electronic music composition—personal or professional—known at the time of publication in early 1967. Listed alphabetically within each geographic region, the studios in New York included (in order), Capitol Records, Carlos's personal studio, the Columbia Broadcasting System (CBS), and the Columbia-Princeton Electronic Music Center.[62]

EMR folded after just eighteen months due to a lack of funding. Further, Raynold Weidenaar, who had served as the magazine's editor, eventually left the R. A. Moog company and moved to Cleveland. Weidenaar recalled that most of *EMR*'s readers were composers: "It was mostly a magazine for specialists, and not really for amateurs."[63] It had more than 1,500 subscribers from all over the world, but it simply couldn't stay afloat on its limited financial resources, especially once its chief editor had left.

Most of the contributors to *EMR* were also composers of electronic music, including Luciano Berio, Alvin Lucier, Henri Pousseur, and Frederic Rzewski. During *EMR*'s short life, Carlos wrote a total of five articles, all of which appeared in the final two issues of the publication. Given the relatively short list of people who could contribute articles, it was not uncommon for an issue of *EMR* to feature multiple articles by the same author or authors. It's unlikely that Moog would have paid her for her contributions, although he probably gave her discounts on additional labor or parts for her custom modules.

Carlos's first two articles, both of which appeared in the April 1968 issue of *EMR*, were co-authored with Benjamin Folkman, a musicologist and fellow engineer at Gotham with whom she would also collaborate on *Switched-On Bach*. Both articles written with Folkman concerned tape music. Together, they reviewed "the big three" American tape recorders of the time, which were Ampex, 3M, and Scully. Carlos and Folkman also wrote an extensive article that was part review, part instructional manual for the practice of multi-track recording in electronic music. Both articles are dense, highly technical in their language and instruction, and were also almost certainly penned by

Folkman and not Carlos. The text lacks any of Carlos's characteristic self-effacing humor and her unabashedly harsh critiques of other people and products.

In the July 1968 issue of *EMR*, Carlos wrote as sole author an article entitled "A Variable Speed Tape Drive." "A Variable Speed Tape Drive," like the articles written with Folkman, is dense and technical but with glimpses of Carlos's personality and wit: Ampex priced its equipment "abortively," and she sought a variable frequency oscillator that was "powerful enough to drive these machines without attendant wow or flutter."[64]

Carlos also reviewed two new albums of electronic music: Morton Subotnik's *Silver Apples of the Moon* and *Panorama of Experimental Music*, a compilation album featuring electronic music by Luciano Berio, Luc Ferrari, and György Ligeti. Subtotnik's *Silver Apples of the Moon*—produced using a Buchla synthesizer, which was one of Moog's main competitors at the time—is arguably the most important album of electronic music to be released before Carlos's own *Switched-On Bach*. Whether she truly disliked *Silver Apples* or whether she was simply knocking down a competitor in advance of her own album's release, Carlos had plenty of negative feedback for Subotnik's album. It was a "bore," it lacked "any sense of performance," and the album was "never musically compelling." And yet she encouraged *EMR*'s readers to purchase the album: she praised Subotnik himself, blaming the Buchla synthesizer for the album's problems. She wrote that *Silver Apples* was "perhaps best described as a poor performance of a very fine composition." Carlos also seems to have foreshadowed the release of her own album while couching her review in terms of her own aesthetic goals: "I still am looking forward to a convincing marriage of performance practice with the new electronic musical art."[65] By the time this review was published in July 1968, she was completing the master of *Switched-On Bach*, an album that many critics and listeners would agree was the first convincing marriage of music and electronics.

At the same time that Carlos was working closely with Bob Moog on developing custom synthesizer modules, she also began seeking medical intervention to help her change her gender. By the time she had entered graduate school at Columbia in the fall of 1962, she was feeling suicidal almost all the time.[66] Carlos recalled feeling incredibly lonely during this period. She had hardly any friends, and she avoided dating and romantic relationships entirely.[67] Some nights, she would ride the subway to Fifth Avenue and simply walk up and down the streets in order to feel surrounded by people.[68] Daily, she considered committing suicide by cutting her wrists with the same razor blade that she used to splice magnetic tape in the studio.[69]

A saving grace was her work, first in the music lab at Columbia and then later as a recording engineer at Gotham and in her side work with Bob Moog on the synthesizer modules, demos, and articles she authored. She has said she used her work with music, science, and technology to escape from her feelings of depression and isolation.[70] Although she could never escape her feelings entirely, her work would have allowed her some refuge. One wonders, then, if her two-hour-long master's thesis project wasn't just a tour de force because she wanted to go bigger and better than her colleagues, but if it was unprecedented in size because she was working on her music to protect herself. The more time she spent in the lab working, perhaps the less time she thought about ending her own life.

She knew that she needed help, but she has said she didn't quite know how to articulate how she felt or what exactly she was seeking.[71] Carlos had seen psychiatrists off and on, but none of them were able to help her much.[72] She recalled that in the early 1960s, she was only just beginning to put the pieces together about what her gender identity was, that she wasn't the only person in the world who felt the way that she did, and that someone out there might be able to help her.[73]

That person who could help her ended up being Dr. Harry Benjamin, a German-American endocrinologist and sexologist who was one of the most respected experts on medical treatments of transgender individuals in the world. Born in Germany in 1885, Benjamin moved to the United States in 1913 and remained there until his death in 1986. He first began working with transgender people in the late 1940s, when the American sexologist and researcher Alfred Kinsey asked Benjamin to consult on the case of a child who identified as female although having been assigned male at birth. Kinsey encountered the child while researching his iconic text *Sexual Behavior and the Human Male*, first published in 1948. Neither Benjamin nor Kinsey had ever met an individual who had expressed their gender in such a way, and they set about to assist the child medically.

Benjamin quickly became one of the primary people in the United States to whom transgender individuals were referred for medical treatment.[74] Before Benjamin, most physicians in the United States had no idea what to do with patients who identified themselves as a gender other than the one they were assigned at birth. These people's doctors advised them to do everything from hypnosis to shock treatments to lobotomies, or they were encouraged to commit themselves to asylums or to live in so-called homo-sexual colonies. None of these interventions could help a person with the real issue of having been assigned a different gender than the gender with which they identified, and they needed a physician who understood medi-cally and physically how they could be helped. The fact that Benjamin was kind and patient was a welcome bonus. He often treated people for little or no payment, and many of his patients remember him for his kindness and for the respect with which he treated them. Indeed, Benjamin corresponded at length with his own patients and with many other people who wrote to him for help but could not, for financial or other reasons, see him in person at his offices in San Francisco and New York.

In 1964, he created the Harry Benjamin Foundation with financial assis-tance from the Erickson Educational Foundation. Based in his New York office, the foundation included a team of experts, including gynecologist Leo Wollman, sexologist Robert E. L. Masters, endocrinologist Herbert Kupperman, and psychologists Wardell Pomeroy and Ruth Rae Doorbar, among others. As a team, they not only treated transgender patients but also studied them from the perspectives of endocrinology, neurology, and psychology. Patients received psychotherapy, hormones, and other kinds of physical and mental interventions.

Gender confirmation surgeries (sometimes referred to reductively as "sex-change operations") were rarely performed in the middle of the 1960s. At this point in time, the medical community, including Benjamin and his colleagues, was skeptical about—not to mention inexperienced in—performing operations on individuals who wanted to have their bodies phys-ically changed to conform to their gender identities. Further, in light of a 1949 legal opinion from California's then-Attorney General Edmund (Pat) Brown that any kind of surgical modification constituted the willful de-struction of healthy tissue, doctors also feared performing surgeries because they could be criminally prosecuted.[75] The first hospital to regularly offer gender confirmation surgeries to patients was Johns Hopkins in Baltimore, and its program was launched in the fall of 1966. The Johns Hopkins pro-gram was headed by a physician named John Money, and although Money was not a member of Benjamin's foundation, the two men worked together closely, with Benjamin frequently referring patients to Money. The first sev-eral patients on whom Money operated in late 1966 were all referrals from Benjamin.

Other physicians and academic researchers were skeptical about the scholarly integrity of Benjamin's research and often refused to support or even acknowledge it. That changed in the summer of 1966, when Benjamin published
the book *The Transsexual Phenomenon*. In *The Transsexual Phenomenon*,
Benjamin summarized his nearly two decades of research with transgender
people, arguing that a person's sex had many different components: anatomical, chromosomal, genetic, germinal, gonadal, hormonal, psychological,
and social. Benjamin wrote that transgender individuals had what he called
"gender disharmony." The text was one of the first to espouse the concept
of gender as opposed to sex, since gender identity could result from many
different factors apart from physical biology. Benjamin explained that a
transgender person's physical body and their sense of self were inconsistent
with each other. He concluded that since a person could not change their
gender identity, it was the physician's responsibility to help their transgender
patients live as fully and happily as possible as the gender with which they
identified.[76] The book earned Benjamin (initially begrudging) praise from
his peers as well as invitations for him and the rest of his team to present
their research at the New York Academy of Sciences and to have their work
published in prestigious journals.

Carlos read Benjamin's book soon after it was published, probably in late
1966 or early 1967.[77] She remembered feeling relief, knowing that while transgender identity was rare, it was not unheard of.[78] Further, she was moved by
Benjamin's descriptions and coverage of the psychological, emotional, and personal needs experienced by other transgender people.[79] She made her first ap-
pointment at the Harry Benjamin Foundation in New York in the fall of 1967.[80]
She has said she wasn't immediately seeking surgery, but she was definitely
interested in exploring all options that would be available to her to help live
authentically.[81] She saw Benjamin himself, and he oversaw her care.[82] She has
called him a "humanist" and credited him with saving her life.[83]

Carlos likely underwent the relatively standard evaluations, tests, and
procedures that were given to other patients at the Benjamin Foundation
at the time. Not all people who sought gender confirmation surgery were
allowed to have the procedure (or multiple procedures, as was often the
case). Nobody was allowed to have it right away. Patients were required to
take hormones for several months or years before they even were considered
candidates for surgery, and they were also required to socially transition, that
is, live as their identified gender, for a period of time. Benjamin began pre-
scribing hormones to Carlos in early 1968.[84] Carlos remembered scolding

Benjamin because she thought he had given her tranquilizers.[85] She was relaxed for the first time that she could ever remember, and it turns out that it wasn't tranquilizers but rather estrogen that had calmed her.[86]

Benjamin and his colleagues had very strict criteria for selecting patients, criteria which were often more indicative of the doctors' and society's biases than they were of the person's need for treatment.[87] In general, they chose as their patients people who would blend into society and not draw attention to themselves. They did not treat patients who had any kind of diagnosed mental illness. Benjamin and his colleagues also limited access to surgery and other treatment to people who could convincingly "pass" as their identified gender and who promised to avoid any kind of publicity or notoriety. Transgender women who had large bodies and deep voices were likely to be rejected under these criteria. Carlos, a small, slim person with fine features and a high voice, would probably have been seen as an ideal candidate, at least physically.

Further, Benjamin and his team sought transgender individuals who were not promiscuous, not homosexual, and who would be able to be employed in "respectable" professions (i.e., not sex work). Carlos's lack of any kind of personal life coupled with her preference to work around the clock in the largely solitary world of electronic music production likely indicated to Benjamin and his team that she would be as isolated and unassuming after her transition as she was before she sought treatment. She wouldn't have seemed like the kind of person who would give transgender people or the foundation a bad reputation. She certainly didn't seem like the type to draw undue attention to herself or to her gender identity.

Carlos was running into a serious problem: she didn't have enough money to take care of her needs.[88] Her medical treatments were probably very expensive, and she was interested in creating music that required very costly equipment to produce. If she chose to move forward with gender confirmation surgery, the cost would likely be a few thousand dollars (upwards of $40,000 in 2018). She also still didn't have all the equipment that she wanted in order to create music that was artistically satisfying to her. To afford what she needed, she was probably going to need more than some side gigs producing commercial jingles and sound effects and a few complimentary or discounted modules from Bob Moog himself.

By late 1967, she had begun thinking about creating an album of music produced on the Moog synthesizer that would also be commercially appealing.

Carlos thought that the right album could change the public image of the synthesizer, taking it from an instrument that produced strange, abstract sounds in an academic laboratory environment to something that was approachable, listenable, and, of course, sellable.[89] The album's commercial appeal, in turn, could earn enough money for her to continue growing and improving her studio and also to continue to see Dr. Benjamin at the foundation. To this end, Carlos began producing renditions of popular tunes using her Moog synthesizer. It would only be after she created some renditions of J. S. Bach's music using her Moog, though, that she would start down the path that would change her life and the reputation of the synthesizer forever.

Notes

1. Information about the Columbia-Princeton Electronic Music Center is drawn from the center's own site, available at http://www.columbia.edu/cu/computinghistory/cpemc.html; Robert Moog, "The Columbia-Princeton Electronic Music Center: Thirty Years of Explorations in Sound," *Contemporary Keyboard* (May 1981); reprinted June 7, 2016, https://www.keyboardmag.com/miscellaneous/the-columbia-princeton-electronic-music-center-thirty-years-of-explorations-in-sound (citations are to the online reprint).

2. Any statements attributed to Milton Babbitt in this chapter are from Moog, "Columbia-Princeton Electronic Music Lab," unless otherwise noted.

3. Thom Holmes, *Electronic and Experimental Music: Technology, Music, and Culture*, 5th ed. (New York: Routledge, 2016), 265.

4. Chuck Miller, "Wendy Carlos: In the Moog," *Goldmine* 613 (January 24, 2004); 48.

5. Jacobson, "The End that Belies the Means," 1.

6. Bell, "*Playboy* interview," 83.

7. Milano, "Wendy Carlos" (1979), 69.

8. Philip Ramey, "Then, Now and In-Between," liner notes to *Sonic Seasonings* (Columbia Records, LP, 1972).

9. Ramey, "Then, Now and In-Between."

10. Milano, "Wendy Carlos" (1979), 69.

11. All information in this paragraph about combining electronic and acoustic music is drawn from Diliberto, "Wendy Carlos," 11.

12. Diliberto, "Wendy Carlos," 11.

13. Gabrielle Zuckerman, "An Interview with Milton Babbitt," *American Public Media* (July 2002), available at http://musicmavericks.publicradio.org/features/interview_babbitt.html.

14. Holmes, *Electronic and Experimental Music*, 203.

15. Zuckerman, "An Interview with Milton Babbitt."

16. Holmes, *Electronic and Experimental Music*, 203.

17. Oteri, "Wendy's World," 4.
18. Oteri, "Wendy's World," 4.
19. Moog, "Columbia-Princeton Electronic Music Lab."
20. Allan Kozinn, unpublished interview with Wendy Carlos and Rachel Elkind (1979), 12 (hereafter "unpublished interview with" Carlos or Elkind). My many thanks to Allan Kozinn for sharing these documents from his personal collection.
21. Moog, "Columbia-Princeton Electronic Music Lab."
22. Moog, "Columbia-Princeton Electronic Music Lab."
23. Diliberto, "Wendy Carlos," 12.
24. Bell, "*Playboy* interview," 83.
25. Jacobson, "The End that Belies the Means," 1.
26. Miller, "Wendy Carlos," 47.
27. Christopher Wren, "Moog is more than a Vogue," *Look* 34, no. 7 (April 7, 1970), 24.
28. Bell, "*Playboy* interview," 83.
29. Kozinn, unpublished interview with Carlos, 39.
30. Trevor Pinch and Frank Trocco, *Analog Days: The Invention and Impact of the Moog Synthesizer* (Cambridge, MA: Harvard University Press, 2002), 18.
31. Unless otherwise noted, all information in this section about Bob Moog and the early Moog modular synthesizers is drawn from Holmes, *Electronic and Experimental Music*, 257–269, Pinch and Trocco, *Analog Days*, 17–31, and Mark Vail, *The Synthesizer: A Comprehensive Guide to Understanding, Programming, Playing, and Recording the Ultimate Electronic Music Instrument* (New York: Oxford University Press, 2014), 16–24.
32. Pinch and Trocco, *Analog Days*, 18.
33. Robert A. Moog, letter to Vladimir Ussachevsky, September 16, 1959. Columbia-Princeton Electronic Music Center Archives, Rare Book & Manuscript Library, Columbia University Libraries. Thanks to Seth Cluett at Columbia University for sharing this document with me.
34. Robert Moog, "On Synthesizers: Why They Don't," *Keyboard* (April 1983), 58.
35. All information in this paragraph is drawn from Moog, "On Synthesizers: What Is a Synthesizer?" *Contemporary Keyboard* (September-October 1975): 45.
36. Carlos, [Wendy]. "On Synthesizers" (letter to the editor. Last Whole Earth Catalog 1160 (June 1971): 330-331.
37. Wendy Carlos, "Bob Moog—R.I.P.," available at http://www.wendycarlos.com/moog/index.html.
38. Milano, "Wendy Carlos" (1979), 69.
39. Carlos, "Synthesizers," *WEC*, 331.
40. Pinch and Trocco, *Analog Days*, 135.
41. Holmes, *Electronic and Experimental Music*, 265.
42. Robert Moog, liner notes to *Switched-On Bach II* (Columbia Records, LP, 1973).
43. Carlos, "Synthesizers," *WEC*, 331.
44. Carlos, "Synthesizers," *WEC*, 331.
45. Pinch and Trocco, *Analog Days*, 136.

46. Bob Moog, undated list of items. Robert Moog papers, #8629. Box 34, folder 9 Division of Rare and Manuscript Collections, Cornell University Library. An invoice in this folder is dated August 6, 1968, so this list was likely written at the same time as the invoice.

47. Carlos, undated letter to Bob Moog. Robert Moog papers, #8629. Box 37, folder 10. Division of Rare and Manuscript Collections, Cornell University Library. The letter was likely written in 1967 because she discusses the test pressings of the demo record she produced for Moog Music, which was released in 1967.

48. Robert Moog, "Rebuilding of Carlos system," Robert Moog papers, #8629. Box 37, folder 2. Division of Rare and Manuscript Collections, Cornell University Library. This page is undated but appears with similar documents dated September 1968.

49. Carlos, sketches for mixer housing. Robert Moog papers, #8629. Box 37, folder 2. Division of Rare and Manuscript Collections, Cornell University Library. The sketches themselves are undated but are placed in a folder with other similar documents that are dated September 1968.

50. Pinch and Trocco, *Analog Days*, 136.

51. Moog, liner notes to *Switched-On Bach II*.

52. Carlos, "Synthesizers," *WEC*, 331.

53. Carlos, "Synthesizers," *WEC*, 331.

54. Carol Wright, "Wendy Carlos: Something Old, Something New: The Definitive Switched-On," *New Age Voice* (November 1999).

55. Robert Moog, "Moog Demo," April 2002, available http://moogarchives.com/moogdemo.htm.

56. Carlos, "Synthesizers," *WEC*, 331.

57. Carlos, "Bob Moog—R.I.P."

58. Carlos, "Synthesizers," *WEC*, 331.

59. Moog, liner notes to *Switched-On Bach II*.

60. Allan Kozinn, "'Switched-On Bach' Creator Returns," *New York Times* (February 17, 1980), D22.

61. For a brief history of *EMR*, see Pinch and Trocco, *Analog Days*, 80–81; 84–85.

62. *Electronic Music Review* 2-3 (April/July 1967): 205–207.

63. Pinch and Trocco, *Analog Days*, 85.

64. Carlos, "A Variable Speed Tape Drive," *Electronic Music Review* 7 (July 1968): 18–19.

65. All *Silver Apples* references are from Carlos's review of it, *Electronic Music Review* 7 (July 1968): 39.

66. Bell, "*Playboy* interview," 83.

67. Bell, "*Playboy* interview," 83.

68. Bell, "*Playboy* interview," 83.

69. Bell, "*Playboy* interview," 83, 86.

70. Bell, "*Playboy* interview," 83.

71. Bell, "*Playboy* interview," 83.

72. Bell, "*Playboy* interview," 83.

73. Bell, "*Playboy* interview," 83.

74. Unless otherwise noted, all information about Harry Benjamin's career is drawn from Meyerowitz, *How Sex Changed*, 132–36; 214–17.

75. Susan Stryker, *Transgender History* (Berkeley, CA: Seal Press, 2008), 44–45.

76. Stryker, *Transgender History*, 73.

77. Bell, "*Playboy* interview," 83.

78. Bell, "*Playboy* interview," 84.

79. Bell, "*Playboy* interview," 83.

80. Bell, "*Playboy* interview," 83.

81. Bell, "*Playboy* interview," 84.

82. Bell, "*Playboy* interview," 86.

83. Wendy Carlos and Annemarie Franklin, letter to Harry Benjamin, December 31, 1979; Harry Benjamin papers, Box 27, Folder 8. Kinsey Institute and Library, Indiana University.

84. Bell, "*Playboy* interview," 86.

85. Bell, "*Playboy* interview," 86.

86. Bell, "*Playboy* interview," 86.

87. Information about gatekeeping and gender norms is drawn from Julia Serano, *Whipping Girl: A Transsexual Woman on Sexism and the Scapegoating of Femininity* (Berkeley, CA: Seal Press, 2008), e-reader pages 155–188.

88. Kozinn, " 'Switched-On Bach' Creator Returns."

89. Baker, "Wendy Carlos," n.p.

3

Switched-On Bach and Undesired Fame
(1968–1969)

In 1967, Wendy Carlos made a new friend who would help change the trajectory of her entire life, both personally and professionally. Rachel Elkind was born in Hong Kong in 1939. When the Japanese invaded Hong Kong during World War II, Elkind and her family were sent to a prisoner of war camp in Shanghai.[1] She came to the United States at the age of eight, after the war ended and the camp where they were being held was liberated. Elkind majored in English and minored in music at the University of California at Berkeley. After graduation, her day job was secretary to Melvin Belli, the attorney who was nicknamed "The King of Torts" for the great number of personal injury cases he pursued.[2] (Belli represented Jack Ruby free of charge after Ruby shot and killed Lee Harvey Oswald in 1963.) At night, Elkind sang in Bay Area jazz clubs.[3]

In 1960, she moved to New York to pursue her dream of being on Broadway.[4] To pay the bills, she became secretary to Goddard Lieberson, who was then the president of Columbia Records. Elkind recalled years later that working for Lieberson gave her a PhD in music, as it were, and her goals changed from performance to recording industry production.[5] Working for Lieberson, Elkind started watching how other producers worked. She became more and more involved in the production process, recording content for Lieberson and observing how other producers edited that content.[6] Elkind eventually left Columbia and worked for the head of A & R at Capitol, where she learned additional production techniques such as overdubbing.[7] She then took her first job as a producer, working at Gotham Recordings. There, she started out by producing spots for the U.S. government, such as campaigns to sell U.S. Treasury savings bonds. The spots she produced featured people including jazz musicians Woody Herman and Louis Armstrong.[8]

Elkind and Carlos have each recalled that their first few meetings were acrimonious.[9] Elkind was having mechanical problems with a console, and a friend told her to contact Carlos, whom the friend called "a genius."[10] Elkind recalled Carlos saying, "I don't like to fix machinery. I'm a composer and physicist."[11] Annoyed, Elkind told the friend that Carlos might have been a genius but was totally arrogant.

At some point, their irritation with each other faded. Their eventual friendship may have begun as a result of finding common ground. Elkind made no secret of the fact that she hated classical music (the music of Johannes Brahms was an exception) and electronic music and much preferred jazz.[12] Carlos took that as a challenge, bringing Elkind project after project to convince her of the appeal of electronic music. Carlos wanted to work with Elkind as a producer and kept trying to win her over with different kinds of sounds.[13] Carlos's Moog synthesizer renditions of popular songs and jazz standards did not sell Elkind on Carlos's skills or on the merits of electronic music, nor did a version of "What's New, Pussycat?" with forty tracks of overdubbing.[14]

The project that eventually piqued Elkind's interest was the synthesizer rendition of a two-part invention in F by Johann Sebastian Bach. More than thirty years after the fact, Elkind recalled,

> I said, well, now, this [Bach recording] is something I could work with, because it had a lot of truth to it, and it had a certain kind of insouciant charm. And [Carlos] said, a whole album of Bach? And I said, yes, I think so, because my thing was music had to sing and dance and had to have truth, and if it did, then it would speak to an audience. I didn't know how big, but I really felt in my naïve days that if I liked something and responded there would be at least a hundred thousand other people in the world who would feel that way.[15]

The singing, dancing, truth-having music Carlos had produced would, with Elkind's help, become the first cut on an album that would eventually be named *Switched-On Bach*. And although Elkind called herself naïve, it would turn out that her estimate of the number of people who would like the music was actually far too low.

To Elkind, the synthesizer enabled the music of Bach to "speak" to her in a way that it simply didn't when played by other kinds of instruments. The synthesizer allowed each line to emerge with a clarity that Elkind found lacking in other kinds of recordings of Bach's music. To Elkind, recordings of Bach's music that were popular in the 1960s were "soggy" because recording engineers insisted on close-miking, that is, placing the microphone less than a foot from the instrument.[16] She has even called cellist Pablo Casals's recordings "mush."[17] For Elkind, these electronic versions of Bach's music that Carlos rendered on the Moog offered dynamic contrast, clarity, and nuance for listeners that she wasn't hearing in recorded acoustic performances at the time.[18]

Both Elkind and Carlos have said the apparent limitations of the Moog synthesizer would actually become assets when recording Bach's music. The Moog synthesizer could only produce one note at a time. The musician had to record each note separately, sequence them into lines, and then stack the lines on top of each other to create harmony and counterpoint. Johann Sebastian Bach's music is made of individual lines in counterpoint that are, in many ways, ideally suited to be rendered on the synthesizer. The average Bach fugue has three or four, and sometimes up to six, individual lines. Another type of Bach counterpoint is the two-part invention, in which just two lines interact for the duration of the piece. This was the type of counterpoint that Carlos first rendered on the synthesizer and that caught Elkind's ear.

At first, Carlos was hesitant to produce an entire album of music that had been composed by another person. She really wanted to release an album of her own original compositions on the Moog synthesizer.[19] Elkind, however, convinced Carlos to move forward with the Bach project for several reasons. Elkind argued that listeners needed to be convinced that the synthesizer was approachable and not just some sort of frightening contraption of the avant-garde. She told Carlos that an album of familiar music rendered on the synthesizer would show listeners that the synthesizer was just another musical instrument and not something to be feared.[20] Elkind's instincts were spot on, perhaps more so than the two of them ever could have imagined at the time. With Elkind's encouragement, Carlos began producing the as-yet-unnamed Bach project in June or July of 1967.[21]

The work took place in Carlos's one-room, walk-up apartment at 410 West End Avenue. A profile of Carlos by Donal Henahan in the *New York Times* described the apartment's contents: "a two-manual Moog synthesizer with additions and refinements of Carlos's own devising, eight-track Ampex tape consoles, a polyphonic generator, a Dolby noise-reducing system, and intestinally convoluted mazes of wires and patch cords."[22] Henahan also wryly noted that Carlos "achieves a homey touch by putting plants atop the cabinets."[23] Another interviewer observed that a stuffed rabbit had been perched on top of the synthesizer.[24] Photos of her studio from this period reveal that the door to the bathroom was right next to the synthesizer.[25]

In response to an interviewer's question about how she got started on the Bach renditions, Carlos replied, "With Bach, I went and bought a score. What a concept!"[26] She has repeatedly said that she did not consider herself a composer in the context of this project but rather an arranger, or even an orchestrator. She has said that she considered her work to be a "re-orchestration" of Bach's music.[27] Carlos approached the music of Bach the way she had imagined the composer Maurice Ravel had approached Modest Mussorgsky's *Pictures at an Exhibition*. Mussorgsky had composed *Pictures* for piano in the 1870s, and fifty years later, Ravel took Mussorgsky's score and turned it into an orchestral piece. Carlos deeply admired Ravel's fidelity to Mussorgsky's piano score as well as his ability to deviate slightly where necessary.[28] Like Ravel had with Mussorgsky, she tried to choose sound colors on the synthesizer that were alive and vivid and faithful to Bach's music in spirit.[29] She acknowledged that there was no way the Moog could imitate the actual instrumental sounds, so they instead sought to evoke a color palette that captured the essence of the music.[30]

All told, the Moog modular setup that Carlos had at the time would have had cost about $12,000 in the late 1960s (upwards of $85,000 in 2018).[31] Each piece of music on the album took weeks to create. Carlos recalled that she spent eight hours a day, seven days a week for five months creating this new album—all in addition to her forty-hour a week job at Gotham.[32] Each sound that Carlos produced on her Moog synthesizer required a unique combination of patch cord routings, knob settings, and switch settings. She selected one of four available wave shapes: pulse wave, sawtooth, sine, or triangle. She could add or decrease envelopes to adjust attack time, decay, sustain, and release for each sound. For example, a harpsichord sound would decay almost immediately, while the sound of an organ would be sustained for much longer, just as would happen by playing the physical instruments themselves.[33] Oscillators were adjusted for octaves, and filters could adjust the high and low ends of the sounds.[34] The process was tedious.[35]

Although Carlos occasionally would write down the combination of settings required to create a particular sound, especially complex sounds like a snare drum, she was more likely to lose the scrap of paper on which the information was written than she was to use the information on it to create a sound. As a result, she more or less kept an entire library of sounds and the settings required to create those sounds in her head.[36] Once a sound was created using the above possible dimensions, that note was recorded. And then the entire process would start over for the next note.

Each line of music was painstakingly constructed note by note. A click track held the individual notes together in a steady tempo.[37] Once all the notes in a single line of music were placed together and completed, she could begin working on the next line of music. Then, when all of the lines had been created, she used overdubbing to stack the lines on top of each other. Carlos had one eight-track tape machine, a unit that she had built herself since she said she couldn't afford a factory-made version. She created her home-made eight-track tape recorder with parts from Ampex models 300 and 351 tape recorders, EMI tape heads, and a control panel for synchronizing the tracks.[38] To synchronize new tracks with tracks she had already recorded, she used Sel-Synching—an Ampex trademark—to monitor the spot on the tape that was recording as opposed to the playback head, which had a slight delay.[39] She mixed the sounds to stereo premasters using a two-track 1/4-inch Ampex. Those mixes were then edited and transferred with equalization and level optimization to the final masters by using Dolby A for noise reduction.[40]

To produce the contrapuntal sounds of J. S. Bach's music, Carlos had to record each line independently and then stack the lines on top of each other and synchronize them. Not only was this a tedious and time-consuming process, but she has said it was also made more challenging by the Moog's limited abilities.[41] Sel-Synching gave her a little bit of room for error in the timing of individual lines that would then be combined to create a contrapuntal section of music.[42] But the layering of individual lines was complicated by the fact that the Moog was very hard to keep in tune. If Carlos was lucky, she has said, she could produce a measure or two of music before the synthesizer went out of tune.[43] She claimed that she sometimes needed to bang on the instrument with a hammer to get it back in tune.[44] Carlos had to check each line meticulously for consistency, because if one line of a contrapuntal section was out of tune, the entire section of music would be ruined.[45]

As much as Carlos valued both Bob Moog and the synthesizers he created, she was very critical of the instrument and its capabilities. She has always acknowledged that the Moog was the best synthesizer option available at the time, and yet she frequently commented on its limitations.[46] She grumbled that the synthesizer was "nasty" to keep in tune and that although the Moog was the best synthesizer on the market, it was still "crude."[47] She found it lacking in expressive capabilities, which she largely owed to its lack of touch sensitivity.[48] She bemoaned its lack of a touch-sensitive keyboard, an option that wouldn't be introduced until the late 1970s.[49]

Nobody in the world probably was more familiar with the Moog synthesizer in the late 1960s than Carlos was, an assessment that Moog, Elkind, and Carlos have all made on separate occasions. Carlos has said repeatedly that she, through her sheer force of will and innovativeness, was able to make the Moog synthesizer do many things that Bob Moog himself could not have envisioned.[50] Further, she has claimed that her inventiveness and cleverness helped cover up what she considered to be the instrument's many deficiencies.[51] In fact, Carlos recalled that the first time she played some of the music on the Bach album for him, Moog asked her how she had come up with so many colors. She replied that she had been able to make it sound as if there were far more colors than there actually were.[52] According to Elkind, they were "always working against the limitations of the synthesizers."[53]

The two-part invention in F major that Carlos had created as a test case for Elkind became the first item that would appear on this new album.[54] Carlos created renditions of two other two-part inventions for the album, one in B-flat major and the other in D minor. Elkind recalled that they selected the remaining pieces by picking a top ten list of sorts from Bach's oeuvre.[55] In addition to the three two-part inventions, Carlos included two preludes and fugues from the *Well-Tempered Clavier*, a book of twenty-four preludes and fugues (one in every major and minor key) that Bach had composed in the 1720s. These five pieces—the inventions and the preludes and fugues—were all works that Bach had composed for keyboard instruments.

The remaining pieces they selected for the new album were all written for orchestras. These included the Sinfonia (or Prelude) to the Cantata no. 29 and the second movement of the Orchestral Suite no. 3, nicknamed "Air on the G String" because the first violinist can play their part entirely on the violin's G string, the lowest string on the instrument. Carlos also included the chorale prelude "*Wachet Auf*" (Sleepers Awake) from the cantata of the same name, as well as "Jesu, Joy of Man's Desiring," a chorale prelude from Cantata no. 147 that she remembered from her childhood because it was played to end the broadcast day on her local FM station.[56] Carlos also chose to include all three movements of Bach's Brandenburg Concerto no. 3.

The Third Brandenburg Concerto was an ambitious choice. Bach had written the piece for three violins, three violas, three cellos, and basso continuo (a grouping that usually includes harpsichord and at least one additional cello or viola da gamba). Carlos followed the first and third movements of Bach's score faithfully, but it is her rendition of the piece's second movement that is so notable. The score left little for Carlos to follow: Bach wrote only two chords. During Bach's lifetime, this type of notation generally suggested that the harpsichord player was to play a cadenza, an improvised passage whose length and complexity was entirely up to the performer. The harpsichordist would play a lengthy trill to indicate to the rest of the musicians that they were finished with the cadenza, and the orchestra would come back in to continue with the piece. Carlos followed the Baroque convention, only she rendered a brilliant section of music using the Moog synthesizer. Although the album was intended to use familiar music to show listeners that the synthesizer was approachable, here in the cadenza of the Third Brandenburg Carlos offered many types of abstract sounds that weren't found in any of the other cuts.

Much in the way that a harpsichordist in Bach's time could have used this cadenza to shine and to show off many tricks and flourishes, Carlos chose to highlight the chromatic abstraction that the synthesizer was capable of producing. She started by paraphrasing Bach's Chromatic Fantasy and Fugue (a piece written specifically for the harpsichord), and then she added three more layers of sound atop the paraphrase.[57] She explained that this cut was her opportunity to show off what the Moog synthesizer could do, and she acknowledged that sounds on this section of the album were far more indebted to her days as a student in the Columbia-Princeton Electronic Music Laboratory than they were to the music of Bach.[58] More than a decade later, she would chuckle at herself, noting that her performance of this movement was the result of her youth and enthusiasm combined with her desire to show off electronic music clichés of the time; the second movement clashed with the first and third movements stylistically, she said, but she'd had a lot of fun putting it together.[59]

Although Carlos was the one creating and assembling all of the sounds, she has said the collaboration with Elkind was 50/50 except for the actual execution of the sounds, which Carlos said was closer to 90/10.[60] With her background in jazz, Broadway, and popular music, Elkind brought a completely different perspective than Carlos had from her own background in classical and academic electronic music. For example, Elkind has said her background in improvisation helped her explain to Carlos how to bring the sounds to life.[61] Although Elkind didn't operate the synthesizer, she could explain what sounds she preferred, allowing Carlos to make the necessary technical adjustments to change the sound accordingly: "Can we get it a little thinner or a little thicker? A little prettier? Could we make it sound more like a French horn? It sounds too trumpet-y."[62] Their communication and their understanding of each other's aesthetics flowed into the sounds on the album. As Elkind explained, "We never know who does what. One of us will have an idea, and the other person helps make that idea live."[63]

Ultimately, it was Elkind who sold the Bach project to Columbia, not Carlos. (Carlos has said she lacks business acumen.)[64] Until the two women dissolved their professional partnership in the early 1980s, Elkind was the one who handled the business aspects of Carlos's music.[65] Despite Elkind's familiarity with the market and her instinct that the Bach album would be saleable, she also knew that a record company was unlikely to accept a pitch from a woman, which is why she didn't initially approach the record companies herself.[66] Instead, Elkind called her friend Ettore Stratta, a classically trained musician who worked in A & R at Columbia Records, and asked him to present the album concept.[67] They were offered a two-album contract on CBS Masterworks.[68]

Accounts differ on how much money was offered for the Bach album. Elkind recalled that they were offered $1,000 for the finished master of the album, and Carlos told an interviewer that they were given approximately $2,500 for the master (around $17,000 in 2018).[69] The saving financial grace would come with the royalties. Elkind negotiated what she called "a very nice royalty" because Columbia didn't appear to take the album seriously enough to expect that it would sell very many copies.[70]

Why would Columbia sign an album it didn't think would sell? According to Elkind, Columbia only accepted the project because the Moog synthesizer renditions of Bach's music fit with an upcoming campaign it was planning called "Bach to Rock."[71] The campaign would include Carlos's Bach album, an album of Terry Riley's early minimalist masterpiece *In C*, and J. Marks and Shipen Lebzelter's *Rock and Other Four Letter Words*, an album of free jazz and psychedelic music mixed with audio clips of rock musicians such as Ginger Baker, Tim Buckley, and Brian Wilson.

Despite Columbia's alleged skepticism about the project, Carlos and Elkind's album would not have been the first surprising interpretation of Bach's music to be released that decade. The 1960s had already seen several unorthodox recorded renditions of Baroque music. In 1963, five years before *Switched-On Bach* was released, Ward Swingle's eight-voice ensemble the Swingle Singers recorded *Bach's Greatest Hits* (called *Jazz Sébastien Bach* in its French-language release). The Swingles' album, featuring vocal renditions of Bach's keyboard and orchestral music, was a surprise hit and earned the group a Grammy award for Best New Artist. Similarly, the 1965 album *The Baroque Beatles Book* was an Elektra/Nonesuch album in which musicologist Joshua Rifkin and an ad hoc group of orchestral musicians created J. S. Bach-style instrumental pieces based on melodies borrowed from Beatles songs.

Yet another surprising but commercially successful approach to Bach's music came from the iconoclastic Canadian pianist Glenn Gould. In recordings, Gould would hum along his own improvised lines of counterpoint, and he often played the music at faster tempi than any other musician had before. Gould's behavior was eccentric as well: he wore heavy winter clothing during recording sessions and insisted on soaking his extremities in very hot water in between takes. He brought his own chair to recording sessions and sat extremely close to the piano. Gould was also signed to Columbia, and the label appears to have tolerated his personality and unprecedented musical interpretations because Gould's music sold well: his 1955 debut album of Bach's *Goldberg Variations* had sold approximately forty thousand copies in its first few years, an outstanding number for a classical album during that period. Although Carlos and Elkind's work would be the first synthesizer rendition of Bach's music, it certainly wouldn't have been the first unusual approach to the repertoire that Columbia or other labels had signed and released.

The team gave the album master to Columbia in the summer of 1968. There was some haggling over what to name the album. Elkind and Carlos wanted to call it "The Electronic Bach," inspired in some part by Rifkin's *The Baroque Beatles Book*.[72] After being presented with several title options from Columbia, Carlos and Elkind eventually warmed to the proposed *Switched-On Bach*. Amused by both the title itself and by its acronym (SOB), Carlos thought the title reflected the fact that the album was all in good fun: "To me, the project had a smile around the corners of the mouth."[73] She didn't want anyone to take it too seriously.[74]

Carlos did not discuss her gender with Elkind until after they had signed the contract with Columbia.[75] Only once they had signed did Carlos disclose to Elkind that she was in the process of transitioning to female. As noted in the previous chapter, Carlos had been seeing Dr. Harry Benjamin since the fall of 1967, and she had begun taking estrogen at some point in 1968. She has said her appearance at the time was "strikingly abnormal" because she was in an awkward phase of her transition.[76] Elkind recalled affectionately that she had simply accepted Carlos as "a wonderful person" without much con-sideration of her gender or appearance.[77] It seems that Carlos disclosed her gender identity to Elkind because she wasn't sure how they should credit and market their album.

Because "Walter Carlos" was practically nonexistent by the summer of 1968, Rachel Elkind recalled that her friend was hesitant to put that person's name on the album.[78] Since Carlos did envision an eventual future in which the album could be credited to her and not to "Walter," she and Elkind devised a workaround: what they called Trans-Electronic Music Productions Inc. or TEMPI.[79] To Elkind, the name was apt because the album and its music were transcending both Bach and electronics.[80]

The album's cover was another story altogether. It featured a bizarre but iconic image of a Bach-like figure, complete with powdered wig. Carlos and Elkind were furious about the first version of the cover, which had the Bach character sitting at the console and listening to his headphones.[81] The image was full of technical errors: the character's headphones were plugged into a 914 filter module, but they were plugged into the input, not the output, and then the module wasn't even connected to anything. In other words, this character had headphones on but wouldn't have had any sound coming through them.[82] Gene Lees of *High Fidelity*, one of the first critics to review the album, wrote, "So much for Columbia's respect for Carlos's curious genius and for the public's intelligence."[83] A subsequent version of the cover, and the version best known, had the figure standing and free of the headphones.

One reason Gene Lees was so disturbed by the inaccuracies on the cover of *Switched-On Bach* was that he knew the album was going to be huge. He lamented that Columbia appeared to be treating the album as a gimmick be-cause, he wrote, "This is one of the most significant classical albums in a long, long time."[84] He was right. *Switched-On Bach* was first released in September of 1968, and the commercial and critical response was beyond anything an-yone working on the project had anticipated. Even Elkind, who thought the record was at least saleable, said she had no idea that it would explode in the way that it did.[85] The result of this kind of overnight success was, for Carlos, both a dream come true and an absolute nightmare come to life.

Listening to *Switched-On Bach* creates a sort of auditory paradox. How can something be so mechanical and so human at the same time? It's motoric without seeming motorized. It's novel without being a cheap novelty. It's an abstraction without being abstract. Nobody could mistake the sounds of the

Moog for those created with acoustic instruments, but the performances on this album cannot be dismissed as purely mechanical or automated. There are no abstract bleeps or chirps, no sense that the music is being spit out by some algorithm. Each individual note from Bach's scores was created and placed with such care that the collective result is richly nuanced and expressive. Despite all of Carlos's concerns that the Moog's lack of a touch-sensitive keyboard was a detriment to her expressivity, the music of *Switched-On Bach* is audibly human.

Carlos did more than just feed another composer's notated music into a machine and record the sonic output. Carlos used Bach's score as if it were an architectural blueprint, but she created all of her construction and building materials from scratch. She realized each individual note that Bach had written down, creating not only its pitch and instrumental color but also its shading, attack, decay, conclusion, and resonance. Isolate any individual note on the album, and that note has a unique personality and sonic character. A single note has its own ebb and flow, its own attack and decay, its own surge and retreat.

Take, for example, the realization of the two-part invention in F major that first captured Elkind's attention. The piece flies by at a breakneck tempo, taking only about forty seconds. Each of the two contrapuntal lines are impeccably clean, allowing the listener to focus easily on a single line or on how the two lines interact. The Moog, in Carlos's hands, makes Bach's contrapuntal lines crystalline. Other pieces on the album have distinct melodies, such as the Sinfonia to Cantata no. 29 and the two chorales, *Wachet auf* and *Jesu, Joy of Man's Desiring*. In these pieces, the melodies are clear but are perfectly balanced with the remaining lines of music. No single line dominates the texture or drowns out any other: the melody is prominent, but the other parts are placed in such a way that they are easy to hear and follow.

More than half a century after *Switched-On Bach* was first released, it is challenging to convey exactly how startling it sounded to audiences at the time. It was stunning, both in its audio quality as well as in its sounds that had never been heard before, at least not in the way that Carlos presented them. *Switched-On Bach* was a novelty in that it was innovative and unprecedented; it was a demonstration of what this kind of synthesizer was capable of doing in the right artistic hands. The synthesizer was not unknown to American audiences in the late 1960s, but nobody had used it quite as Carlos had. Most of the music produced on synthesizers at the time was still abstract, eschewing conventional ideas of melody and harmony. The goal Carlos and

Elkind had was to create an album that would show listeners that music produced on the synthesizer was accessible. To say that they achieved their goal
would be an understatement.

The critical and commercial success of *Switched-On Bach* cannot be
overstated. Critics were agog, and sales went through the roof. Harold
C. Schonberg, Donal Henahan, Leonard Feather, and other leading music
critics of the day called it "sophisticated," "stunning," "serious," "legitimate,"
"exciting," "genius," "valuable," "sheer joy," "fun," "electrifying," "brilliant,"
and many other superlatives. Thomas Willis of the *Chicago Tribune* said he
would take the album with him to a desert island.[86] Schonberg wrote in the
New York Times that he would be buying up Moog stock if it wasn't a conflict
of interest with his position as a music critic.[87]

Music critics weren't the only people blown away by this new album. Even
some of the most famous classical musicians of the era were impressed. Sir
Georg Solti, the conductor of the Chicago Symphony Orchestra, expressed
his skepticism for electronic music to an interviewer while in the same breath
praising *Switched-On Bach* as "fascinating" and "quite extraordinary."[88]
Leonard Bernstein used the album and its title as the inspiration for an entire
Young People's Concert television episode called "Bach Transmogrified." In
fact, according to his handwritten script for the April 1969 episode, Bernstein
initially wanted to call the episode "Switched-On Bach," but he later struck
out that title and replaced it with "Bach Transmogrified."[89] Bernstein told
his viewers that the episode would include Bach "switched-on, turned on,
rocked, rolled, shaken, and baked."[90] Even if people weren't talking about
or listening to *Switched-On Bach*, they were hearing about it: the interview
with Solti appeared on the front page of the *Chicago Tribune*, and Bernstein's
Young People's Concerts were broadcast on CBS and syndicated in some forty
countries around the world.

Perhaps no one was a greater fan of *Switched-On Bach* than Glenn Gould.
In December 1968, before most of the public had even heard of *Switched-On
Bach*, Gould wrote a massive piece for the Canadian magazine *Saturday Night*
entitled "The Record of the Decade." For pages and pages, he gushed about
the album's attributes, the Moog synthesizer, the recording techniques, and
the ways in which the album effortlessly seemed to push back at the current
performance practice movement. He praised its "unflagging musicality" and
hailed it as "an inkling of the future."[91] Moreover, he found it to be one of the
greatest feats every achieved in the history of keyboard performance, noting

that the keyboard in this context was "the three-octave, electric-action, one-note-at-a-time keyboard of the Moog synthesizer."[92]

Carlos suspected that some of Gould's affection for the album was related to his own choice to perform only in the recording studio, because *Switched-On Bach* had demonstrated that Bach, and really any music, could be rendered exquisitely without necessarily requiring any type of live performance.[93] Gould wrote that *Switched-On Bach* provided sure evidence that "live music never was best."[94] To Gould, the album was "one of the most startling achievements of the recording industry in this generation."[95] The enormous musical and artistic success of *Switched-On Bach* would have provided ample evidence for Gould's idea that music did not have to be made live and, in fact, was usually better off if created in the recording studio.

Glenn Gould's approach to Bach, with his hummed improvisations and breakneck tempos, was inconsistent, to say the least, with the approaches espoused by proponents of what is called performance practice. The movement is also sometimes called historically informed practice, or HIP. In the 1950s and 1960s, some classical musicians began to advocate that Bach's music should only be played exactly the way that it would have been played in Bach's time. Musicians and historians went to great lengths to research exactly what types of instruments the musicians in Bach's orchestras would have played, and they tried to get those exact types of instruments themselves or else create replicas. Rosters and pay records at the churches where Bach's music was played were scrutinized to determine exactly how many people played and sang on each part. Musicians meticulously worked to recreate the dynamics, tempi, and tunings of Bach's time in order to perform the music as close to its original context as possible.

A few critics echoed the values of performance practice in their reviews of *Switched-On Bach*. Schonberg, despite his desire to buy Moog stock, wasn't actually a fan of the album, at least in terms of how Bach's music was presented. He wrote, "As an indication of what can be done with the Moog synthesizer, *Switched-On Bach* is breathtaking. As an example of Bach style it is pretty bad."[96] Later in the same review, Schonberg said that although the album was being hailed as a modern approach to Bach, "I do not want a modern approach to Bach. I want Bach's approach to Bach."[97] A reviewer for the *Washington Post* who signed only "P. H." to their review claimed, "If you are at all concerned with music, and especially with Bach . . . then I say it stinks and I say that if Bach were here today he'd throw up."[98] Like Schonberg, P. H. praised the album as "a phenomenal demonstration of what today's synthesizer can do" but was not impressed with its interpretation of Bach's music. In fact, these two critics were actually echoing Elkind and Carlos's stated intention for the album, which was that Bach's contrapuntal music would make the ideal vehicle for demonstrating just exactly what a synthesizer was capable of doing.

As they had been putting the album together, Carlos and Elkind knew that performance practice advocates and other classical music experts or purists might be disturbed by this synthesized approach to Bach.[99] In anticipation of these critiques, they had partnered with the musicologist Benjamin Folkman during the album's production. Carlos and Folkman had worked together at Gotham and co-authored pieces for Moog's *Electronic Music Review* journal. According to Elkind, Folkman was an expert in ornamentation in Baroque music.[100] His knowledge would help them make the sounds on the album as "authentic" as possible, keeping in mind, of course, that the sounds were being rendered on an instrument that Bach likely never could have even imagined might one day exist.[101]

Folkman wrote extensive liner notes for *Switched-On Bach*, explaining every piece in the context of Bach's original composition and what sounds the listener could expect to hear on Carlos's album. An excerpt from his description of the first movement of the Brandenburg Concerto no. 3, for example, reads: "A querulous second theme keeps intruding and getting shouted down, until the cellos and bass at last invert it, turn it into a nightmare, and exorcise it." Folkman's role, Elkind asserted years later, helped insulate the album from criticism by classical music scholars and critics.[102]

Critics such as Schonberg and P. H. were very much in the minority in terms of their negative responses to the album: virtually everyone else was enamored with it. *Switched-On Bach* shattered every sales record for classical music in history. It quickly ousted Van Cliburn's 1958 RCA Victor recording of Peter Ilyich Tchaikovsky's Piano Concerto no. 1 as the bestselling classical album of all time. It stayed at the top of *Billboard*'s Classical chart for more than three years, from 1969 into 1972. It even spent some time high on the *Billboard* 200 chart. It finished 1969 as the twenty-first bestselling album of the year in any genre; number one that year was Iron Butterfly's *In-A-Gadda-Da-Vida*.

What happens when you're the artist behind the most popular classical album in the history of recorded music but you can't appear in public without fear of being the object of ridicule or the victim of physical violence? Wendy

Carlos would later describe this period of her life to *Keyboard* magazine's Dominic Milano in Dickensian terms: "It was a terrible and a wonderful time."[103] In the spring of 1969—when *Switched-On Bach* was only being out-sold by the *Hair* soundtrack, Blood, Sweat & Tears' eponymous album, and Iron Butterfly's *Ball*—Carlos socially transitioned to female.[104] After that, she would only dress as "Walter" if she absolutely had to appear in public for the sake of promoting her music.[105] She would turn thirty in November of that year.

Despite the use of the TEMPI acronym on the album's cover, journalists and listeners had every reason to believe that a man named Walter Carlos was the person behind the project. Rachel Elkind's notes on the back of the record sleeve gush about "the genius of Walter Carlos," and the album credits "Walter Carlos with the assistance of Benjamin Folkman." Folkman's notes also detail the role that Carlos played in the production of sounds the listener was hearing. A note on the album from Bob Moog praised "Walter Carlos's realizations" as a "dazzling display of virtuosity." A clever acronym couldn't hide Carlos's predominant role in the album. Perhaps if the album hadn't been so successful, the acronym would have helped Carlos obfuscate her transition. Unfortunately for her, there was a clamor for interviews with and demonstrations by "Walter Carlos" at the same time that "he" was fading from existence.

Carlos never expected *Switched-On Bach* to have the kind of success that it did.[106] The last thing she wanted during this period was any kind of publicity, let alone any notoriety.[107] All she wanted was to hide away and transition, or, as she said, "undergo my transformation."[108] But just as she transitioned, she became one of the most in-demand people in American popular culture. "Walter Carlos" had been left behind, and yet she still had to dredge him up if she wanted to appear in public at all to promote her music.[109] Carlos was trapped: her album was more successful than she ever could have imagined, and she wasn't able to promote it because of her gender and the risk it posed for her to disclose who she was.

If Carlos had disclosed her gender identity following the release of *Switched-On Bach*, such a move would have been almost without precedent. In the late 1960s, many people in the United States were only vaguely acquainted with the notion of a person being transgender. Dr. Harry Benjamin's *The Transsexual Phenomenon* had been published in 1966, but it wasn't a book that the average American household would have had on its bookshelves or coffee table. People in the United States were probably more likely to have purchased a copy of Christine Jorgensen's autobiography, first published in 1967. Jorgensen had transitioned to female in Copenhagen in the late 1940s and was the public face of transgender identity in the United States for decades. As Rachel Elkind recalled, in the late 1960s, Jorgensen was the only transgender person most Americans had ever heard of.[110] Jorgensen's fame is considered by historians to be a watershed moment in the history of transgender rights because she brought an unprecedented amount of attention to the issues surrounding gender identity.

Christine Jorgensen was young, blonde, beautiful—and a former GI. She had been drafted (under her birth gender and name) and served in World War II, and then she stayed in Europe after the war in order to transition. The first major news outlet to run a story about her was the *New York Daily News*, and she earned a front-page story with the headline "Ex-GI Becomes Blonde Beauty."[111] As transgender historian Susan Stryker has noted, Christine Jorgensen was the most written-about topic in the media in 1953, even as hydrogen bombs were being tested, a war in Korea was ongoing, Queen Elizabeth II was crowned, and Jonas Salk invented the polio vaccine.[112]

Stryker suggests that the media attention surrounding Jorgensen was consistent with anxieties about gender, gender roles, and sexuality in American culture during the 1950s:

> With millions of women who had worked outside the home during the war being steered back toward feminine domesticity, and millions of demobilized military men trying to fit themselves back into the civilian social order, questions of what made a man a man, or a woman a woman, and what their respective roles in life should be, were very much up for debate. The feminist movement of the 1960s took shape in reaction to social conservative solutions to these questions, and transgender issues have been a touchstone for those debates ever since fate thrust Christine Jorgensen into the spotlight.[113]

Christine Jorgensen's identity, and particularly the notion that gender itself and all of a gender's associated social roles were not ironclad, tapped directly into these postwar cultural attitudes.

Jorgensen did try to make a career for herself. She starred in her own cabaret show for many years and frequently appeared in stage productions. She toured widely and gave lectures at college campuses. By and large, her role was as the face of and spokesperson for transgender identity in its entirety.

She opened many doors and shed light on an aspect of identity that many people did not even know existed. Jorgensen would receive thousands of letters from other transgender people thanking her for her courage and praising her as a champion or a liberator of sorts. At the same time, much of the media attention surrounding her ranged from curious to exploitative, from making her the butt of jokes to framing her as some kind of monster. In 1970, her autobiography was adapted into a film called *The Christine Jorgensen Story*; text on the film's poster included pull quotes such as, "Did the surgeon's knife make me a woman or a freak?"

The precedent Jorgensen had set was that a transgender woman would be splashed all over the media, scrutinized, and potentially mocked or even worse. It doesn't seem surprising, then, that Carlos felt she needed to protect herself, her friends, and her music after she transitioned.[114] Carlos was also terrified about her personal safety; she has spoken about physical assaults that she experienced as a child, and in the twenty-first century, she has written about being afraid of being beaten or even killed.[115] In a 2015 survey of transgender individuals conducted by the National Center for Transgender Equality, almost half of respondents had been verbally harassed and 10 percent had been physically attacked because of their gender identity—in the previous year only.[116]

Further, transgender women were frequently sexualized by mainstream culture. As Joanne Meyerowitz as shown, sex became an increasingly popular topic in mainstream magazines during the 1960s, no longer relegated to tabloids and pulp paperbacks. The sex lives of transgender women, especially transgender women who were sex workers, were a favorite topic.[117] One popular example was Gore Vidal's novel *Myra Breckinridge*, which was published in 1968, the same year *Switched-On Bach* was released. *Myra Breckinridge* was one of the first appearances in mainstream fiction of a transgender character, although it wasn't exactly the type of positive representation that many transgender people might have hoped for. After transitioning to female, Myra seeks revenge against all men for the torture she had previously endured as the gay male Myron. She exacts her revenge by humiliating, assaulting, and raping men, events that Vidal depicted in graphic detail. Many transgender people were horrified by Vidal's novel; Christine Jorgensen said it was tasteless garbage. She lamented that the progress she had made over the past fifteen years for increasing positive visibility for transgender people was likely to go down the drain thanks to *Myra Breckinridge*.[118]

Carlos didn't just have threats of physical violence and verbal harassment to consider: she could very well have been evicted from her apartment and never been hired anywhere again, with absolutely no legal recourse for either scenario. Even in the twenty-first century, there are no anti-discrimination laws in the United States protecting the rights of transgender people for housing, medical care, and employment. Like Jorgensen, Carlos's career might potentially be limited to "professional transgender spokesperson" if nobody would hire her and people focused only on her gender identity. Any article about her from that point forward could have been accompanied by "before" and "after" photos and lengthy discussions of her gender identity instead of information about her music.

Because Carlos thought she would be perceived as some kind of oddity, she expressed concern that her gender transition might complicate interpretations of her music.[119] Both she and Elkind have repeatedly used the term "circus" when discussing the types of responses they wanted to prevent in the context of Carlos's gender identity.[120] As Elkind recalled, "We didn't want the music to get confused. This was already very, very different, this music."[121] Carlos was afraid that people who were looking for ways to denigrate the synthesizer would find it easy to do if the instrument's new poster child suddenly turned out to be a "clown."[122] If Carlos was a clown, then the music she had created and the technology she had used to create it might also be categorized as a circus, which was a risk she decided she couldn't afford to take.[123] The stakes were too high, so she decided to hide the fact that she had transitioned in order to protect herself, her career, and her music.

As a result, she and Elkind set about maintaining the illusion of the existence of Walter Carlos for the next decade. The extents to which they went to keep up the charade were exhausting for the both of them and strained their friendship and professional relationship nearly to the breaking point.[124] For a few months, Carlos tried to appear publicly as "Walter" in order to promote her music, but this approach turned out to be unsustainable. Maintaining the illusion of "Walter" after she had transitioned nearly drove Carlos to attempt suicide.[125] In the very few photos of Carlos from this era, she looks as if she's wearing some sort of ill-fitting costume and appears anywhere from uncomfortable to miserable.

Any appearance as "Walter Carlos" by early 1969 required a wig, fake sideburns, and elaborate makeup. When Hugh Downs interviewed Carlos for a February 1969 episode of the *Today* show on NBC, Elkind overheard people arguing backstage about whether Carlos was a man or a woman; one person guessed that she was a woman dressed as a man.[126] During an appearance on *The Dick Cavett Show*, Carlos recalled that Cavett and the other guest, actor Peter Ustinov, kept looking her up and down suspiciously and seemed very uncomfortable in her presence.[127] Makeup artists noticed and commented on Carlos's glued-on sideburns and lack of facial hair, so she started doing her own makeup before any television appearances to keep makeup artists away from her face.[128]

A low point for her came after an appearance with the St. Louis Symphony in 1969.[129] She had been invited to perform a concert and demonstration of synthesizer music and be interviewed onstage by the conductor. Carlos and Elkind traveled to St. Louis together, and Carlos wept the entire time. Elkind feared that Carlos would have a nervous breakdown, and Carlos considered committing suicide rather than going through with the live event. At one point, she locked herself in her hotel room and told Elkind, "Let Walter go and do it."[130] Elkind pleaded with her to make the appearance, so Carlos put on her "Walter" costume with its wig and fake sideburns, filling in her pores with eyebrow pencil to create the illusion of five o'clock shadow.[131] She said she lowered her voice as deep as she could and attempted to adopt a "macho" persona for the event.[132] That was one of the last times she appeared in public as "Walter." Since she was afraid to appear in public as herself, too, she effectively went into hiding for the next decade.

Carlos gave up many opportunities during this period in order to protect herself. Although she went into isolation to protect her music and her career, she separated herself from the world just when she was getting to be known as an artist. For example, although the Moog synthesizer and *Switched-On Bach* were at the center of the drafts for Leonard Bernstein's "Bach Transmogrified" *Young People's Concert* episode, Carlos was nowhere to be found. Early scripts of the episode suggest that Bernstein wanted Carlos to participate—Bernstein's drafts of this episode have him introducing and welcoming Carlos to the program as the Moog's "most famous interpreter."[133] But the episode that eventually aired did not mention Carlos at all. Several men wheeled a Moog synthesizer on the stage in front of the orchestra, and Bernstein spoke with equal parts affection and bewilderment about the instrument. He told his audience that it had produced the sounds on *Switched-On Bach*, "a very popular album which I'm sure most of you have listened to."[134] Bernstein then shared with his audience the sounds of a Bach fugue that had been rendered on the Moog synthesizer, but it was not a fugue Carlos had created or one that appeared on *Switched-On Bach*. Instead, it was a fugue created by Walter Sear, another early adopter of the Moog and a composer whose most famous credit at that point was the soundtrack to the Dustin Hoffman and Jon Voigt film *Midnight Cowboy*. Carlos was completely absent from the discussion in the episode. For a musician to not want to participate in a *Young People's Concert* episode, extraordinary circumstances would likely have to be at work.

The tides for transgender people were beginning to change in the late 1960s, although not nearly quickly or dramatically enough to have helped Carlos much at this point. In June 1969, at the same time that *Switched-On Bach* had settled in at the top of the classical charts and was holding its own on the pop charts, the Stonewall Riots were taking place not far from Carlos's home and studio. The Stonewall Inn in Greenwich Village was a bar where gay, lesbian, transgender, and gender-variant people could gather for cheap beer, good music on the jukebox, and a crowded dance floor.[135] Stonewall was frequently raided by the police, who usually left once bribes were paid. Sometimes the bar's occupants were arrested, beaten, and raped.

Accounts vary about what happened in response to the police raid that took place late on June 28, 1969: some accounts say they were resisting arrest, other accounts say that Sylvia Rivera, a transgender woman and one of the leading activists of the time, threw a beer bottle (some accounts say it was her shoe) at the police. Other bar patrons joined in, yelling and throwing things at the police, and the police responded by grabbing people out of the crowd and beating them. The balance of power tipped, however, as neighborhood residents emerged and joined the bar patrons in confronting the police. Many accounts claim that at least two thousand people had gathered at one point. The police were quickly outnumbered, and they barricaded themselves inside the Stonewall Inn and called for reinforcements. It took until dawn for the Tactical Patrol Force officers to break up the crowds, but the next night, even more people gathered at the Stonewall Inn to protest. More police came, and more violence ensued. The protests and police attempts to contain them lasted for several days, but the events at the Stonewall Inn galvanized activists in the area to take political action.

Stonewall is viewed as a landmark moment in LGBT history, but the role of transgender people is often written out of the story, as is the role of people of color. Within a month of the Stonewall Riots, Sylvia Rivera and others formed the Gay Liberation Front (GLF), but transgender people were quickly shut out of many gay activist organizations, even if they had helped found them. In response, Rivera—who was just seventeen at the time—and her friend Marsha P. Johnson, both transgender women of color, founded STAR, or Street Transvestite Action Revolutionaries. STAR's primary goal was to provide safety, housing, education, and food for transgender kids who had been kicked out of their own homes. They wanted to help protect young transgender people from the same kinds of danger they themselves had experienced; they even taught some of the young people how to read and write, since their educations had been disrupted by bullying or by being kicked out of their homes at a young age.[136]

Stonewall was just one beginning in the struggle for LGBT rights in the United States. It certainly wasn't the first time people had fought back, but Stonewall galvanized many movements that would advocate for LGBT rights for decades. Although transgender people had been on the front lines of the Stonewall riots themselves, transgender people were not necessarily included in the front lines of the activism and advocacy that would follow those riots. Nor did Stonewall or the activist groups that formed in its aftermath effect any immediate change. The slog for LGBT rights in the United States was extremely slow. Only with the Supreme Court ruling in *Obergefell v. Hodges* in June of 2015 were same-sex couples granted legal right to marry in the United States. As of this writing, a half-century after Stonewall, transgender people are still largely unprotected legally from discrimination in hiring, housing, and medical treatment. Some states have passed protective laws, but there are currently no federal laws on the books designating transgender people as a protected class or requiring equal treatment for transgender people.

Carlos likely heard about the Stonewall Riots, since they were happening in her own city, but there is no record that she got involved in any kind of the activism that followed. She has said that she was never interested in any kind of fellowship with other transgender people; she stayed away from what she called the transgender "pipeline," referring to everything from dance clubs to support groups, all in the service of protecting her career.[137] She was too afraid of what consequences she might face professionally if people knew who she was. So Carlos, with Elkind's help, settled into hiding for the next decade. She continued to create and release music under Walter's name, but she had to release it out into the world with absolutely no ability to go out and speak about it unless she revealed who she was. It would take a decade before she was finally ready to disclose her transition.

Notes

1. Mary Campbell, "Recording Surf is Slippery Job," *Associated Press* (August 1972), n.p.
2. No author, "Rachel Elkind—Biography," 1. Allan Kozinn personal collection.
3. No author, "Rachel Elkind—Biography," 1.
4. Trevor Pinch, "unpublished interview with Rachel Elkind," (October 10, 1999), n.p. (hereafter Pinch, "Rachel Elkind"). Many thanks to Trevor Pinch for sharing this document with me.
5. Campbell, "Recording Surf is Slippery Job," n.p.
6. Pinch, "Rachel Elkind," n.p.
7. Campbell, "Recording Surf is Slippery Job," n.p.
8. Campbell, "Recording Surf is Slippery Job," n.p.
9. Pinch, "Rachel Elkind," n.p.
10. Campbell, "Recording Surf is Slippery Job," n.p.
11. Campbell, "Recording Surf is Slippery Job," n.p. Carlos has recounted their first meeting similarly.
12. Pinch, "Rachel Elkind," n.p.
13. Campbell, "Recording Surf is Slippery Job," n.p.
14. Pinch, "Rachel Elkind," n.p.
15. Pinch, "Rachel Elkind," n.p.
16. Dominic Milano, "Rachel Elkind," *Contemporary Keyboard* (December 1979): 36 (hereafter "Milano, "Rachel Elkind").
17. Pinch, "Rachel Elkind," n.p.
18. Milano, "Rachel Elkind," 36.
19. Kozinn, unpublished interview with Carlos, 38–39.
20. Pinch, "Rachel Elkind," n.p.
21. Pinch, "Rachel Elkind," n.p.
22. Donal Henahan, "A Tale of a Man and a Moog," *New York Times* (October 5, 1969), HF1.
23. Henahan, "A Tale of a Man and a Moog," HF1.
24. Wren, "Moog Is More Than a Vogue," 26.
25. Contact sheet of photos in Carlos's studio by an unidentified photographer can be found in the Robert Moog papers, #8629. Box 41, folder 2. Division of Rare and Manuscript Collections, Cornell University Library.
26. Wright, "Something Old, Something New," n.p.
27. Kozinn, " 'Switched-On Bach' Creator Returns," D22.
28. Milano, "Wendy Carlos" (1979), 33.
29. Kozinn, " 'Switched-On Bach' Creator Returns," D22.
30. Kozinn, " 'Switched-On Bach' Creator Returns," D22.
31. Wright, "Something Old, Something New," n.p.
32. Wright, "Something Old, Something New," n.p.
33. Wright, "Something Old, Something New," n.p.
34. Wright, "Something Old, Something New," n.p.
35. Pinch, "Rachel Elkind," n.p.

36. Vail, *The Synthesizer*, 327–329.
37. Kozinn, " 'Switched-On Bach' Creator Returns," D22.
38. Holmes, *Electronic and Experimental Music*, 534, note 23.
39. Holmes, *Electronic and Experimental Music*, 534, note 23.
40. All information about the recording equipment used for *Switched-On Bach* is drawn from Wendy Carlos, "Audio note," available at http://www.wendycarlos.com/+sob.html.
41. Baker, "Wendy Carlos," n.p.
42. Holmes, *Electronic and Experimental Music*, 267.
43. Wright, "Something Old, Something New," n.p.
44. Baker, "Wendy Carlos," n.p.
45. Wright, "Something Old, Something New," n.p.
46. See, for example, Baker, "Wendy Carlos," n.p.
47. Carlos, "Synthesizers," *WEC*, 330.
48. Baker, "Wendy Carlos," n.p.
49. Wright, "Something Old, Something New," n.p.
50. Baker, "Wendy Carlos," n.p.
51. Baker, "Wendy Carlos."
52. Milano, "Wendy Carlos" (1979), 62.
53. Milano, "Rachel Elkind," 37.
54. Pinch, "Rachel Elkind," n.p.
55. Pinch, "Rachel Elkind," n.p.
56. Carlos, liner notes to *Switched-On Bach 2000*, 16.
57. P.R. [possibly Philip Ramey], unpublished interview with Wendy Carlos (1979), 13. Allan Kozinn personal collection.
58. Kozinn, unpublished interview with Carlos, 2.
59. Carlos, liner notes to *Switched-On Bach 2000*, 19.
60. Milano, "Wendy Carlos" (1979), 35.
61. Pinch, "Rachel Elkind," n.p.
62. Pinch, "Rachel Elkind," n.p.
63. Kozinn, unpublished interview with Elkind, 40.
64. Bell, "*Playboy* interview," 102.
65. Pinch, "Rachel Elkind," n.p.
66. Pinch, "Rachel Elkind," n.p.
67. Pinch, "Rachel Elkind," n.p.
68. Pinch, "Rachel Elkind," n.p.
69. Elkind's recollection of $1,000 is quoted in Pinch, "Rachel Elkind," n.p.; Carlos's memory of $2,500 appears in Susan Reed, "After a Sex Change and Several Eclipses, Wendy Carlos Treads a New Digital Moonscape," *People* (July 1, 1985).
70. Pinch, "Rachel Elkind," n.p.
71. Pinch, "Rachel Elkind," n.p.
72. Pinch, "Rachel Elkind," n.p.
73. Blinx, "From Bach to the Future," 60.
74. Blinx, "From Bach to the Future," 60.

75. Pinch, "Rachel Elkind," n.p.

76. Bell, unpublished interview notes.

77. Pinch, "Rachel Elkind," n.p.

78. Pinch, "Rachel Elkind," n.p.

79. Pinch, "Rachel Elkind," n.p.

80. Pinch, "Rachel Elkind," n.p.

81. Pinch, "Rachel Elkind," n.p.

82. Pinch and Trocco, *Analog Days*, 142.

83. Gene Lees, "The Electronic Bach: Johann Sebastian in a Wild, Wild Breakthrough," *High Fidelity* (December 1968), 3.

84. Lees, "The Electronic Bach," 3.

85. Pinch, "Rachel Elkind," n.p.

86. Thomas Willis, "*Tribune* Interview Music Meteor Solti," *Chicago Tribune* December 22, 1968), A1.

87. Harold Schonberg, "A Merry Time with the Moog?" *New York Times* (February 16, 1969), D17.

88. Willis, "Music Meteor Solti," A1.

89. Leonard Bernstein, "Bach Transmogrified" script (1969), 1. Library of Congress Music Division. Box 112, Folder 7.

90. Bernstein, "Bach Transmogrified," 2.

91. Glenn Gould, "Record of the Decade," *Saturday Night* (December 1968). Reprinted in *The Glenn Gould Reader*, ed. Tim Page (New York: Knopf, 1984), 432, 434 (citations are to the 1984 reprint).

92. Gould, "Record of the Decade," 431.

93. Oteri, "Wendy's World," 2.

94. Gould, "Record of the Decade," 430.

95. Gould, "Record of the Decade," 430.

96. Schonberg, "Merry Time with the Moog," D17.

97. Schonberg, "Merry Time with the Moog," D17.

98. P. H., "The Switched-On Bach Bit," *Washington Post* (February 9, 1969), 171.

99. Pinch, "Rachel Elkind," n.p.

100. Milano, "Rachel Elkind," 36.

101. Pinch, "Rachel Elkind," n.p.

102. Pinch, "Rachel Elkind," n.p.

103. Milano, "Wendy Carlos" (1979), 68.

104. Bell, "*Playboy* interview," 91.

105. Bell, "*Playboy* interview," 91.

106. Milano, "Wendy Carlos" (1979), 68.

107. Milano, "Wendy Carlos" (1979), 68.

108. Milano, "Wendy Carlos" (1979), 68.

109. Bell, "*Playboy* interview," 91.

110. Pinch, "Rachel Elkind," n.p.

111. Ben White, "Ex-GI Becomes Blonde Beauty: Operations Transform Bronx Youth," *New York Daily News* (December 1, 1952), 1..

112. Stryker, *Transgender History*, 47–50.

113. Stryker, *Transgender History*, 48.

114. Bell, "*Playboy* interview," 81.

115. Bell, "*Playboy* interview," 82; Carlos, "Hall of Shame," available at https://web.ar-chive.org/web/20141110014545/http://www.wendycarlos.com/ouch.

116. National Center for Transgender Equality, "The Report of the 2015 U.S. Transgender Survey," available at https://www.transequality.org/sites/default/files/docs/usts/USTS%20Full%20Report%20-%20FINAL%201.6.17.pdf. More than 27,000 individuals responded to the survey.

117. Information about the increased sexualization of transgender women in the 1960s is drawn from Meyerowitz, *How Sex Changed*, 202–204.

118. Meyerowitz, *How Sex Changed*, 204.

119. Bell, unpublished interview notes with Wendy Carlos, 1978–79. Arthur Bell papers, Billy Rose Theatre Division, New York Public Library.

120. Bell, unpublished interview notes; Pinch, "Rachel Elkind," n.p.

121. Pinch, "Rachel Elkind," n.p.

122. Bell, unpublished interview notes, 1979.

123. Bell, unpublished interview notes, 1979.

124. Bell, "*Playboy* interview," 82.

125. Bell, "*Playboy* interview," 100.

126. Bell, "*Playboy* interview," 99–100.

127. Bell, "*Playboy* interview," 100.

128. Bell, "*Playboy* interview," 100.

129. Bell, "*Playboy* interview," 100.

130. Bell, "*Playboy* interview," 100.

131. Bell, "*Playboy* interview," 100.

132. Bell, "*Playboy* interview," 100.

133. Bernstein, "Bach Transmogrified," 5.

134. *Young People's Concerts: Bach Transmogrified* (original air date April 27, 1969), 15:00–20:45.

135. Unless otherwise noted, the information in this section about Stonewall is drawn from Stryker, *Transgender History*, 82–89.

136. For more information about early activist movements among transgender people in New York, Los Angeles, and other major American metropolitan areas during the 1960s and 1970s, see Meyerowitz, *How Sex Changed*, 235–241.

137. Bell, "*Playboy* interview," 86.

4

Something Went Wrong (1970–1978)

The cultural impact that *Switched-On Bach* had in the late 1960s and early 1970s cannot be overstated. It brought an entirely new perspective for how music could be created and heard. The album and Carlos won three Grammy Awards in 1969: Best Engineered Recording, Classical; Best Classical Performance—Instrumental Soloist or Soloists (With or Without Orchestra); and Album of the Year, Classical. The album's enormous commercial success inspired dozens of copycat albums.[1] RCA Victor released *The Moog Strikes Bach... (To Say Nothing of Chopin, Mozart, Rachmaninoff, Paganini and Prokofieff)*, whose title suggests that it was a direct response to *Switched-On Bach*. Charles Lishon and Hans Wurman used a Moog synthesizer and several other musical instruments, such as the Clavinet, to render music of J. S. Bach, Sergei Rachmaninoff, Wolfgang Amadeus Mozart, Frederic Chopin, and Sergei Prokofiev. Another album was Columbia's *Switched-On Rock*, in which Kenny Ascher and Alan Foust, as "The Moog Machine," created Moog synthesizer renditions of top 40 hits of the era, including the Rolling Stones' "Jumpin' Jack Flash," Ohio Express's "Yummy Yummy Yummy," and The Beatles' "Hey Jude." Albums of *Switched-On* renditions of music by Frederic Chopin, George Gershwin, the Beatles, Christmas music, Nashville country, and dozens of others were released.

Critics almost universally agreed that none of these albums even came close to *Switched-On Bach* in terms of technical complexity or musical artistry. Of Columbia's *Switched-On Rock*, Robert Hilburn of the *Los Angeles Times* wrote, "Rarely has rock sounded so bad."[2] An unnamed critic for *Melody Maker* called it a "bore" and "an artistic failure."[3] Most of these albums were simply trying to cash in on the popularity of *Switched-On Bach* and the sounds of the Moog synthesizer. Many of these albums attempted to play on Bob Moog's name in the title, but a lack of due diligence on the musicians' or promoters' parts meant that many record titles' wordplay were based on a mispronunciation of Moog's name: following its Dutch origin, "Moog" rhymes with "vogue." There was *Music to Moog By, Moog Indigo*, perhaps most painful of all, *The Plastic Cow Goes MOOOOOOG*.

Carlos and Elkind appear not to have been immune to the financial lure of this newfound popularity of the Moog synthesizer and its sounds. The second album of their contract with Columbia was called *The Well-Tempered Synthesizer*, a play on the title of a book of keyboard music by Johann Sebastian Bach called *The Well-Tempered Clavier*. It was released in November 1969, almost exactly a year after the initial release of *Switched-On Bach*. Like *Switched-On Bach*, *The Well-Tempered Synthesizer* included Moog synthesizer renditions of familiar Baroque music, such as selections from George Frederic Handel's *Water Music Suite* and Claudio Monteverdi's early opera *L'Orfeo*. They also featured four different keyboard sonatas by Domenico Scarlatti. The only piece on the album by Johann Sebastian Bach was the Brandenburg Concerto no. 4, of which Glenn Gould said it was no less than "the finest performance of any of the Brandenburgs—live, canned, or intuited—I've ever heard."[4] At the same time, Carlos has said she believes that *The Well-Tempered Synthesizer* would not have sold as well if it had been released first.[5]

Carlos later recalled that she told herself at the time that she was doing a second album in the vein of *Switched-On Bach* because she was trying to refine her techniques and produce music that was more precise and less coarse than *Switched-On Bach*.[6] Carlos also expanded into the creation of vocal sounds using the Moog, realizing Monteverdi's choral piece *Domine ad adjuvandum* from his *Vespers*. Both Elkind and Thomas Frost, then the music director at Columbia Masterworks, assured listeners in *The Well-Tempered Synthesizer*'s liner notes that this album was far more refined than its predecessor.

Carlos and Elkind hadn't wanted to do another Baroque album, though. Carlos still wanted to do an album of her own original compositions, but both Columbia and Elkind convinced her that it wasn't yet the right time.[7] Carlos and Elkind also really wanted to create their own version of Modest Mussorgsky's *Pictures at an Exhibition* with the Moog synthesizer, but Columbia turned down their proposal.[8] Carlos and Elkind were devastated when first Keith Emerson and then Isao Tomita released their own synthesizer versions of *Pictures at an Exhibition* during the 1970s.[9] Even though Emerson's and Tomita's versions were very different than what Carlos and Elkind had envisioned for their interpretation, they would eventually scrap their idea for a *Pictures* album because they felt it had already been done.[10] In fact, Elkind claimed that Peter Munves at Columbia had suggested the idea of *Pictures* to Tomita because Munves knew that Carlos and Elkind wanted to do it.[11]

Columbia and the record-breaking sales of *Switched-On Bach* eventually convinced them to do another album of Baroque music. By the time *The Well-Tempered Synthesizer* was released in late 1969, *Switched-On Bach* had already sold more than four hundred thousand copies. *Switched-On Bach* did not budge from its position at the top of the classical music charts until February 1972, when it was finally bumped to number two by the premiere recording of Leonard Bernstein's *MASS: A Theatre Piece for Singers, Players, and Dancers.*

Benjamin Folkman, Carlos's colleague at Gotham who had been a collaborator on *Switched-On Bach* and had authored the liner notes, was not part of the production of *The Well-Tempered Synthesizer*. It's not clear why he didn't participate in any subsequent Carlos productions. He does not appear to have ever spoken on the record about these projects. Elkind has said that Folkman left for France soon after the release of *Switched-On Bach* because he didn't want to work with them anymore.[12] Elkind and Carlos have suggested that it was probably for the best that Folkman left, though: Elkind went so far as to call Folkman's presence a "crutch" because he had done all of the research for them, but once he withdrew, the two women were forced to do the research themselves.[13] It was with Folkman's departure, both Carlos and Elkind have agreed, that Elkind was able to step up and became more of a collaborator and less of a producer.[14]

The Well-Tempered Synthesizer followed the same formulas as *Switched-On Bach*. It is impeccably clean and precise, and the paradoxical mix of mechanical sound and human expression are omnipresent. It is more of the same, which is both its greatest strength and its biggest weakness. Those who were hoping to hear major innovations and improvements in what the Moog synthesizer could do in the year since *Switched-On Bach* came out were going to be disappointed. Those who wanted to hear more "hits" of the seventeenth and eighteenth centuries rendered with great artistry on the Moog synthesizer would be pleased. The four sonatas by Domenico Scarlatti on the *Well-Tempered Synthesizer*, for example, offer the same type of contrapuntal clarity and precision as the three two-part Bach inventions on *Switched-On Bach*.

The most substantial addition to the *Well-Tempered Synthesizer* was Carlos's attempt to create vocal sounds with the Moog. On *Switched-On Bach*, Carlos had rendered the lines that Bach had written for singers as instrumental sounds, such as in the two chorales. The choral passages on the *Well-Tempered Synthesizer* aren't nearly as effective as the instrumental sounds are. Using the Moog, Carlos allowed the contrapuntal instrumental lines of Bach, Handel, Scarlatti, and their contemporaries to sparkle. The music of the vocal parts is not the problem, but Carlos just couldn't seem to get the Moog to enunciate words with much precision. The end result is muffled and sounds not unlike the voice of Charlie Brown's teacher, which Vince Guaraldi created using trombone "wah-wahs" and first introduced to audiences in the 1967 *Peanuts* special *You're in Love, Charlie Brown*.[15]

Because she was rarely appearing in public by late 1969, Carlos said very little about the *Well-Tempered Synthesizer* on the record when the album was released. In a short interview with Donal Henahan of the *New York Times*, Carlos mentioned that she was still struggling to get the Moog to produce consonants in the vocal passages.[16] Moreover, she complained to Henahan about the Moog synthesizer's shortcomings: "You have to fight with the instrument to get any musicality out of it."[17] By this time, however, Carlos had almost entirely withdrawn from the public eye, so she said practically nothing at the time about this new album.

The Well-Tempered Synthesizer was nominated for, but did not win, two Grammy Awards in 1970: Best Engineered Recording, Classical, and Best Classical Performance—losing to Pierre Boulez and the Cleveland Orchestra's recording of Igor Stravinsky's *The Rite of Spring*—and Instrumental Soloist or Soloists (With or Without Orchestra)—losing to violinist David Oistrakh and cellist Mstislav Rostropovich and their recording of the Concerto for Violin and Cello (also called the Double Concerto) of Johannes Brahms. Although *Switched-On Bach* had won the Classical Album of the Year the previous year, *The Well-Tempered Synthesizer* was not nominated in that category. That award went to (now Sir) Colin Davis and the Royal Opera House, Covent Garden Orchestra and Chorus for their recording of the massive *Les Troyens*, an opera by Hector Berlioz.

In her liner notes for *The Well-Tempered Synthesizer*, Rachel Elkind wrote, tongue in cheek, about everything that had "gone wrong" with the release of *Switched-On Bach*. "Something went wrong," she explained. "*Switched-On Bach* was meant to be an artistic experiment, a learning and testing vehicle, not the marked commercial success it has so clearly become."[18] Most who read the note probably found it funny, but for Carlos, this probably wouldn't have seemed like an ironic statement that Elkind made. Something had indeed gone wrong, because now she was famous and in demand, and she thought that revealing her identity would likely have devastating consequences for her music, her relationships, and her career.

Carlos's isolation prevented her not only from promoting her own music but also from working with other musicians on projects that involved the synthesizer. Popular music artists were inspired by *Switched-On Bach* to include the sounds of the Moog and other synthesizers into their music. Although a few artists such as the Monkees and the Doors had used synthesizers in their songs before *Switched-On Bach*, the instrument's popularity exploded in the late 1960s and early 1970s. Some artists pressed Bob Moog to create a synthesizer that could be played live, most notably Keith Emerson of Emerson, Lake, and Palmer (ELP). Bob Moog eventually created the so-called Monster Moog for ELP to use in live performances, a massive piece of equipment that was 17 square feet in size and weighed 550 pounds.[19]

Other musicians were fascinated with the sounds of the synthesizer and wanted to learn how to incorporate those sounds into their studio albums. Some of these artists tried to consult with Carlos, but she refused to meet with them. She recalled hiding in her own home when Stevie Wonder came over to check out her synthesizer and setup; she was afraid to even speak to him because she knew that her voice would give away the fact that she was a woman.[20] Wonder would go on to release album after album that featured the synthesizer, including *Music of My Mind* and *Talking Back*. For these and several other albums in the 1970s, Wonder worked with TONTO, the acronym of the self-proclaimed "Moogists in Residence" Malcolm Cecil and Bob Margouleff.[21] We can only speculate about what might have happened if Carlos had been able to work with Wonder on these or other projects.

Carlos may have missed an opportunity to work with Stevie Wonder, but she did find a way to collaborate with another one of the most respected artists of the era, film director Stanley Kubrick. Music was a crucial part of Kubrick's filmmaking and film editing process, and he often chose what music he wanted very early in the production process, sometimes even before the cameras rolled. Kubrick's musical choices for his films were lauded critically, perhaps most notably in *2001: A Space Odyssey*. The iconic soundtrack of *2001* featured existing pieces of classical music, such as the opening section of Richard Strauss's *Also sprach Zarathustra*, Johann Strauss II's *The Blue Danube Waltz*, and several pieces by György Ligeti.

MGM had rejected Kubrick's idea when he said he wanted to use a score of existing music for *2001*, so he commissioned a completely new score from Alex North. North had worked with Kubrick earlier on the film *Spartacus*. Although Kubrick had cautioned North that a few bits of his new score might end up being replaced with existing classical music, Kubrick didn't use a note of North's music, ignoring MGM and going through with his original plan of using existing music. North didn't find out that Kubrick hadn't included any of his music until he attended the film's premiere in April 1968.[22]

Kubrick had an encyclopedic knowledge of classical music recordings, and music played a greater role for him in the production process than it did for many film directors.[23] For example, he would play music for the actors and crew while filming scenes in order to help establish a mood. During the film editing process, Kubrick would use existing recordings of classical music in the temporary (temp) tracks, before the new score was added and the rest of the sound was edited. He often had a specific piece of music in mind for a particular scene even before he began to film it, so in many instances the temp tracks were more than just placeholders—they were the music Kubrick had wanted for that scene all along.

Kubrick's next film after *2001* was an adaptation of Anthony Burgess's 1962 dystopian novel *A Clockwork Orange*. In the novel, the character Alex is obsessed with the music of Ludwig van Beethoven—whom he affectionately calls "Ludwig Van"—a fact that is used to punish him later. Alex leads a gang of "droogs" in everything from reckless driving to burglary to assault to rape to murder. After Alex commits and is arrested and jailed for several violent crimes, he is reconditioned (tortured) using the Ludovico Technique to make him hate the violence that he once loved; a side effect is that he is also reconditioned against Beethoven's music. Alex now becomes violently ill when he hears the music of his once beloved Ludwig Van.

Carlos and Elkind were both familiar with Burgess's novel and the prominent role that Beethoven's music played in the story.[24] They had already been working on a synthesizer rendition of Beethoven's Symphony no. 9, the fourth movement of which includes the famous choral setting of Friedrich Schiller's poem "Ode to Joy." When they heard that Kubrick was going to direct the film adaptation of *A Clockwork Orange*, they knew they had to contact him and tell him about their music; Elkind recalled, "You know how you sometimes feel that somebody is just going to love you?"[25]

Things moved quickly. Elkind contacted their agent, Lucy Kroll, who knew Kubrick's attorney in Los Angeles.[26] The attorney was interested in their proposal and agreed to send Kubrick copies of *Switched-On Bach*, *The Well-Tempered Synthesizer*, the synthesized Beethoven that Carlos and Elkind had just created, and their new original composition called *Timesteps*.[27] Kubrick was clearly impressed with what he heard and acted immediately: Elkind recalled that Kubrick's assistant called them on a Thursday and asked them to fly to London to meet with him that Saturday.[28] They consulted with Kubrick in London for a few days and returned to New York to begin producing additional music for the film.[29]

It seems that Carlos met and worked with Kubrick as "Walter Carlos," despite the fact that it had been at least two years since she had socially transitioned; she did assume "Walter's" identity for the sake of her career, which is likely what happened with Kubrick. She told an interviewer later that Kubrick had seemed relatively uninterested in her identity at first, but that as time passed during their collaboration, he seemed more and more curious about her and kept trying to find out more about her and who she was.[30] Carlos recalled that Kubrick would casually bring up the names of his gay friends in conversation, as if to gauge whether "Walter" was gay.[31] She said she gave Kubrick enigmatic answers suggesting she was not gay and that he seemed "disturbed" by her responses.[32] Further, she claimed that during the last couple of days of their collaboration on *A Clockwork Orange*, Kubrick took many photos of her with his own camera.[33] She chalked his behavior up to his own curiosity and the fact that he seemed to find her interesting.[34] Carlos wouldn't disclose her gender to Kubrick until she began working on music for his 1980 film *The Shining*.

Regardless of what Kubrick thought about Carlos's gender identity, sexual orientation, or physical appearance, he was eager to include her music in *A Clockwork Orange*. Elkind recalled that Kubrick cut their synthesized rendition of Beethoven's Ninth Symphony and their original composition *Timesteps* into the film almost immediately.[35] Both of these pieces used the vocoder, an envelope-following audio processing system where two different audio signals are merged. The vocoder imparts the characteristics of one audio signal onto another input signal, creating an output sound in which the pitch of one signal has most of the sonic characteristics of the other signal. The most common application for the vocoder is the human voice merged with a synthesized sound. A person (Rachel Elkind, in this case) speaks or sings into a microphone. Then the vocoder breaks the audio signal into a series of adjacent frequency bands, after which it uses those bands to build a new signal that has similar characteristics to the inputted signal. The result is a sort of talking instrumental sound, or a synthesized vocal sound, depending on how one hears it.[36]

Elkind's voice, as filtered through the vocoder, produces far more recognizable words compared with Carlos's attempts to make vocal music with the Moog on the *Well-Tempered Synthesizer*. The German-language text of Schiller's "Ode to Joy" ("*Freude, schöner Götterfunken/Tochter aus Elysium/ wir betreten feuertrunken/Himmlische, dein Heiligtum*") is much easier to hear than is the Latin text of the Monteverdi piece from the *Well-Tempered Synthesizer*. This is not a one-to-one comparison, however: the text of the Beethoven piece is far more familiar to most listeners than is the text of the Monteverdi piece, meaning that a listener is more likely to be able to fill in words that they don't understand. Further, Carlos was using different approaches in the Beethoven and the Monteverdi. The Beethoven includes the sung text in Elkind's voice but filtered through the vocoder, while the Monteverdi included Carlos's attempt to create sung text from scratch using the Moog synthesizer.

Although vocoders had been around since the 1930s, their sound was still largely unfamiliar to most listeners. Carlos had composed *Timesteps* as a kind of warm-up or introduction to the vocoder for listeners.[37] A number of listeners had reacted negatively to the sounds of the vocoder in their realization of the fourth movement of Beethoven's Ninth Symphony, so Elkind suggested that Carlos create a piece that slowly and gently introduced the vocoder so as not to startle listeners.[38] According to Carlos, Elkind thought that once a listener had become acclimated to the sounds of the vocoder in *Timesteps*, they would be far more receptive to the instrument's sound in the Beethoven arrangement.[39]

Timesteps is almost fourteen minutes in length, and it is a tour de force. Carlos created a Moog fantasia using the instrument's entire color palette. Some sections are abstract, floating in and out of sonic focus. Distant chants, created using the vocoder, fade into the sonic texture and then fade back out as quickly as they appeared. Other sections have a strong rhythmic drive, propelled forward by motoric ostinatos. Fanfares announce themselves from the highest registers as musical thunderstorms crash and rage at the surface. *Timesteps* was the first completely original piece that Carlos had created since releasing *Switched-On Bach*, and it is also the most abstract in terms of its melodic and harmonic structure.

Carlos and Elkind had already produced the Beethoven and *Timesteps* when they heard that Kubrick was working on *A Clockwork Orange*, so he added them to the film right away.[40] Kubrick also asked Carlos and Elkind to produce synthesizer versions of some pieces of classical music. He already had plans to incorporate music of Henry Purcell and Gioachino Rossini in specific scenes of the film, and so he requested new Moog synthesizer realizations of these pieces.[41] In fact, Elkind recalled that Kubrick simply replaced his temp tracks of orchestral versions of the pieces with Carlos's synthesizer versions of the same pieces as soon as they were ready.[42] According to Carlos, Kubrick had originally planned to use a rather "stodgy British performance" (her words) of Henry Purcell's *Funeral Music for Queen Mary* in the opening of the film.[43] After Kubrick heard Carlos's electronic rendition of the piece, however, he not only incorporated the music but also adjusted the film's opening sequence to better suit Carlos's realization.[44]

Carlos and Elkind have both acknowledged how fortunate they were that their musical aesthetic matched so closely with Kubrick's goals for the film's music. They knew about his affinity for pre-existing classical music in his films as well as his outright rejection of Alex North's original score for *2001: A Space Odyssey*.[45] Elkind commented that they were extremely lucky they were able to create realizations of Kubrick's chosen music that were in line with his existing vision for specific scenes.[46] For example, Rossini's overture to the opera *William Tell* is heard in the scene where Alex has sex with the two young women he has just met in the arcade, and Rossini's overture to *La gazza ladra* (*The Thieving Magpie*) is heard as Alex and his droogs stop a rival gang from raping a woman and then start a fight with the other gang members. As Carlos said of her Moog synthesizer renditions of Rossini's overtures, Kubrick was essentially having his cake and eating it too, because he was still getting to have the music that he'd already had in mind for the film while also having it presented with new, exciting sounds.[47] In a sense, Carlos and Elkind were creating new arrangements of the temp tracks that Kubrick had already chosen for specific scenes in *A Clockwork Orange*.

Kubrick didn't include every piece of music that Carlos created in his final version of *A Clockwork Orange*. Only an excerpt of *Timesteps* was cut into the film, and a shortened version of the second movement of Beethoven's Ninth Symphony accompanies the scene in which Alex attempts suicide. Carlos also composed "Orange Minuet," an original minuet in 5/8 time that was intended to accompany the scene in which an auditorium full of spectators watch as the "cured" Alex retches as he is tempted with physical violence and a nude woman.[48] Carlos claimed that although a number of people on the production team loved her minuet and wanted to include it in the film, ultimately Kubrick kept the temp track that he had been using throughout the production process.[49] She said he liked the music enough, though, that he suggested she release "Orange Minuet" as a single.[50]

But Carlos's original compositions for the film weren't relegated to obscurity once Kubrick rejected them. The official film soundtrack on Warner Brothers did have a few excerpts of Carlos's music from *A Clockwork Orange*, such as excerpts of the Rossini overtures and about four minutes of *Timesteps*. It also contained orchestral versions of music by Beethoven, Rossini, and Edward Elgar, plus pop songs like "Singin' in the Rain" and "I Want to Marry a Lighthouse Keeper." A couple of months after Warner Brothers released the official film soundtrack, called *Stanley Kubrick's A Clockwork Orange*, Columbia released its own version of the film's soundtrack, called *Walter Carlos's A Clockwork Orange*. According to Carlos, she and Elkind cut a "special deal" with Columbia for this album because it was a "digression" from what they had been planning to do next.[51]

The Carlos soundtrack on Columbia included the uncut, fourteen-minute version of *Timesteps* as well as extended versions of realizations of music of Beethoven and Rossini that had appeared only in short excerpts on Warner Brothers' soundtrack album. Columbia's soundtrack album of *A Clockwork Orange* also included "Country Lane," another original piece Carlos had written for the film that Kubrick chose not to include; "Country Lane" had been written for the scene in which Alex's former droogs, now corrupt police officers, attempt to drown him.[52] A quarter of a century later, Carlos would reissue her music from *A Clockwork Orange* with even more original compositions for the film that Kubrick had not used, including "Orange Minuet" and "Biblical Daydreams."[53]

A Clockwork Orange was a box office success in the United States and also earned generally positive reviews from critics (with notable detractors such as Roger Ebert and Pauline Kael). The success of *A Clockwork Orange* meant that once again, Carlos was in demand but could not appear in public to speak about or promote her music. She recalled one elaborate stunt in which she and Elkind were supposed to be guests on the CBS television program *Camera Three*.[54] Carlos had been invited to appear on camera with Anthony Burgess and the film's star, Malcolm McDowell. When Carlos refused, *Camera Three*'s producers compromised by sending a still photographer to her home studio in New York to take pictures of Carlos, Elkind, and their equipment.[55] Film historian William Everson appeared with Burgess and McDowell in the thirty-minute program instead of Carlos. During the ninety-second discussion of the music in *A Clockwork Orange*, excerpts of Carlos's realization of Beethoven's "Ode to Joy" plays underneath a series of still photographs taken in Carlos's home studio.[56]

Both Elkind and Carlos appear in these photos, and although Carlos is shown only in profile and from above, she does not appear to be wearing fake sideburns, a wig, painted-on facial hair, or any of the other accoutrements she had previously donned in public appearances as "Walter." Her shoulder-length hair, enormous glasses, and baggy clothes are very much in style for the early 1970s; indeed, Malcolm McDowell's hair is as long as hers. A casual observer of these photos would probably just think "Walter Carlos" was a typical long-hair of the period. This glimpse of her in a montage of still photographs was the most substantial appearance she had made on television since *Switched-On Bach* was released three years earlier.

Timesteps, both in its abridged version on Warner Brothers' official Kubrick soundtrack and its complete version on Columbia's Carlos soundtrack, was Carlos's first original composition to be released commercially. Both *Switched-On Bach* and *The Well-Tempered Synthesizer* were synthesizer renditions of existing Baroque music. Both the Warner Brothers and Columbia soundtracks for *A Clockwork Orange* included Carlos's realizations of other people's music in far greater proportions than they included her original compositions. Her next project, *Sonic Seasonings*, would break this mold, as it was an album of entirely original compositions.

Carlos had moved from her one-room studio apartment to a brownstone on Manhattan's Upper West Side, the first floor and basement of which she and Elkind transformed into a production studio. Elkind actually owned the brownstone, having purchased it with her mother in the middle of the 1960s, before she and Carlos had first met.[57] Part of the main floor had been dropped by several feet into the basement in order to create a high enough ceiling for Carlos to monitor audio.[58] Michael Barrett of the *Washington Post* reported that Carlos's studio was the most sophisticated recording laboratory in the city.[59] It was outfitted not only with Carlos's Moog synthesizer modules but also with four enormous Cornwall speakers that hung from the ceiling, four Ampex tape recorders, and a mixing console with eighteen separate faders. She had also upgraded from 8-track to 16-track recorders between *The Well-Tempered Synthesizer* and *A Clockwork Orange*, although she kept 2-, 4-, 8-, and 16-track Ampex recorders on hand. She purchased a small used Moviola to watch the film scenes from *A Clockwork Orange* that she and Elkind were scoring, and they borrowed a mono audio dubber from a friend to play back the film dialogue track in sync and to help them locate the sync points.[60] Carlos also had a Steinway concert grand piano, an electronic organ, and a Novachord, a 1930s synthesizer that was already a collector's item by the early 1970s.[61]

Elkind and Carlos would spend the better part of a decade living and working together in the brownstone. It does not seem that the two were ever romantically involved with each other. Friends and observers recalled that the two were more like sisters, sharing deep affection as well as many irritations and concerns. Elkind has said that by the time they moved in together in the late 1960s, they were both in their early thirties and more or less planned to grow old together as "two old maids."[62] The two women's relationship would begin to change in 1973, when Elkind met Yves TourréTourré, whom she would marry by the end of the decade. Carlos would meet her own partner, Annemarie Franklin, in 1979. But for the first part of the 1970s, Carlos and Elkind were a team in every sense of the word, living and working together.

Another interest that Elkind and Carlos shared was eclipse photography. Carlos saw her first total solar eclipse in Maine in July of 1963.[63] She recalled that the weather that day was terrible but that the clouds parted for a total of sixty-two seconds. That was enough time to completely hook her. It took a few years before she had the time and the financial resources to travel around the world to view the eclipses and to purchase the appropriate equipment to photograph them at a high quality. Between 1972 and 1985, she saw and photographed every total solar eclipse that occurred on planet Earth. Her photos of these eclipses would appear frequently in full-page features and even on the covers of magazines including *Sky & Telescope* and *Astronomy*.[64]

In July of 1972, Carlos and Elkind sailed into the northern Atlantic Ocean (southeast of Nova Scotia) on the *SS Olympia* to view and photograph a total solar eclipse. In June 1973, they traveled to the Air Mountains in Niger to photograph what was the longest totality ever recorded, at seven minutes and two seconds (Rachel Elkind met her future husband, Yves Tourré Tourré, during this trip to Niger). During the 1970s, Carlos would also capture total solar eclipses from planes (June 1974, off the coast of southwestern Australia in the Indian Ocean) and ships (October 1977, in the middle of the Pacific Ocean west of Panama). On April 7, 1976, Carlos was able to capture a solar eclipse that occurred not by the moon but by the planet Mars blocking the sun; amazingly, she photographed this event from the roof of her own building in Manhattan using a telescope.[65] For Carlos, chasing and photographing eclipses was a hobby in that she didn't do it professionally, but she has freely admitted that it is a very important part of her life.[66]

In 1972, Carlos had gender confirmation surgery, which at the time was re-ferred to with the oversimplified term "sex-change operation." This procedure (or multiple procedures, in many cases) involves changing a person's physical features to conform to their gender identity.[67] In the 1970s, to change one's sex legally, one had to have undergone such surgery. Public conceptions of transgender identity often place far more stock in these medical procedures than many transgender people themselves do, including Carlos. She saw this surgery as a final corrective step in her transition. Even in the twenty-first century, journalists and scholars would use male names and pronouns for anything that happened in Carlos's life until 1972, and then, as if a switch was flipped by a medical procedure, begin using female pronouns for her after 1972. In reality, Carlos had transitioned years earlier and the surgery was one of the last items she needed to check off of her list.[68] To her, the procedure was inevitable and comfortable, and she has said that while the public may have found that part of her life to be the most interesting thing about her, she thought it was the least important aspect of her story.[69]

The soundtrack to Kubrick's *A Clockwork Orange* was not the only pro-ject Carlos and Elkind worked on in 1971. They also embarked on their first album of entirely new compositions, which would eventually be titled *Sonic Seasonings*. They created what Elkind called "an aural tapestry" using recorded nature sounds and electronic sounds. In the album's liner notes, Elkind explained that *Sonic Seasonings* was "designed to be a part of the décor, a sonic ambience that enhances the listener's total environment." At the same time, Elkind pitched the album as a way for listeners to leave behind their current sonic environment and instead travel into "the countryside of their fantasy." Examples she gave included a mountain dweller listening to the sounds of the ocean and a "weary urbanite" listening to birdsong.[70]

Sonic Seasonings included recorded nature sounds (fire, waves, rain, and wind), Elkind's imitations of nature sounds (including insects, wolves, frogs, and birds), sounds created with a laboratory oscillator, and sounds created with tape splices.[71] There was a mix of newly generated sounds created in the studio and natural sounds that had undergone varying degrees of ma-nipulation; Carlos has said some of the sounds that seemed the most "live" on the album were actually synthesized and vice versa.[72] She described the album as an organic process in which she created audio collages using all of these various sounds.[73] She began by recording and manipulating con-crete sounds, and then she added the synthesizer where appropriate. *Sonic Seasonings* included a total of seven tracks. "Spring," "Summer," "Fall," and

"Winter" were each about twenty minutes in length; Carlos also included two twenty-minute cuts called "Aurora Borealis" and "Midnight Sun," as well as a five-minute outtake from "Winter."

Carlos said the album began as an irreverent project: since her isolation was keeping her from getting fresh air, she and Elkind began emulating the sounds of nature and the outdoors in their studio.[74] They were, in fact, the "weary urbanites" Elkind mentioned in the liner notes who were desperately seeking the sounds of a more rural environment. Elkind did leave the apartment to record some of the sounds, however; in a 1972 interview with Mary Campbell of the *Associated Press*, Elkind said she had almost fallen in the ocean while standing on slippery rocks with a microphone in each hand, trying to record the sounds of the surf at midnight.[75] The thunderstorm heard in the "Spring" movement was recorded at their brownstone, although Elkind was quick to point out that the recorded storm had occurred in August.[76] Carlos recalled that this project started as a sort of joke because it was so far removed from the other projects that they had been doing, but they eventually realized that the direction it was taking was something they wanted to share commercially.[77] *Sonic Seasonings* also seemed to encapsulate some of Carlos's cynicism about urban life. Evoking the paved paradise in Joni Mitchell's "Big Yellow Taxi," Carlos told an interviewer in 1972, "Soon the only source of nature sounds will be our records."[78]

Carlos and Elkind also included several poems in the album's liner notes. Each poem mentioned the changing of seasons, and the poems were arranged in order as to take the reader through an entire year. Emily Dickinson's "The Sky is low" captures the final moments of winter, followed by a couple of lines from chapter 2 of "The Song of Solomon" that praise the passing of winter and the arrival of flowers and singing birds. Spring passes by in "Sheltered from the Spring wind," a poem by Chu Shu Chen. "The old sun went down," a poem by Carlos's friend Philip Ramey, depicts summer fading into autumn. The final poem in the sequence, "The mountain receives the last rays of autumn" by Wang Wei and Pei Ti, conveys the final moments before autumn becomes winter again.

Columbia's response to *Sonic Seasonings* isn't quite clear. Carlos has given different accounts of how Columbia responded to the concept. In one interview, she claimed that Columbia had more or less written her off before *Sonic Seasonings* was even conceived, likely due to the fact that she wouldn't be photographed or perform live.[79] In response to Columbia's lack of enthusiasm for her, Carlos said she decided to make an album of whatever she wanted since Columbia wouldn't have been interested in or supportive of it anyway.[80] But in another interview given at almost the same time, she said that Columbia was expecting another *Switched-On Bach* from them and were annoyed when she and Elkind delivered the master of *Sonic Seasonings* instead.[81] According to Carlos, Columbia was so disenchanted with *Sonic Seasonings* that the company reneged on its original contract and made Carlos and Elkind take a lower advance.[82]

Sonic Seasonings was largely unprecedented in its approach to sound. It wasn't exactly music, and it wasn't exactly a nature album, either. The movement "Summer," for examples, features the sounds of crickets, frogs, and mosquitos placed atop more abstract-sounding synthesizer passages that fade in and out, back and forth through the sonic landscape. The mosquito sounds (and their irregular buzzing through the left and right channels) are convincing enough to warrant a preemptive slap, but the other sounds have very plainly been produced using the Moog and other electronic media. As Michael Barrett of the *Washington Post* commented, "Although nature records are nothing new, this one is exceptional."[83] In hindsight, historians and critics often term *Sonic Seasonings* a "proto-ambient" or "pre-ambient" album because it embodied a number of the same concepts that Brian Eno would later include in his music and textual manifesto *Ambient 1: Music for Airports*.[84] Eno coined the term "ambient music" in the middle of the 1970s, referring to music "on the cusp of melody and texture" that could be actively listened to or ignored.[85] Eno's terminology and music came well after the release of *Sonic Seasonings*.

The upgraded studio and its equipment allowed Carlos to mix all of her music in quadraphonic (Carlos sometimes called it quadrasonic) sound. In the 1970s, quad sound was the first consumer product available that created surround sound. Before that time, standard stereo recordings were made in just two channels, so anything in quad required special equipment both to produce the music and to listen to it. Carlos had fallen in love with the concept of quadraphonic sound more than a decade earlier when she was a graduate student in the Columbia-Princeton lab.[86] She had eagerly anticipated the day when commercial quad sound would be available to the general public, but she was absolutely horrified at what happened when it did.[87]

Since the early 1970s, Carlos has called commercial quadraphonic sound everything from a "fiasco" to "catastrophic" to a "rip-off" to "bullshit." She has railed against the fact that commercial matrix quad sound was nothing

like "real" or "genuine" quad sound, and she has excoriated record companies for trying to cash in on such an inferior concept.[88] Soon after Columbia
released the quad version of *Switched-On Bach*, she and Elkind asked the
company to withdraw it. Carlos even came out of hiding to submit a massive
letter to the editor of *Billboard* magazine decrying commercial quad sound.
The letter, printed in the magazine's August 5, 1972 issue, was nearly three
pages in length and used extensive technical language that was likely to make
the head of the average reader spin. She wrote (all italics are hers), "*Every matrix quad system has an infinite number of signal combinations which cancel
out when the matrix master is encoded and can never again be recovered.*"[89] In
essence, quad mixes would always have some sounds missing, by nature of
the technology used to create a quad mix.

Carlos explained that even though she had mixed the master of the quad
version of *Switched-On Bach* using the best matrix system she could possibly
find, the commercial versions fell completely short of her master. She noted
that the balance had been "irrevocably bastardized" to the point that solo
lines could not be heard over the accompaniment.[90] Carlos was so unhappy
with how the quad version of *Switched-On Bach* sounded that she not only
asked Columbia to withdraw it but also implored *Billboard*'s readers not to
buy it, or any other quad recording, for that matter.[91]

As she noted in her letter to the editor, it probably seemed foolish that she
was encouraging people not to buy her music, but she felt so strongly about
the artistic and acoustic shortcomings of commercial matrix quad sound that
she would rather people not purchase it at all than purchase what she thought
was an inferior product.[92] Indeed, when the quad version of *Switched-On
Bach* was released in early 1972, the original *Switched-On Bach* had only
just recently been bumped from the number one spot on the classical music
sales charts by Leonard Bernstein. Here was an opportunity to re-up sales
of *Switched-On Bach* with the new quad version, but it was too important to
her to keep the integrity of the sound as opposed to sell more copies of something she couldn't stand behind.[93] Carlos closed her letter by predicting the
failure of quad and literally imploring buyers to beware ("Caveat emptor!").[94]

She was right. Commercial matrix quad sound collapsed soon after, a
point that would irritate her for many years. In 1979, she told an interviewer
that matrix quad was "bullshit" and that as she had predicted, the industry
had "cut off our noses and spite our faces" and ruined any chance at ever
getting real quadraphonic sound.[95] To her, the matrix quad wasn't even quad
at all, and since nobody ever heard "real quad," they ultimately abandoned

the concept without even having heard the real thing.[96] She lamented the fact that she thought genuine quadraphonic sound would probably have been successful but was never given a chance; to her, quad was run off by an inferior commercial attempt that lacked fidelity to the studio-produced quad masters.[97]

This letter to the editor of *Billboard* was not Carlos's first lengthy letter to the editor published in a magazine. The previous year, she had written a multipage letter to the editor of the counterculture magazine *Whole Earth Catalog* in response to an inquiry in an earlier issue asking readers to write in about the merits of various synthesizers. This *Whole Earth Catalog* letter is one of the first documents Carlos had written for publication following the pieces she had written for Bob Moog's *Electronic Music Review* magazine. It was certainly the longest piece she had written since the release of *Switched-On Bach*. In fact, she even acknowledged that this letter marked the first time she had left her "hermitting" to speak publicly.[98]

The letter, including a lengthy postscript, takes up almost two entire pages in the issue of the *Whole Earth Catalog*. In the first paragraph, Carlos said she had been meaning to write in for a long time, and given the magazine's direct call for content about synthesizers and the fact that people were telling her she was "the ultimate sage" of synthesizers and electronic music, she had chosen this moment to "get off her ass" and write them.[99] The letter is verbose, salty, and sharply opinionated. She stated that there was no good literature available on the subject of the synthesizer, period.[100] The one publication she gave any positive credit to was Moog's *Electronic Music Review* (*EMR*), which had shuttered in 1968 after only eighteen months in print. Even *EMR*, Carlos said, had many shortcomings. She wrote that every other publication on the topic of electronic music stank and had an axe to grind.[101] She called out the new periodical *Synthesis* by name, calling it stuffy and faddist and grumbling that it would probably be very successful as a result of these characteristics.[102]

Carlos didn't spare anyone from critique in her *Whole Earth Catalog* letter. She stated outright that no synthesizers on the market were sufficient.[103] The Moog was workable but crude, and it was a nightmare to keep in tune.[104] The Tonus, the Buchla, and mini versions of any other synthesizer brands were "cash-in-on-ignorance rip-offs."[105] Others were "clatter machines," "contrived," "wonder toys," "dull," "awful," "flimsy," and "imbecilic." She railed against the trendiness that popped up surrounding the Moog synthesizer as a result of her *Switched-On Bach* album, complaining about everything from the "bullshit artists" that tried to cash in on the synthesizer's appeal to the ignorance of those who pronounced "Moog" as if it were a sound a cow was making.[106]

An ad for the new periodical *Synthesis* appears on the same page of the *Whole Earth Catalog* as Carlos's critique of it, so the magazine's editors had to have seen her low opinion of their new venture.[107] Further, she noted in her letter that many of the synthesizers she found to be so crummy were the same synthesizers that were regularly advertised in the pages of the *Whole Earth Catalog*; indeed, beneath the first page of her letter are ads for synthesizers by Moog, ARP, and Buchla.[108] As early as this 1971 letter, Carlos was publicly and vehemently criticizing some of the very individuals and institutions that might have been allies or potential collaborators.

Both *Whole Earth Catalog* and *Billboard* gave Carlos wide berth to air her grievances about synthesizers in the former and quad sound in the latter. In her letter to *Whole Earth Catalog*, she commanded, "TELL THEM: That none of the existing hardware really does the job."[109] In her letter to *Billboard*, she provided a list of twelve points, most of which contained several sub-points, of future possibilities for quadraphonic sound.[110] Both letters are substantial critiques of existing systems as well as pleas for equipment that was better suited to her own artistic needs.

Despite the fact that Carlos found so many shortcomings in existing equipment, despite the fact that "Walter Carlos" existed primarily on bank statements, and despite her desire to record her own original compositions, Carlos created two more albums in the 1970s that followed the *Switched-On Bach* model: *Switched-On Bach II* and *Walter Carlos: By Request*.

Switched-On Bach II was released by Columbia in 1973. It closely followed the model of the original *Switched-On Bach*, including Moog synthesizer renditions of familiar J. S. Bach compositions: two two-part inventions, the chorale "Sheep May Safely Graze" from the Cantata no. 208, four pieces from the *Notebook for Anna Magdalena Bach*, three movements from the Orchestral Suite no. 2 in B minor, and the complete Brandenburg Concerto no. 5. The album's cover featured a Bach-like character in outer space, his crude space suit connected to a synthesizer that floats nearby. Bob Moog wrote the album's liner notes, praising Carlos's first *Switched-On Bach* and lauding Carlos's music for having "redefined the boundaries of the electronic music medium."[111]

Carlos and Elkind were particularly pleased with how their version of the Brandenburg came out.[112] Carlos sent Bob Moog an advance copy of that side (one of the first five copies of the album, she told him), and she called it the "breakthrough side."[113] She wrote to him that she hoped the piece (what she affectionately termed the "Fifth Brandy") would bring him and his family a similar sense of excitement that she and Elkind had experienced while creating it.[114] After all, she wrote to Moog, he was one of the very few people who understood just how much work went into creating this kind of music.[115]

As with the *Well-Tempered Synthesizer*, *Switched-On Bach II* didn't offer the listener any new innovations or major changes in what Carlos could do with the Moog synthesizer. Carlos did not attempt to render any vocal music on *Switched-On Bach II* with the Moog, perhaps disappointed at how the vocal music on the *Well-Tempered Synthesizer* had sounded. Instead, she returned to the same model of the original *Switched-On Bach*: a chorale whose vocal parts were rendered using instrumental sounds. Placed next to its 1968 counterpart, *Switched-On Bach II* sounds as if it could have been produced a month later; it had been five years. For *Switched-On Bach II*, like the *Well-Tempered Synthesizer*, the good news and the bad news were the same: they sounded more or less interchangeable with Carlos's first album in terms of the types of music and how the music was rendered on the Moog synthesizer.

Walter Carlos: By Request came two years later, also on Columbia. The repertoire on this album is by far the most eclectic of any of Carlos's solo albums to this point. *By Request* contains Moog versions of a variety of classical pieces, including several popular dances from Peter Ilyich Tchaikovsky's ballet *The Nutcracker*, the first movement of Bach's Brandenburg Concerto no. 2, Bach's "little" G minor fugue, and the Wedding March from Richard Wagner's *Lohengrin*. For the first time, Carlos also offered Moog realizations of popular songs, including John Lennon and Paul McCartney's "Eleanor Rigby." She also included the rendition of Burt Bacharach's "What's New, Pussycat?" with forty layers of overdubbing that she had created several years earlier when she was trying to sell Rachel Elkind on the synthesizer's merits.

In 2002, when *By Request* was reissued, Carlos recalled that listeners in the 1970s wrote to her asking for "more Bach" and "less Bach" in equal measure; the "less Bach" camp also wanted to hear more of her original compositions.[116] This album was an attempt to satisfy both demands.[117] In addition to "Pompous Circumstances," *By Request* included three more original pieces. Two had been written more than a decade earlier during Carlos's graduate study at Columbia: *Dialogues for Piano and Two Loudspeakers* and *Episodes for Piano and Electronic Sound*, both of which featured pianist Philip

Ramey. *Geodesic Dances* was a new composition that translated geodesic ratios into dance rhythms, all while experimenting with spatial placements in quadraphonic sound.[118]

By Request was Carlos's most stylistically varied album. *Dialogues* and *Episodes* sound like a lot of music that was produced at the Columbia-Princeton lab in the 1960s: the electronic sounds are abstract, and the piano's melodies are atonal. "What's New, Pussycat?" and "Eleanor Rigby" are whimsical takes on popular tunes. The remaining pieces of classical music by Tchaikovsky, Wagner, and Bach are predictable in their clarity, their vivid coloring, and their precision. *Geodesic Dances* has a strong rhythmic drive, with passages strongly reminiscent of *Timesteps*. The highlight of *By Request*, though, is the album's B-side, a piece Carlos called "Pompous Circumstances."

"Pompous Circumstances" is Carlos's electronic fifteen-part fantasy and variations on Sir Edward Elgar's most famous Pomp and Circumstance march—the piece often heard during graduation ceremonies in the United States. Carlos had realized Elgar's march on the Moog for the soundtrack of *A Clockwork Orange*, remaining faithful to the score. But "Pompous Circumstances" uses the march's melody as a point of departure. The piece showcases not only of Carlos's skill with the Moog but also her wit and her encyclopedic grasp of others composers' musical styles—not to mention her love of wordplay. It is a delightful romp through multiple centuries and continents of music.

Over the course of twelve minutes, the melody of Elgar's iconic Pomp and Circumstance march is presented in the styles of several different composers and genres, including Modest Mussorgsky ("Pomp and Pictures"), Scott Joplin ("Pomp Rag"), bagpipe playing, Maurice Ravel ("Bolero Pomp"), Gioachino Rossini ("Pomp of Seville" and "Pomp and William Tell"), Johann Sebastian Bach ("Brandenpomp"), and John Philip Sousa ("Hail to the Pomp").[119] The piece concludes with "Pompasthustra," a juxtaposition of the march's melody with the familiar brass and timpani sounds of the opening of Richard Strauss's tone poem *Also sprach Zarathustra*—a work that had become familiar to audiences through Stanley Kubrick's use of it in the initial moments of the film *2001: A Space Odyssey*.

Although Carlos was still using the same Moog modular setup that she had been for years, the music of "Pompous Circumstances" indicates that she was still trying to innovate and get new sounds out of the instrument. The movement "Piper Pomp," for example, emulated the sounds of bagpipes.

Carlos played that part at a very slow, sloppy tempo in order to create the correct sounds for the bagpipe's grace notes; to ensure that the timbre was correct once it was sped up to the correct tempo, Carlos and Elkind played their slow synthesizer version against a record of actual bagpipe playing that had been slowed down.[120] She even got the Moog to produce some convincing consonant sounds, namely "oh, the doo-dah day" from "Yankee Doodle," heard as the piece transitions from "Pomp and Pictures" to "Pomp Rag." The consonants are less clear in the brief quotation of "Largo al factotum," Figaro's entrance aria from Rossini's *The Barber of Seville*.

Throughout the 1970s, Carlos and Elkind entertained a number of ideas that never materialized into new commercial artistic ventures. At one point in the early 1970s, for example, they considered creating a feature film about eclipses that seems not to have gone much of anywhere.[121] The "little" G minor Bach fugue that ended up on *By Request* was created for a television program that never came to fruition.[122] Carlos also wrote a piece for a church as a commission that she claimed was inspired by *Forbidden Planet* but that she said ultimately came out sounding nothing like the source.[123] Carlos claimed she had been approached about creating scores for several different science fiction films in the late 1960s.[124] One specific film she said she had been approached about was the 1969 film Gregory Peck outer space thriller *Marooned*, but the director ultimately went with a soundtrack made entirely of sound effects instead.[125] Carlos and Elkind even discussed starting their own record label, a project that Carlos would later joke was a saga whose telling needed to be accompanied by the sounds of a Hammond organ.[126]

Carlos and Elkind worked closely with their agent, Lucy Kroll, during this time, and Kroll's letters to Elkind and notes from phone conversations with Elkind leave a trail of clues with regard to some of these potential projects. Kroll put Carlos and Elkind in touch with other potential collaborators. For example, several letters between Kroll and Elkind in late 1969 pertain to a museum exhibit of a *Switched-On Bach*-like project of famous film music excerpts rendered on the Moog synthesizer.[127] At one point, Kroll called the project "Movie Theme Song Album," although it does not to appear to have had a more formal title.[128] Kroll and Elkind each took several production meetings with museums and other venues, and Carlos and Elkind compiled a list of nearly one hundred different possible film music excerpts that they could realize on the synthesizer for the exhibit.[129] This project never came to fruition, likely due to rights issues with the film music as well as the fact that

Richard Griffith, the art critic and historian who was the impetus behind the project, died in 1969 and no one else picked it up after his passing.

Kroll also wrote several letters on behalf of Carlos and Elkind to John Lewin about a project called *The Emperor's Clothes*, an animated film for adults that Carlos could score as soon as she completed work on *The Well-Tempered Synthesizer*.[130] After *The Well-Tempered Synthesizer*, however, Carlos went on to create the music for Kubrick's *A Clockwork Orange* instead of this other film project. Dozens of other potential ideas are bounced around in Kroll's notes from the 1970s, but nothing else apart from *A Clockwork Orange* took root until 1977, when Kubrick reached out to Carlos asking her about possibly scoring his latest project, a film adaptation of Stephen King's novel *The Shining*.[131]

In the late 1970s, Carlos began working on an album of all six of J. S. Bach's Brandenburg Concertos. She had already released the Concerto no. 3 on *Switched-On Bach*, the Concerto no. 4 on *The Well-Tempered Synthesizer*, the Concerto no. 5 on *Switched-On Bach II*, and one movement of the Concerto no. 2 on *By Request*. Carlos and Elkind were not particularly excited about the project, but they have both spoken about it as a necessary evil, a burden, an oppression, and a terrible record that they hated doing.[132] According to Carlos, once she had released the complete Brandenburgs, perhaps then she would be released from the expectation (from listeners and from Columbia) that she needed to keep producing Bach's music using the synthesizer.[133] Elkind was less kind in her assessment. She said they only did the Brandenburgs album to fulfill part of their contract obligation with Columbia and that the project was "painful" and "took about 20 times longer than it should have" because it required them to go backwards in time in terms of their innovation and production.[134] They were both ready to look to the future, to new kinds of music and production.

In preparation for this new album, Carlos said she revised anything that she and Elkind didn't feel "right" about from their previous Brandenburg renditions using the Moog.[135] She kept the Fourth Concerto almost exactly as it had appeared on *The Well-Tempered Synthesizer*, claiming that it could not have been made any better.[136] Similarly, she only "partially remixed" some sounds on the Fifth Concerto from its realization on *Switched-On Bach II*.[137] She kept the first and third movements of the Third Concerto, but completely reworked the second movement, which she now called "unsatisfactory."[138] That movement had been an electronic extravaganza and a showcase of the synthesizer's possibilities on *Switched-On Bach*, but Carlos reeled it in for *Switched-On Brandenburgs*. She explained that she found it "unconvincing" and that it was barely any more than a paraphrase of Bach's Chromatic Fantasy.[139] For *Switched-On Brandenburgs*, she replaced the second movement of the Third Concerto with a short interpolation based on the single cadence that Bach had written in the score.[140] She had included one movement from the Second Concerto on *By Request*, but she was unhappy with it and scrapped it for a completely new version in *Switched-On Brandenburgs*.[141]

For *Switched-On Brandenburgs*, then, Carlos had to create the First, Second, and Sixth Concertos from scratch while also reworking the movements mentioned above. She and Elkind tried to follow Bach as closely as possible, consulting many different editions of the scores.[142] However, any time they departed from Bach, they argued that they were doing so for good reason.[143] Hence the change in the second movement of the Third Concerto: they reduced the size, length, and complexity of the synthesizer fantasia because they felt it wasn't representative of Bach.[144] They also wanted to use the newer capabilities and techniques that the most recent synthesizers allowed, but they needed to make similar updates in all of the concertos in order to maintain consistency across the album.[145] For example, Carlos was pleased with the sound of the violin-piccolo in the third movement of the First Concerto because she thought it was the most idiomatic and truest to the sound of the original instrument of any of the sounds on the album.[146] She was also delighted with how truly legato her legato phrases came out in the second movement of the Second Concerto, a sound that she said took a very long time to achieve.[147]

The greatest strength of *Switched-On Brandenburgs*, like *The Well-Tempered Synthesizer* and *Switched-On Bach II* (and, to a certain extent, *By Request*), was the fact that it sounded a whole lot like *Switched-On Bach*. The music is familiar and well-loved, and Carlos's Moog realizations are painstaking in their precision and nuance. Of course, this sameness was also the album's greatest weakness. It's predictable in its quality, which was wonderful news for listeners who wanted to hear more music from the eighteenth century performed using the Moog synthesizer. But for those who wanted to know what else the Moog could do, this album wasn't really giving them much.

Further, thanks in large part to the success of *Switched-On Bach* a decade earlier, the sound of the Moog synthesizer (and other brands) had become omnipresent in all kinds of music. By the time Carlos and Elkind were working on *Switched-On Brandenburgs*, the Moog and other analog synthesizers had been used in music by everyone from ABBA to ELP (Emerson, Lake, and Palmer) to Giorgio Moroder to Tangerine Dream to Stevie Wonder to Yes. The sounds of the analog synthesizer were no longer novel for most listeners. The synthesizer was now a lingua franca in many genres of music. What had made *Switched-On Bach* so successful was its use of a new instrumental sound to perform familiar, existing music. She was creating the same kind of music that she had been for a decade, but the audiences' knowledge and tastes had changed drastically during that time. Now that the Moog's sound was familiar, the freshness of Carlos's Bach realizations was drastically decreased.

As Carlos was working and reworking the Brandenburg Concertos for release, she also began seriously considering disclosing her gender identity publicly. She felt that her isolation was holding her back artistically and creatively.[148] She couldn't go out and talk about her music, and she couldn't talk to other people about their music, either.[149] Every letter between Elkind and Lucy Kroll about potential projects in the 1970s mentions conversations, lunches, and meetings that Elkind took, but Carlos was never there. There's no evidence that Carlos and Kroll communicated directly with each other. If Carlos wasn't communicating with her agent, she probably wasn't communicating with anyone whom her agent wanted her to meet, either. Apart from *Sonic Seasonings* and a few selections on *By Request*, all of her music that had been released commercially followed the same mold, a mold she perhaps could not break in part because she couldn't reach out directly to anyone to talk about new directions she was taking.

Carlos gave a few interviews in the 1970s, none of which appear to have been published anywhere. One lengthy unpublished 1975 interview with Robert M. Jacobson calls her "Walter," but Jacobson had to have known the truth.[150] His interview has lengthy quotes from her and from Elkind, as well as detailed descriptions of their home, their furniture, and Carlos's recording studio. It's not clear if Jacobson's interview was intended for publication in *Opera News* (the classical music magazine published by the Metropolitan Opera Guild and to which Jacobson was a regular contributor) or elsewhere. It was written as a promotion for *By Request*, so its content would likely have been beyond the scope of *Opera News*. Perhaps Jacobson was planning a follow-up volume to his 1974 book *Reverberations*, a collection of interviews he had conducted with leading names in classical music, and he wanted to include Carlos.

Carlos wanted to compose original music, but she has said her isolation was stifling her creativity as well as her options for composing new music for live ensembles.[151] The nature of her isolation kept her from interacting with musicians in a way that would have made a commission for a live piece nearly impossible. Symphony orchestras or chamber music ensembles weren't likely to commission a piece from a composer who wouldn't meet them in person, appear in any promotional materials, or make public appearances to discuss the new piece they had written. She told an interviewer that she found it difficult to compose new music if she didn't have a real purpose for doing so; she needed artistic direction or inspiration in order to compose something new.[152] To Carlos, composition was about having a challenge to meet or being given a commission to create a specific, interesting idea.[153] She wanted to create something that performers would want to play and that audiences would want to hear, something that would inspire musicians and audiences to ask her for more and something that would fulfill her enough to make her want to create more.[154]

Her isolation seems to have kept her from being able to engage in real, ongoing conversations about the developments in electronic music. The letters to the editor she had sent to *Whole Earth Catalog* and *Billboard* didn't exactly change anything: commercial matrix quadraphonic sound had been abandoned, and synthesizers were still far below her expectations. She would eventually claim that the artistic growth of synthesizers and of the music created with synthesizers in the 1970s had been stunted. She would speculate that had she been able to be more present, she might have been able to push the field further and in a more progressive direction.[155]

Her few attempts in the early 1970s to discuss ways synthesizers could be improved, however, were critical to the point of being vitriolic. She may have thought her letters to the editor were full of constructive criticism for the creators of synthesizers and electronic music instruments, but they read as criticism, bordering on insult, of both the products and the people who bought the products. Synthesizer and other electronic music instrument manufacturers were likely uninterested in consulting with a musician who (1) was well known to be a Moog loyalist, (2) harshly criticized the Moog synthesizer in print despite being known as the instrument's main champion and Bob Moog's friend and colleague, and (3) trashed their products and the consumers of their products without qualification in print.

Due to the popularity of *Switched-On Bach*, most synthesizer companies weren't exactly having any difficulty selling their products, regardless of what Carlos had to say about them. Why would a company spend thousands of hours (and untold amounts of research and development money) tweaking the product to the specifications demanded by one of the world's very few specialists when the average person with a bit of disposable income found the present iteration of the synthesizer well suited to their needs and their budgets? Although Carlos may have attributed a lack of dialogue about electronic music to her isolation, it seems just as likely that her few attempts to discuss electronic music publicly were not greeted as invitations to productive conversations but rather as isolated soapbox speeches from an eccentric recluse.

Even Bob Moog seems to have had little time for Carlos during this period. Although Moog and Carlos exchanged some correspondence during the 1970s, it seems that her orders for custom pieces had dwindled. Moog was inundated with orders in the wake of *Switched-On Bach* and likely couldn't produce many custom items, even from the person who had helped his product become so famous. At the end of the fiscal year in June 1967 (about eighteen months prior to the release of *Switched-On Bach*), Moog reported sales of $96,000. In a report filed in early 1970, Moog reported that in the fiscal year ending June 1969, he had sales of $526,000 (a fivefold increase), and he was projecting $1 million in sales by the end of the fiscal year ending in June 1970.[156] He even received the New York State Small Businessman of the Year Award from the U. S. Small Business Administration in 1970.

Moog was so busy trying to keep his business going that he didn't have time or space to make custom items for Carlos any more. At some point in the early 1970s, she had asked him for a frequency follower. He wrote to her to apologize that Moog Music had yet to even invent such an item, and he referred her to a similar pitch to voltage converter designed by Bob Easton.[157] He told her that he had heard an earlier prototype of Easton's product but not the latest version, although he vouched for Easton and said that he had no hesitation recommending the product to Carlos.[158]

In 1979, Carlos and Elkind claimed that *Sonic Seasonings*, Carlos's *A Clockwork Orange* soundtrack, *Switched-On Bach II*, and *By Request* had not been reviewed in the United States.[159] Carlos thought that the critical responses to her recent albums were limited, at least in part, because she wasn't available to give interviews or promote the music.[160] Certainly, none of the albums received even a fraction of the press that *Switched-On Bach* had in the late 1960s. *Sonic Seasonings* was mentioned favorably in several periodicals, including the *Chicago Tribune*. Although not American, Roy Hollingworth of the British weekly magazine *Melody Maker* called *Sonic Seasonings* "the most remarkable book of recorded sound I've ever heard."[161] Carlos's soundtrack to *A Clockwork Orange* was mentioned in *Time* and *Variety* magazines, and Jacobson did conduct a lengthy interview with her about *By Request* (that went unpublished), but critics do seem to have largely overlooked almost all of her albums from the 1970s.

One periodical that did review *By Request* was *Contemporary Keyboard*. Founded in 1975, *Contemporary Keyboard* (renamed to just *Keyboard* in the early 1980s) was dedicated to keyboard music, instruments, and musicians of all types. A typical issue might include articles about pianos, harpsichords, accordions, organs, and synthesizers in jazz, popular, classical, electronic, and every genre in between. Each issue included reviews, how-to columns, seminars, and opinion pieces, plus full-length feature interviews with an astonishing array of keyboard players, manufacturers, and composers. The magazine published features on everyone from Keith Emerson to Andre Watts to Chick Corea to Jan Hammer. Bob Moog contributed a regular column called "On Synthesizers" each month from the magazine's inception. Until the early 1980s, *Contemporary Keyboard* included reviews of the latest albums, and this is where one of the few American reviews of *By Request* did appear. Taylor Young wrote that Carlos's versions of existing music were "interesting, if unimpassioned" but had high praise for the original "Pompous Circumstances," calling it "bizarre" and "hilarious."[162]

Contemporary Keyboard's readers wanted to hear from Carlos. She regularly placed highly in their annual polls of favorite musicians. A separate survey that asked readers whom they wanted to see profiled include Carlos as well as Morton Subotnick, Bob James, Sun Ra, and Isao Tomita.[163] The magazine's editors repeatedly reached out to Carlos for interviews during the 1970s, but they were told that interviews wouldn't be possible.[164] We can only speculate about what the case might have been if she had been available at the magazine's inception. Perhaps she, like Bob Moog, Tom Rhea, and Leonard Feather, might have been invited to contribute a monthly column.

Although Carlos had gone into hiding in the late 1960s in order to protect her career, a decade later, she realized that her career was probably hurting even more specifically because she was so isolated. It had to have seemed like a terrible kind of Catch-22: she couldn't promote her music unless she left the house and people knew who she really was, but if people knew who she really was, they might treat her like a sideshow freak or worse. If she remained in isolation, though, she wouldn't even have the opportunity to be rejected for reasons that had nothing to do with her music. She and Elkind began testing the waters with some of their friends and looking for a sympathetic journalist or other figure who might be the right fit for helping Carlos make her story public.

Elkind ended up telling some of their friends the truth and asking them for help because she couldn't keep Carlos's secret by herself much longer. Elkind went to the home of their friend Elly Stone without Carlos; it's not clear if she did this with Carlos's knowledge and consent or if she simply couldn't handle the secret anymore and had to tell someone before she exploded.[165] Elkind blurted out to Stone that Wendy was actually the same person once known as "Walter Carlos" and that they had been keeping her secret together for almost a decade. Stone was shocked and delighted by the information—she loved a good bit of gossip, but she also realized what a terrible predicament her friends were in.[166] Elkind told Stone that they needed help finding someone sympathetic, someone who would get to know the real Carlos and tell her story simply and honestly. They wanted truth, not sensation.

For years, their cover story for their friends had been that Wendy was Walter Carlos's sister.[167] Wendy and Rachel claimed that they were handling all of Walter's business dealings because he kept such a low profile, which was also why none of their friends had ever met him. To explain away Wendy's exceptional prowess with electronics and her expertise with the Moog, they told friends that Wendy had worked with Walter on *Switched-On Bach* and other projects but that Walter had taken all the credit on the final product. The friend recalled thinking that Walter had to be some kind of bum to not give any credit to his sister because she was clearly very knowledgeable about the Moog synthesizer and other electronics, probably just as knowledgeable as Walter himself was, if not more so.[168] Eventually, after reading about transgender tennis player Renee Richards, this friend began to suspect the truth; Carlos and Elkind confessed when he confronted them.[169]

This friend and others accepted Carlos as she was and set about trying to help her find the right way to share her identity publicly.[170] Ultimately, Elly Stone would connect Elkind and Carlos with the person who would help Carlos tell her story, the journalist Arthur Bell.[171] By 1978, Carlos had decided to release *Switched-On Brandenburgs* as herself and to obliterate "Walter Carlos" from existence.

Notes

1. For more information on the explosion of Moog-related albums in the late 1960s, see Pinch and Trocco, *Analog Days*, 149–154.
2. Robert Hilburn, "Many Discs Suited as Time Killers," *Los Angeles Times* (October 19, 1969): U36.
3. "New Pop Albums," *Melody Maker* (November 8, 1969), 34.
4. Gould, liner notes to *The Well-Tempered Synthesizer* (Columbia, 1969).
5. Kozinn, unpublished interview with Carlos, 38.
6. Kozinn, unpublished interview with Carlos, 1.
7. Rachel Elkind, liner notes to *The Well-Tempered Synthesizer* (Columbia, 1969).
8. Milano, "Rachel Elkind," 35.
9. Milano, "Rachel Elkind," 35.
10. Milano, "Rachel Elkind," 35.
11. Kozinn, unpublished interview with Elkind, 38.
12. Milano, "Rachel Elkind," 36.
13. Milano, "Rachel Elkind," 36.
14. Milano, "Rachel Elkind," 36.
15. On the voice of Charlie Brown's teacher, see, for example, Lance Ulanoff, "The Story of Wah Wah and Other 'Peanuts' Specials Secrets," *Mashable* (October 26, 2015), available at https://mashable.com/2015/10/26/peanuts-wah-wah/#456OB7Tiwuqn.
16. Henahan, "Man and a Moog," HF1.
17. Henahan, "Man and a Moog," HF1.
18. Elkind, liner notes to *The Well-Tempered Synthesizer*.
19. On Keith Emerson and the Moog, see Pinch and Trocco, *Analog Days*, 200–213.
20. Bell, "*Playboy* interview," 101.
21. On TONTO and their relationship with Stevie Wonder, see Pinch and Trocco, *Analog Days*, 182–186.
22. For more information about Kubrick, North, and the music of *2001*, see Christine Gengaro, "'It Was Lovely Music that Came to My Aid': Music's Contribution to the Narrative of the Novel, Film, and Play, *A Clockwork Orange*," PhD dissertation (University of Southern California, 2005), 109–118.
23. All information in this paragraph about Kubrick's process is drawn from Gengaro, "*Clockwork Orange*," 111–112.
24. See, for example, Chris Twomey, "Wendy Carlos: Still Switched On," *Exclaim!* (December 1998/January 1999), n.p.
25. Campbell, "Recording Surf is Slippery Job," n.p.
26. Justin Bozung, "Interview: The Shining and A Clockwork Orange Co-Composer Rachel Elkind Talks about Stanley Kubrick," *TV Store Online* (September 2, 2017), available at https://web.archive.org/web/20160403031854/http://blog.tvstoreonline.com/2014/09/interview-shining-and-clockwork-orange.html .
27. Campbell, "Recording Surf is Slippery Job," n.p.
28. Campbell, "Recording Surf is Slippery Job," n.p.
29. Campbell, "Recording Surf is Slippery Job," n.p.

30. Bell, "*Playboy* interview," 100.
31. Bell, "*Playboy* interview," 100.
32. Bell, "*Playboy* interview," 100.
33. Bell, "*Playboy* interview," 100.
34. Bell, "*Playboy* interview," 100–101.
35. Pinch, "Rachel Elkind," n.p.
36. For more on how a vocoder works with a synthesizer, see Vail, *The Synthesizer*, 18, 200–201 and Moog, "On Synthesizers: Vocal Sounds Part II: Vocoders," *Contemporary Keyboard* (May 1978): 54.
37. Twomey, "Wendy Carlos," n.p.
38. Campbell, "Recording Surf is Slippery Job," n.p.
39. Twomey, "Wendy Carlos," n.p.
40. Twomey, "Wendy Carlos," n.p.
41. Pinch, "Rachel Elkind," n.p.
42. Pinch, "Rachel Elkind," n.p.
43. Jeff Bond, "A Clockwork Composer: Wendy Carlos Switches Back on Soundtracks and Revisits her Premiere Score," *Film Score Monthly* (March 1999), 21.
44. Bond, "A Clockwork Composer," 21.
45. Bond, "A Clockwork Composer," 21.
46. Pinch, "Rachel Elkind," n.p.
47. Bond, "A Clockwork Composer," 21.
48. Bond, "A Clockwork Composer," 20.
49. Bond, "A Clockwork Composer," 20.
50. Carlos, liner notes to *Wendy Carlos's A Clockwork Orange* (Columbia, 1972; East Side Digital, 2000), 11. (All citations are to the 2000 reissue.)
51. Oteri, "Wendy's World," 6.
52. Carlos, "Wendy Carlos's *Clockwork Orange* (complete original score)," available at http://www.wendycarlos.com/+wcco.html.
53. Oteri, "Wendy's World," 6.
54. Bell, "*Playboy* interview," 100.
55. Bell, "*Playboy* interview," 100.
56. John Musilli, "An Examination of Kubrick's 'A Clockwork Orange,'" *Camera Three* (Creative Arts Television: 1972): 20:20–22:00.
57. Carlos, "Rachel," available at http://www.wendycarlos.com/rachel.html.
58. Carlos, "About the Studio," available at http://www.wendycarlos.com/+wcco.html.
59. Michael S. Barrett, "An Electronic Studio in a Box," *Washington Post* (October 8, 1972), L6.
60. Carlos, liner notes to *Wendy Carlos's A Clockwork Orange*.
61. Jacobson, "The End that Belies the Means," 1.
62. Pinch, "Rachel Elkind," n.p.
63. Unless otherwise noted, all information about Carlos's eclipse chasing and photography is taken from "Confessions of a Coronophile," available at http://www.wendycarlos.com/eclipse.html.

64. See, for example, Fred Espenak and Jay Anderson, "Eclipse 2002: Africa or Australia?" *Sky and Telescope* (October 9, 2003), available at https://www.skyandtelescope.com/astronomy-news/observing-news/eclipse-2002-africa-or-australia/.

65. Wendy Carlos, "Mars Occultation," available at http://www.wendycarlos.com/marsoclt.html.

66. Bell, unpublished interview notes.

67. For a medical and cultural history of gender confirmation surgery in the United States, see chapter 4, "A 'Fierce and Demanding Drive,'" in Meyerowitz, *How Sex Changed*.

68. Bell, "*Playboy* interview," 90.

69. Bell, "*Playboy* interview," 91.

70. Elkind, liner notes to *Sonic Seasonings* (Columbia, 1972).

71. Milano, "Wendy Carlos" (1979), 35.

72. Kozinn, unpublished interview with Carlos, 27.

73. Milano, "Wendy Carlos" (1979), 35.

74. Milano, "Wendy Carlos" (1979), 35.

75. Bell, "*Playboy* interview," 76.

76. Kozinn, unpublished interview with Carlos, 27.

77. Milano, "Wendy Carlos" (1979), 35.

78. Barrett, "Studio in a Box," L6.

79. Milano "Wendy Carlos" (1979), 37.

80. Milano "Wendy Carlos" (1979), 37.

81. Kozinn, unpublished interview with Carlos, 36.

82. Kozinn, unpublished interview with Elkind, 36.

83. Barrett, "Studio in a Box," L6.

84. See, for example, Keith Phipps, "Review: *Sonic Seasonings*," *The AV Club* (April 19, 2002), available at https://music.avclub.com/wendy-carlos-sonic-seasonings-1798196599.

85. Eno, quoted in Michael Jarrett, *Sound Tracks: A Musical ABC* (Philadelphia: Temple University Press, 1998), 11.

86. Milano, "Wendy Carlos" (1979), 74.

87. Milano, "Wendy Carlos" (1979), 74.

88. Milano, "Wendy Carlos" (1979), 74.

89. Carlos, "Moog Soundings" (letter to the editor), *Billboard* (August 5, 1972), 6.

90. Carlos, "Moog Soundings," 6.

91. Carlos, "Moog Soundings," 6.

92. Carlos, "Moog Soundings," 6.

93. Carlos, "Moog Soundings," 6.

94. Carlos, "Moog Soundings," 86.

95. Milano, "Wendy Carlos" (1979), 74.

96. Milano, "Wendy Carlos" (1979), 40.

97. Milano, "Wendy Carlos" (1979), 40.

98. Carlos, "Synthesizers," *WEC*, 331.

99. Carlos, "Synthesizers," *WEC*, 330.

100. Carlos, "Synthesizers," *WEC*, 330.

101. Carlos, "Synthesizers," *WEC*, 330.
102. Carlos, "Synthesizers," *WEC*, 330.
103. Carlos, "Synthesizers," *WEC*, 330.
104. Carlos, "Synthesizers," *WEC*, 331.
105. Carlos, "Synthesizers," *WEC*, 330.
106. Carlos, "Synthesizers," *WEC*, 331.
107. Carlos, "Synthesizers," *WEC*, 330.
108. Carlos, "Synthesizers," *WEC*, 330.
109. Carlos, "Synthesizers," *WEC*, 330.
110. Carlos, "Moog Soundings," 6, 10, 86.
111. Moog, liner notes to *Switched-On Bach II* (Columbia, 1973).
112. Carlos, letter to Bob Moog, December 1973. Robert Moog papers, #8629. Box 60, folder 15. Division of Rare and Manuscript Collections, Cornell University Library.
113. Carlos, letter to Bob Moog, December 1973.
114. Carlos, letter to Bob Moog, December 1973.
115. Carlos, letter to Bob Moog, December 1973.
116. Carlos, "By Request," available at http://www.wendycarlos.com/+br.html,
117. Carlos, "By Request."
118. Folkman, liner notes to *By Request* (Columbia, 1975).
119. Carlos, "By Request—Track List," available at http://www.wendycarlos.com/+br. html.
120. Milano, "Wendy Carlos" (1979), 28.
121. Moog, letter to Carlos and Elkind, September 24, 1973. Robert Moog papers, #8629. Box 60, folder 15. Division of Rare and Manuscript Collections, Cornell University Library.
122. Folkman, linter notes to *By Request*.
123. Milano, "Wendy Carlos" (1979), 72.
124. Bond, "Wendy Carlos," 20.
125. Bond, "Wendy Carlos," 20.
126. Kozinn, unpublished interview with Carlos, 31.
127. Lucy Kroll Client File 1916–1998, Library of Congress, Box 109: Elkind, Rachel, 1969–1980, 1986, undated. All citations of correspondence between Elkind and Kroll are found in this collection, as are Kroll's notes about projects related to Carlos and Elkind.
128. Kroll, letter to Elkind, August 14, 1969.
129. Kroll, letter to Elkind, August 14, 1969.
130. Kroll, letter to John Lewin, August 14, 1969.
131. Kubrick, letter to Carlos, September 5, 1977.
132. Kozinn, unpublished interview with Carlos and Elkind, 42.
133. Milano, "Wendy Carlos" (1979), 70.
134. Milano, "Rachel Elkind," 36.
135. Kozinn, unpublished interview with Carlos, 1.
136. P.R., unpublished interview with Carlos, 15.
137. Kozinn, unpublished interview with Carlos, 2.

138. Kozinn, unpublished interview with Carlos, 1.
139. P.R., unpublished interview with Carlos, 13.
140. P.R., unpublished interview with Carlos, 13.
141. P.R., unpublished interview with Carlos, 10.
142. Kozinn, unpublished interview with Carlos, 42.
143. Kozinn, unpublished interview notes, 41.
144. Kozinn, unpublished interview notes, 1.
145. Kozinn, unpublished interview notes, 41–42.
146. P.R., unpublished interview with Carlos, 6.
147. P.R., unpublished interview with Carlos, 12.
148. Milano, "Wendy Carlos" (1979), 69.
149. Bell, "*Playboy* interview," 100.
150. Jacobson, "The End that Belies the Means," 1.
151. Bell, "*Playboy* interview," 100.
152. Milano, "Wendy Carlos" (1979), 75.
153. Milano, "Wendy Carlos" (1979), 69.
154. Milano, "Wendy Carlos" (1979), 69.
155. Kozinn, unpublished interview with Carlos, 6–8; 18–19.
156. Moog, "History of the Business," from his application for SBA Small Businessman of the Year Award for Fiscal Year 1970, 5. Robert Moog papers, #8629. Box 31, unnumbered binder. Division of Rare and Manuscript Collections, Cornell University Library.
157. Moog, letter to Carlos, September 24, 1973. Robert Moog papers, #8629. Box 60, folder 15. Division of Rare and Manuscript Collections, Cornell University Library.
158. Moog, letter to Carlos, September 24, 1973.
159. Kozinn, unpublished interview notes, 28–29.
160. Kozinn, unpublished interview notes, 29.
161. Roy Hollingworth, "The Walter Carlos Sonic Boom," *Melody Maker* (September 23, 1972), 42.
162. Taylor Young, "Review: *By Request*," *Contemporary Keyboard* (January/February 1976): 75.
163. Editors' note, *Contemporary Keyboard* (January 1977): 4.
164. Jim Crockett, "From the Publisher," *Contemporary Keyboard* (December 1979): 3.
165. Bell, unpublished interview notes.
166. Bell, unpublished interview notes.
167. Bell, unpublished interview notes.
168. Bell, unpublished interview notes, 1979.
169. The responses from Elly Stone and from other friends of Carlos's appear in Arthur Bell's interview preparation notes from 1978 and 1979. Elly Stone is the only friend whose full name is given. Other friends mentioned by first name are Matthew and Eric.
170. Bell, "*Playboy* interview," 76.
171. Bell, "*Playboy* interview," 76.

5

"Welcome Back, Wendy!" The *Playboy* Interview (1979)

In the winter of 1977, Wendy Carlos and Rachel Elkind began exploring the idea of disclosing Carlos's transition to the general public. Their friend Elly Stone suggested the journalist Arthur Bell as a possible interviewer.[1] Bell, a regular columnist for the *Village Voice* and a previous contributor to *Playboy*, told Stone he'd be interested in the interview.[2] Carlos and Bell began meeting in the fall of 1978, conducting several interviews between October and January. Bell's interview with Carlos appeared in the May 1979 issue of *Playboy* magazine, just a few months before Carlos turned forty. After the interview was published, her life would never be the same. The interview helped Carlos kick open the closet door, so to speak—she frequently referred to being "closeted" or "in the closet."[3] At the same time, she learned some difficult and embarrassing lessons about giving interviews to seasoned professional journalists who were more than willing to make all kinds of promises about what the printed interview would look like and ultimately print something else. Her secret would finally be out, but on the journalist's terms, not her own. This imbalance deeply upset her, leaving her hurt and confused.

Carlos was in an unusual position because the public already knew her as one gender but she was about to reveal that she was, in fact, another gender. From Christine Jorgenson in the 1950s to Renee Richards in the 1970s, most transgender people in the public eye had only become famous after their transitions. To reveal that the person known publicly as the male Walter Carlos was in fact the female Wendy Carlos was a risky, largely unprecedented move. At the same time, Carlos's career was stuck: she couldn't promote her own music if she couldn't leave the house. Plus, she struggled to compose music if she didn't have a specific audience or goal in mind; her years in isolation had started to affect her creativity.[4] She had hidden from the public to protect her career, but now her career was suffering because of that isolation.[5]

As she told Bell in the interview, she was terrified about disclosing her transition for several reasons. She didn't want to become the object of scorn or ridicule by those who were disgusted by her transition.[6] Although she didn't say so explicitly, it's likely she wanted to protect herself from physical violence, as well; when discussing her childhood with Bell, she mentioned several incidents of bullying, beatings, and sexual assault perpetrated by teenage boys who perceived her as a gay or effeminate boy.[7] As a transgender woman, it is not surprising that she anticipated even more severe violence and abuse than she had endured when perceived as a gay male child. In the interview with Bell, Carlos recounted an incident from 1968 or 1969 in which a woman verbally assaulted her in a Fifth Avenue Chock Full o' Nuts. She recalled that the woman was horrified, yelling at Carlos and demanding that she explain whether she was a man or a woman.[8] By the late 1970s, though, she felt some of the danger she had initially feared had subsided.[9]

In addition to the fear of humiliation or physical assault, Carlos was also very protective about her career. She feared never being taken seriously again by the public.[10] She told Bell that she never participated socially with other transgender people out of a need to protect her career; she seems to have assumed that if anyone knew who she was, her career would have been ruined.[11] She was also afraid for her friends' safety, particularly for Rachel Elkind, noting that they might be targeted by angry people who thought Carlos was sick or evil.[12]

At the same time, she explained, lying had exhausted her, Elkind, and their friends.[13] Carlos no longer wanted to hide, and she no longer wanted the people closest to her to be burdened by having to lie for her any more.[14] Elkind would tell callers and visitors that "Walter" was unavailable because he was on tour or was visiting his parents.[15] (Carlos joked to Bell that while "Walter" might have been close to his parents, Wendy certainly wasn't close to hers.[16]) When Stevie Wonder showed up at Carlos's home to play the synthesizer, she hid from him and didn't speak to him, certain that he would know her secret right away from the sound of her voice.[17] In the *Camera Three* episode about *A Clockwork Orange*, both Malcolm McDowell and Anthony Burgess helped cover for her, claiming that they had visited Walter Carlos's studio when they had done no such thing.[18] Carlos had grown tired of maintaining the illusion of "Walter's" existence and was finally ready to become free of him.

A few months after the *Playboy* interview was published, Carlos told Allan Kozinn that American music critics had chosen to pretend that she and her music didn't exist. She claimed that critics (what she called a "New York music mafia") had ignored her for several (seemingly contradictory) reasons: her music angered them, her music disappointed them, her music made too much money, her music didn't make enough money, and they thought she should be out in public more, promoting her music.[19] This final point probably weighed the most heavily on Carlos's mind in terms of her career: she could allow "Walter Carlos" to continue releasing albums, but "he" was not available to give interviews, promote the music, or meet fans. She told Bell that she effectively lost an entire decade of her career because she couldn't concertize, travel, or even have conversations with other musicians during that period.[20]

Carlos's decision to disclose her transition was also facilitated by a changing tide with regard to public attitudes toward transgender people.[21] As mentioned earlier, Carlos was extremely unusual in that she had already been known before her transition. At the time she transitioned, the doctors who treated transgender people operated under a strict gatekeeping system that was, ostensibly, to protect the patients but likely was in place to protect the doctors' reputations as well. For example, doctors preferred to treat patients who could "pass" as both in appearance and behavior, and they wanted patients who wouldn't make a scene or otherwise sensationalize their transitions.[22]

Following their transition (which often but not always included surgery), a transgender person was expected to live quietly and to not disclose the fact that they had been assigned another sex at birth. Many were encouraged to move away from their old lives, jobs, and homes and start over somewhere else. As Julia Serano writes:

> The gatekeepers' requirement that transsexuals so completely hide their trans status created innumerable obstacles for trans people: the shame and self-loathing that is associated with living in the closet; having to cut off relationships with family and friends, thus eliminating any possible social support system they have had had previously; having to look for a new job, in a new location, without being able to reference their past employment history and while continuing to pay for therapy and medical bills necessary to complete their transition—all this on top of having to navigate their way through the world in their identified gender for the first time. Because of the combination of all of these stresses, it was not uncommon for transsexuals to become highly depressed or suicidal post-transition.[23]

Carlos has acknowledged that while her isolation might have been hellish, it was perhaps strangely beneficial to her career, at least in the early stages. She explained to Bell that her utter lack of a personal life before her transition facilitated her complete immersion in her professional life; she noted that her highly polished work on the Moog synthesizer was due, in part, to the fact that she really had nothing else taking up her time apart from her work.[24] Carlos was fortunate in that she managed to stay in the same apartment with the same best friend and support system after her transition. At the same time, her professional life suffered throughout the 1970s because she could not appear publicly to promote her work.

Fortunately for Carlos, the culture was shifting, making the disclosure of her transition seem more plausible than it might have been ten years earlier. Courts were finding in favor of transgender people's rights. In 1971, Deborah Hartin sued the Bureau of Records and Statistics in New York when she was prevented from changing the sex listed on her birth certificate.[25] Hartin had made headlines the previous year when she and her wife divorced after Hartin transitioned to female. Her case was dismissed in 1973, after the Bureau of Records and Statistics opted to remove sex designation from transgender people's birth certificates.

Ophthalmologist and tennis player Renee Richards sued the U.S. Tennis Association (USTA) in 1976 when the organization refused to allow her to play tennis because she would not undergo a test to prove that she had XX chromosomes.[26] The court found that such a test was invasive and unfair, and Richards was allowed to play in the women's division. The USTA feared that men would begin undergoing sex reassignment surgeries at rapid rates in order to infiltrate women's tennis and other sports; no such trend ever took off.[27] Further, Richards lost many of the games she played, thereby lessening anxiety that a transgender woman would have some sort of an unfair advantage over a cisgender woman. The 1977 court decision that found in favor of Richards would certainly have indicated to Carlos that the culture was becoming increasingly amenable to accepting a transgender woman on her own terms.

Transgender people were appearing in the news relatively regularly and were being treated, if not warmly, at least respectfully. Most news outlets appear to have worked hard to take their transgender subjects seriously and respectfully during this period. The year 1974 saw the publication of *Conundrum*, British journalist Jan Morris's autobiography about her transition to female. The book was reviewed positively in mainstream outlets such as *Time* and *Newsweek*.[28] Magazines such as *Cosmopolitan* and *Good Housekeeping* published sympathetic pieces about transgender individuals; notably, most articles that appeared in these types of publications were about transgender men, not transgender women.[29] Deborah Hartin appeared on Phil Donahue's TV show, and NBC News played segments about transgender people in its science segments. Carlos noted during her interview with Bell that transgender people were placing personal ads in gay newspapers in the late 1970s, something that would have been unheard of a decade earlier when she was transitioning.[30]

Carlos may also have been familiar with the composer, conductor, and arranger Angela Morley. Born Wally Stott in England in 1924, Morley made a name as a bandleader, composer, and arranger beginning in the 1940s. In 1972, she transitioned to female. Morley continued her remarkable career, earning two Academy Award nominations for her arrangements on the soundtracks to *The Little Prince* (1974) and *The Slipper and the Rose* (1977) and serving as an arranger for some of John Williams's best-known film scores, including *Star Wars* (1977) and *The Empire Strikes Back* (1980). Although Morley does not appear to have ever acknowledged her transition publicly, it seems that the people in her personal and professional circles accepted her transition and continued to collaborate with her. In fact, her greatest professional and commercial successes came after her transition.

There is no evidence that Carlos knew Morley personally or had even ever heard of her. At the same time, Carlos had provided music for Stanley Kubrick's *A Clockwork Orange*, which was nominated for four Academy Awards in 1972 (although none of those awards pertained to the score). It does not seem a stretch to think that Carlos would have closely followed the film music Oscar nominees in the years following her own work in film music. Further, Carlos had definitely seen *Star Wars* and critically appraised the soundtrack, lamenting the clichéd use of vocoders in the film.[31] If Carlos did know of Morley's transition, it seems as if Morley's situation would have been the most similar to Carlos's, in that both were known and respected musicians before their transitions; Morley's continued acceptance and success in the industry following her transition would have looked encouraging to Carlos.

Renee Richards's successful challenge to the USTA, Morley's second Academy Award nomination and her work on the blockbuster film *Star Wars*, and the increasing presence of transgender people in mainstream media outlets all indicated a more hospitable environment for transgender people than Carlos had experienced in the late 1960s. The improved cultural reception of transgender people, coupled with the lack of attention that her music was receiving, all seem to weight the scale in favor of Carlos disclosing her transition.

It is not as though transgender people had achieved any kind of universal tolerance or acceptance during the 1970s, however. A set of cruel experiments under the moniker of the Feminine Boy Project were undertaken at the University of California, Los Angeles UCLA and overseen by Richard Green, Ole Ivar Løvaas, and George Rekers. In his work with autistic children, Løvaas would strike, yell at, withhold attention from, or use electric shocks on children who exhibited common autistic behaviors such as avoiding eye contact, using echolalia, or engaging in self-stimulating behavior. Drawing on the operant conditioning techniques Løvaas had developed for autistic children, the researchers in the Feminine Boy Project worked to eliminate what they called "sissy boy syndrome." They argued that operant conditioning could help "confused" children early enough in life that they would be prevented from becoming gay or transgender later—yet another erroneous conflation of gender identity and sexual orientation.

Rekers and his team would punish young boys who exhibited "feminine" behaviors such as preferences for dolls and dresses, interest in dresses or makeup, or certain ways or walking or talking ("swishy gait" and "limp wrist"). "Masculine" behaviors were rewarded with treats such as candy or attention.[32] The goals of the Feminine Boy Project were similar to those of the gatekeepers who advised transgender people to leave behind any aspect of their lives and start over somewhere new. Løvaas and Rekers claimed that they had the children's best interests at heart, arguing that it was easier to force a few individual children to conform to specific gender roles and behaviors than it was to change society's attitudes toward people who did not conform to those gender roles. In the end, they likely caused far more harm than good to the children. Kirk Murphy, the main subject of Rekers's experiments in the 1970s, was claimed to have been cured of his "sissy" behavior. Murphy died by suicide in 2003 at the age of 38.[33] Rekers himself was found in the company of a male escort in 2010.

Feminist scholars were not universally in support of transgender women. In 1979, the same year Carlos's *Playboy* interview was published, feminist scholar Janice Raymond published *The Transsexual Empire: The Making of the She-Male*. In her book, Raymond claimed transgender women did not exist,

that they were merely men who were practicing deception based on patriarchal structures. Raymond argued that "all transsexuals rape women's bodies"
because they were "appropriating this body for themselves."[34] Further, she
reduced transgender women's identities to the characteristics of their physical bodies, claiming, "Transsexuals merely cut off the most obvious means
of invading women so that they seem non-invasive."[35] To Raymond, transgender women were just men in disguise, taking advantage of female spaces
and bodies in the same way that a patriarchal culture would dictate that all
men should do to women's spaces and bodies. Although Raymond's writings
have, in large part, been discredited as examples of transphobia and hate
speech, at the time of their publication they were widely read and respected.
According to feminist scholar Carol Riddell, for example, Raymond's book
didn't invent prejudice against transgender women, but Raymond did more
to perpetuate and justify that prejudice than anything else that had ever been
published.[36]

Although the tides were turning in a positive direction, it was still not completely safe for a transgender person to disclose their identity. There was still
plenty of prejudice, anger, and even violence directed toward transgender
people, and transgender women in particular. Carlos continued to waffle
until late 1978, when she and Elkind first made contact with Arthur Bell. She
told Bell that she viewed her gender transition as a social barometer in the
same way she had viewed *Switched-On Bach* as a cultural barometer a decade
earlier: each phenomenon inspired strong reactions among people and easily
separated those who were open-minded from those who were not.[37]

Arthur Bell (see Figure 5.1) was a journalist and gay rights activist in
New York. Bell was an active member in the Gay Liberation Front in the
organization's early days following the Stonewall Riots in June 1969. His first
piece for the *Village Voice* was an account of the Stonewall Riots published
in 1969. He contributed pieces to the *Village Voice* off and on throughout the
1970s, becoming a regular contributor in 1976 with the "Bell Tells" column
about show business and New York nightlife. He published two books during
his lifetime: *Dancing the Gay Lib Blues* (1971) and *Kings Don't Mean a Thing*
(1978).

Although Bell himself was gay and most of his work focused on gay issues and interests, he also supported and advocated for transgender individuals. He maintained a friendship with transgender activist Sylvia Rivera,
and he published articles advocating for transgender individuals' rights. In

Figure 5.1 Journalist Arthur Bell outside the offices of the *Village Voice* in 1978. Photo by Jack Mitchell. Getty Images. Used by permission.

pieces for the *Village Voice*, Bell not only respectfully profiled a transgender woman named Bebe, but he also explained the differences between female impersonators, drag queens, transvestites, and transsexuals. Further, he alerted transgender readers to their legal rights and encouraged them to contact organizations such as Transvestite Information Service and Transsexual Action Organization for assistance.[38]

Bell first met Carlos and Elkind on Halloween of 1978, and he recalled that the first meeting was largely the two women interviewing him.[39] They grilled him about his credentials, experience, and background, clearly trying to determine whether he was the right person to interview Carlos for publication. According to Bell, Carlos seemed to have been sold on him when he explained that viewed himself as a writer who was also gay, rather than as a gay writer; he thought she identified with this assessment because she desperately wanted to be known as a human and a musician, not as some sideshow attraction.[40] The three decided together that *Playboy* was an ideal forum in which to publish the interview.[41] After securing a publication agreement with *Playboy*, Bell began conducting the interview in late 1978. He interviewed Carlos multiple times over a couple of months, and the end result was more than eight hundred pages of transcribed text.[42]

Why did Bell, Carlos, and Elkind think *Playboy* was the ideal forum in which to publish the interview? In the published interview, Carlos told Bell that *Playboy* was a publication concerned with liberation and that the interview was the chance for her to liberate herself.[43] As David Ulin, book critic for the *Los Angeles Times*, has written, *Playboy*'s cultural zeitgeist was a mixture of pinup photos, articles on fine living, and in-depth conversations with remarkable figures, including Malcolm X, Jimmy Carter, Martin Luther King Jr., and Marshall McLuhan.[44] Indeed, one reader wrote to *Playboy* to tell the editors that the interview with Carlos, coupled with his "number one favorite girl from the Playmate search" had made that particular issue worth the entire year's subscription price.[45]

Playboy's interviews have featured some of the most striking cultural, political, and intellectual figures, many of whom speak more candidly in those interviews than they have in any other forum, a prime example being Carter's admission in the November 1976 issue that he had committed adultery in his heart. In the months preceding Carlos's interview, *Playboy*'s interviews included Marlon Brando, Bob Dylan, Neil Simon, and Ted Turner. *Playboy* was a distinguished venue for famous people to be interviewed, and Carlos joined prestigious ranks when her interview was published in the May 1979 issue of the magazine. Elkind recounted that they thought *Playboy* would treat Carlos with dignity, avoid turning her into a freak show, and discuss her gender and music in appropriate proportions.[46]

Bell's interview transcripts were more than 800 pages in length, but the published interview spanned pages 75 to 109 of the magazine, including plenty of advertisements, resulting in approximately 10 full pages of text. The vast majority of the interview, at least in published form, focused on Carlos's gender identity and the medical procedures she had undergone in her transition. Most mentions of her music were brought back to her transition; for example, a brief discussion about the early days of the Moog synthesizer were quickly turned into a discussion of Carlos's decision at the same time to transition. Approximately two columns of text are devoted to Carlos's music without any mention of her gender identity or transition; the rest of the interview, including her interactions with Kubrick, her relationship with her family, and the reception of *Switched-On Bach*, were all presented in the context of her transition.

The detail with which Carlos describes her past and present anatomy and the medical procedures she underwent is startling. She enumerated the hormone treatments and the operation she had undergone.[47] The graphic details of the physical changes she experienced are only a small part of the interview, however; Bell pressed her for details about her sex life, her gender identity, her sexual orientation, and how she experienced the world both before and after her transition. She discussed everything from her tortured childhood, in which she feared her parents would withhold their love if they discovered her wearing dresses, to the joy she felt when she donned a bikini for the first time.[48] On one page, Bell asked her to respond to those who might claim she had been castrated, and on another, she explains the feeble attempts at publicity she made when *Switched-On Bach* was first released.[49] What emerges is a portrait of a woman who is just now coming into her own, a woman who was now free to be herself. She comes across at times as preciously naïve, such as in her discussions of sex and relationships, but other times, like when she describes her distaste for disco, her New England saltiness gets the best of her. With one deeply personal interview, Wendy Carlos threw off the veil of secrecy under which she had been hiding for more than a decade.

Several aspects of the interview are notable in terms of understanding both how Carlos viewed herself and how society viewed transgender individuals at the time. The article is extensive and was a source of humiliation for Carlos following its publication. It is not necessary here to quote or summarize her statements about the medical and anatomical portion of her transition. She did, however, offer valuable information that helps us understand both her transition as well as how she would relate to journalists and the media for the rest of her life.

Carlos explained that she preferred the term "transgender" to "transsexual" because, in her experience, the latter term focuses exclusively on sexuality and the former term is more inclusive.[50] She also explained the difference between sexual orientation (she used the term "sexual preference," which was relatively standard nomenclature at the time) and gender identity, distinctions which *Playboy*'s readership may not have fully understood until they read the interview.[51] The interview was not only Carlos's opportunity to explain her gender identity to the readership, but it was also an opportunity for the readership to understand one transgender person's specific set of experiences. At the same time, she stressed that her story was only one, and it was not necessarily to be understood as either typical or as an example for others to follow.[52]

Bell focused his questions and the trajectory of the interview around her gender confirmation surgery, perpetuating the misconception that she was not female until the "sex-change operation" or "transsexual operation" was completed. Further, Bell's questions conflated cross-dressing behavior with transgender identity, even though he knew the difference because he had published a piece in the *Village Voice* that had made those very distinctions among various gender identities and behaviors. In the first question posed in the printed interview, he stated, "In 1972, after cross-dressing for a number of years, you underwent a transsexual operation and became a female . . . Since that date, you've kept the operation a secret from all but a few close friends."[53] Either he or the editors ignored the dates and facts Carlos had provided; she had begun hormone therapy in early 1968 and had socially transitioned in the spring of 1969. The surgery came years later, in 1972.

As she told Bell, although the public might have seen the surgery as the most important part of her transition, to her, it was both the least interesting and least important because she had already transitioned in terms of her physical appearance and secondary sex characteristics.[54] She explained that she was female by the time of the surgery, which she called "corrective," noting that it was necessary in terms of the final physical correction to her body as well as in allowing her to change her name and gender legally.[55] Despite the facts that Carlos had given about her transition and the role surgery played in her experience, Bell maintained the problematic narrative that she was male until the day of surgery.

Carlos made it very clear that once this interview was published, she was finished talking about her transition.[56] She had no interest in being a spokesperson or an advocate for the transgender community; she was a "normal" woman, and that was the end of it.[57] In fact, she wanted to forget that she had ever been known by any other name because her earlier life had been so excruciating.[58] She told Bell that she hoped readers would yawn after finishing the article.[59] She also was adamant that her gender identity was not something that could be read or interpreted in her music. When Bell asked her whether her biography was detectable in her music, she scoffed and said no way: "Can you imagine writing *The Transsexual Symphony*?"[60] She wanted to move on and live her life without further discussion of her gender identity.

Unlike women such as Renee Richards and Christine Jorgensen, who published autobiographies, gave lectures, and appeared on talk shows to discuss their own transitions and lives, Carlos had no interest in being known for her gender transition or for any other part of her private life. The paradox here is that Carlos announced her transition in a very public way and then asked the public to promptly forget that she had ever been known by another name and to never bring up the topic again. The interview with Bell was the last time she ever discussed her gender identity in print, apart from very brief, oblique mentions in two other interviews that she would give in 1979.

The response to the publication of Carlos's interview seems to have been largely positive and supportive. Of the dozens of letters sent to Arthur Bell and/or the editors of *Playboy*, most praised her courage, intellect, honesty, erudition, beauty, and "intestinal fortitude."[61] Bell's papers at the New York Public Library include about twenty letters addressed either to him or to the editors of *Playboy*, four of which were published in a subsequent issue of the magazine. Carlos mentioned that the few letters she had received following the interview were generally kind and supportive.[62] Although Bell and the magazine undoubtedly received negative feedback, Bell appeared only to have saved the letters of praise or admiration. One writer went so far as to ask for Carlos's address in hopes that the "beautiful" and "pretty" composer would like to be his friend.[63] Another letter writer said Carlos was probably the most intelligent and sensitive person *Playboy* had ever interviewed.[64]

Many of the letter writers were delighted to learn that Carlos was still alive, well, and creating music. They could finally get some answers about her music directly from her. Several people asked when her next album was coming out—a point that Bell and *Playboy* had neglected to include in the published version of the interview. One reader wrote to ask Carlos why she had withdrawn the quadraphonic version of *Switched-On Bach*.[65] Another corrected her harmonic analysis of the taunts she had endured as a child: she had mentioned the harmonic interval of a minor sixth in the singsong, "Carlos is a sissy," but the reader noted that the interval was actually a major sixth.[66]

Multiple letters asked Carlos about a hair removal procedure that she had mentioned in the article that involved cutting the nerve endings to hair follicles; notably, she had not actually undergone this procedure herself and in fact mentioned in the interview that the thought of the subdermal process made her extremely uncomfortable.[67] Whether Bell passed along the contact information for her admirers or for those interested in the hair removal is uncertain; if he did share the information with Carlos, it is highly unlikely that she would have replied to the messages, particularly those written by transgender people looking for advice, mentorship, or friendship. As she told Bell, she didn't want to know about the cliques, pipelines, or clubs to which transgender people belonged; she wanted to leave that part of her past behind, avoiding any reminders of who she had been and what she had undergone to confirm her gender identity.[68] Despite her own isolation for the last decade, she seemed uninterested in associating with anyone who may have been going through a similar experience.

One of the more vitriolic reactions came from Carlos herself. She wrote Bell a letter in May 1979, seven weeks after the publication of the interview.[69] She was horrified that the printed interview included so much "medical stuff" about her physical transition and so little about her personality and interests, and she accused Bell of presenting her as two-dimensional, as a shadow of a person. Carlos told him that she felt betrayed by both Bell and *Playboy* because the printed interview had included so much material about her transition and so little information about what she called her "soul."[70] She claimed that both Bell and *Playboy* had violated their promises that the interview would be as much about her music as it was about her gender. She lamented that any readers who already knew about transgender issues would have been terribly bored by the entire article, since that subject was almost the exclusive focus.

Despite Carlos's concerns that Bell had presented her as a simplistic figure, the letters readers sent to Bell and to *Playboy* suggest that most readers saw her as anything but simplistic. One reader wrote that Carlos was a rare type: a warm, non-phony, honest human being who inspired compassion and who would be welcome at their house for dinner any time she liked.[71] Another reader confessed that they had thought transgender people were "mentally deranged" until reading the interview, and their perspective shifted in response to what they called "the most dramatic personal revelation" *Playboy* had ever published.[72] Another transgender woman wrote that when she interacted with people, she hoped they came away with the impression that she was interesting and not weird, which was the same impression she had gotten of Carlos in the interview.[73] Even though the published interview had focused almost exclusively on Carlos's gender identity and the medical interventions she had experienced, her personality did shine through to the extent that a number of letter writers commented on her intelligence and warmth.

Carlos also felt that Bell had deceived her to get the information from her that he wanted to publish and then made that information the focus of the printed interview. According to her letter, Bell had asked her to clarify or explain some medical articles and books about gender confirmation surgeries to her, and he then quoted her explanations about gender reassignment surgery in the printed interview as if she had been explaining the procedures she had undergone.[74] She wrote that she forgave him for the deception with a jab that he probably didn't even realize how immorally he was acting because he was a journalist who would do anything for a story.[75] Despite the fact that Bell had identified himself as a writer who was also gay (rather than a gay writer) and Carlos had inferred that he would present her as a composer who was also transgender, she felt he had misrepresented her and focused far too much on the transgender part of her identity.

Ultimately, Carlos seemed crushed that Bell wasn't her friend. She was humiliated that in his introduction to the printed interview, he had referred to parts of their conversation as "rambling" and "irrelevant."[76] She told him that she felt like a fool for believing that the interviews had constituted a friendship, and she blamed her own desperation and naiveté for trusting a journalist in the first place.[77] Among Bell's interview notes, there is a page in Carlos's hand with Bell's address and a date and time. Bell had been hit by a car in late December 1978 in the midst of their interview sessions. Carlos agreed to meet him at his apartment instead of her own for the next session since he was still recuperating. In addition to the address, date, and time, she wrote in large letters "GINGER ALE," clearly a reminder to herself to pick up the remedy for the bedridden Bell. She trusted him and wanted to help him, and she perhaps was too earnest. As she wrote in her letter, Bell probably liked and respected her—he even hand-delivered an advance copy of the magazine to her with a bizarre handwritten comment that had to have been some kind of inside joke from their conversations.[78] He just didn't see her as a friend, and she was embarrassed that she had thought otherwise.[79]

Carlos desperately wanted to control the content of the interview, how the interview was received, and what kind of relationship she had with Bell before and after the interview was published. In an early draft of his introduction to the interview, Bell wrote that Carlos clearly had no understanding of how an interview with a journalist was conducted.[80] Carlos had given very few interviews in the late 1960s when *Switched-On Bach* first came out, so she may very well have been unprepared for what to expect in an interview. Further, the few interviews she had given a decade earlier had focused entirely on her music and not on any aspect of her personal life. Both *Whole Earth Catalog* and *Billboard* had published massive letters to the editor that she had written during the early part of the 1970s, perhaps leading her to the assumption that she would be able to dictate the content of the published interview with Bell in the same way that she had composed her letters to the editor.

Bell seemed charmed by her lack of awareness as they were conducting the interviews, noting that she had even brought along her own outline of the questions that she wanted him to ask and the answers she planned to provide.[81] Fragments of Carlos's handwritten outline are among Bell's notes; she included at least twelve pages of questions that she wanted Bell to ask her about, and her main topic headings start with letter A and go through at least letter S.[82] She clearly had a lot to say about many parts of her life and a specific idea of how she wanted to say those things, but, as she learned, a journalist was conducting the interview with her and would decide what questions were asked and what answers would be printed. Carlos may have had a chance to discuss all of her prepared topics with Bell during their conversations, but he clearly thought *Playboy*'s readership would prefer a different focus for the version of the interview that he ultimately published.

Carlos's outline suggests that she wanted to focus almost exclusively on her music, including her previous albums, her forthcoming albums, and the new technology she was exploring. She wanted to talk about how *Sonic Seasonings* transcended category, why she loved scoring films, and her desire for a touch-sensitive synthesizer keyboard. An entire page of notes in her hand is devoted to her hobbies, including her interest in photographing eclipses and a prize she had recently won for an eclipse photo. Of one eclipse photo, she had jotted [all text is *sic*], "A big trophy for me (as Wendy) helps afirm my identity and self worth."[83] Her gender is only mentioned once in the pages of notes and even then, only in the context of her career: she wondered how a first album by a woman would have been received.[84] Had *Playboy* published her autobiography instead of an interview with her, the content would have had a very different focus.

As Carlos learned the hard way, nothing is ever off the record with a journalist, and if he has an agenda, he will do everything in his power to achieve that agenda. Bell wrote in his manuscript draft that Carlos was resistant to discussing her medical procedures and claimed that the medical part of her transition was both boring and available in textbooks for those who were truly interested in the subject.[85] Carlos's letter to Bell indicates that he finally got her to discuss the details of the surgery by asking her to clarify what he had read about the procedure.[86] In the introduction to the interview that was ultimately printed in *Playboy*, Bell claimed that Carlos, moved by his vulnerability following the car accident, finally opened up to him about the surgery.[87] (He did note that she described the procedures "utterly without emotion, as if she were lecturing on the best way to prune an avocado tree."[88]) Despite his promise to Carlos that the interview would treat her and her music thoroughly and respectfully, he seems to have employed some deceptive tactics to get her to talk about the one topic that she resisted and that would likely be most titillating to *Playboy*'s readership.

As unhappy as she was with what was published in *Playboy* as well as with Bell and the magazine's editors, Carlos was relieved and grateful that her secret was out at last.[89] She told Bell that her anger had dissipated since the interview's initial publication, leaving only hurt and confusion behind.[90] This statement was not entirely true; Carlos would continue to carry a grudge against the magazine for decades, lambasting it and its editors on her website more than twenty years after the interview was first published. Bell died in 1984 at the age of 44, reportedly of complications of diabetes. Whether Carlos truly had forgiven Bell or whether she simply didn't want to speak ill of the dead, she has never publicly criticized Bell by name.

Bell was not the only journalist with whom Carlos thought she had forged a friendship only to discover that the relationship was professional, not personal, as would happen later in the context of her relationship with Allan Kozinn. Perhaps her relationship with Elkind—which began as a professional consultation and morphed into an intimate friendship as well as a rich musical partnership—had given her unrealistic expectations of the typical boundaries in professional relationships.

The *Playboy* interview was the end of Carlos's period of hiding. She had learned the hard way that no matter how she wanted to be portrayed in print or what she said in an interview, she had no control over what was ultimately published. At the same time, there was now nothing preventing her from promoting her music publicly. The *Playboy* interview left Carlos with a healthy dose of skepticism about journalists and the interviews they conducted with her. Although she would give dozens of interviews in the 1980s, her dissatisfaction and distrust gradually increased as she tried, usually unsuccessfully, to dictate what appeared in print about her. The published interview in *Playboy* was also the beginning of the end of several other parts of her life, including her use of analog sound and her personal and professional relationship with Rachel Elkind. Within a couple of years of disclosing her gender identity, she would make some huge changes in her life and music.

Notes

1. Bell, "*Playboy* interview," 76.
2. Bell, "*Playboy* interview," 76.
3. Carlos, letter to Bell, May 1979. Arthur Bell papers, Billy Rose Theatre Division, New York Public Library.
4. Milano, "Wendy Carlos" (1979), 69.
5. Bell, "*Playboy* interview," 100.
6. Bell, "*Playboy* interview," 77.
7. Bell, "*Playboy* interview," 82.
8. Bell, "*Playboy* interview," 100.
9. Kozinn, unpublished interview with Carlos, 37; Bell, "*Playboy* interview," 77.
10. Bell, "*Playboy* interview," 77.
11. Bell, "*Playboy* interview," 84.
12. Bell, "*Playboy* interview," 77.
13. Bell, "*Playboy* interview," 77.
14. Bell, "*Playboy* interview," 77.
15. Bell, "*Playboy* interview," 96.
16. Bell, "*Playboy* interview," 96.
17. Bell, "*Playboy* interview," 101.
18. Bell, "*Playboy* interview," 100.
19. Kozinn, unpublished interview with Carlos, 29.
20. Bell, "*Playboy* interview," 100.
21. Bell, "*Playboy* interview," 77.
22. See Meyerowitz, *How Sex Changed*, 224–226; Serano, *Whipping Girl*, 143–152.
23. Serano, *Whipping Girl*, 151.
24. Bell, "*Playboy* interview," 83.
25. On the history of court decisions regarding transgender individuals' name changes, see Meyerowitz, *How Sex Changed*, 241–253; 274.
26. Carlos mentioned Richards's chromosomal test in her interview with Bell. See Bell, "*Playboy* interview," 103.
27. See Meyerowitz, *How Sex Changed*, 252, 277. See also Renee Richards and John Ames, *Second Serve: The Renee Richards Story* (New York: Stein & Day, 1983).
28. On the increased presence of transgender people in mainstream media in the late 1970s, see Meyerowitz, *How Sex Changed*, 274–279.
29. No author, "My Daughter Changed Sex," *Good Housekeeping* (May 1973): 87, 152–158; Robert Jennings, "Women Who Dare to Become Men," *Cosmopolitan* (August 1975): 136.
30. Bell, "*Playboy* interview," 84.

31. Bell, "*Playboy* interview," 101.

32. See, for example, Steve Silberman, *Neurotribes: The Legacy of Autism and the Future of Neurodiversity* (New York: Avery, 2015), e-reader edition: 719–727.

33. See, for example, Scott Bronstein and Jessi Joseph, "Therapy to change 'feminine' boy created a troubled man, family says," AC360° (CNN), June 10, 2011, available at http://www.cnn.com/2011/US/06/07/sissy.boy.experiment/index.html.

34. Janice Raymond, *The Transsexual Empire: The Making of the She-Male* (Boston: Beacon Press, 1979), 104.

35. Raymond, *The Transsexual Empire*, 104.

36. Carol Riddell, "Divided Sisterhood: A Critical Review of Janice Raymond's *The Transsexual Empire*," in *The Transgender Studies Reader*, ed. Susan Stryker and Stephen Whittle (New York: Routledge, 2006), 144–158.

37. Bell, "*Playboy* interview,"101.

38. See, for example, "How a Transvestite Lives" and the accompanying "TV [Transvestite] Guide," *Village Voice* (October 24, 1974), 12.

39. Bell, unpublished article draft, Arthur Bell papers, Billy Rose Theatre Division, New York Public Library.

40. Bell, unpublished article draft.

41. Bell, unpublished article draft.

42. Bell, "*Playboy* interview," 77.

43. Bell, "*Playboy* interview," 77.

44. David L. Ulin, "Revisiting classic Playboy interviews with e-books," *Los Angeles Times* (September 6, 2012), available at http://articles.latimes.com/2012/sep/06/news/la-jc-the-reading-life-return-of-the-playboy-interview-20120906.

45. Eben Atwater, letter to *Playboy*; Arthur Bell papers, Billy Rose Theatre Division, New York Public Library.

46. Pinch, "Rachel Elkind," n.p.

47. Bell, "*Playboy* interview," 86–92.

48. Bell, "*Playboy* interview," 82, 96.

49. Bell, "*Playboy* interview," 95, 100.

50. Bell, "*Playboy* interview," 82.

51. Bell, "*Playboy* interview," 82.

52. Bell, "*Playboy* interview," 109.

53. Bell, "*Playboy* interview," 77.

54. Bell, "*Playboy* interview," 87, 92.

55. Bell, "*Playboy* interview," 92, 95.

56. Bell, "*Playboy* interview," 86.

57. Bell, "*Playboy* interview," 86.

58. Bell, "*Playboy* interview," 86.

59. Bell, "*Playboy* interview," 109.

60. Bell, "*Playboy* interview," 101.

61. Arthur Bell papers, Billy Rose Theatre Division, New York Public Library.

62. Carlos, letter to Bell, May 1979. Arthur Bell papers, Billy Rose Theatre Division, New York Public Library.

63. Miguel Biegh, letter to *Playboy*, Arthur Bell papers, Billy Rose Theatre Division, New York Public Library.
64. Ed DeJesus, letter to *Playboy*, Arthur Bell papers, Billy Rose Theatre Division, New York Public Library.
65. Jay L. Rudko, letter to *Playboy*, Arthur Bell papers, Billy Rose Theatre Division, New York Public Library.
66. Gary Bouton, letter to *Playboy*, Arthur Bell papers, Billy Rose Theatre Division, New York Public Library.
67. Bell, "*Playboy* interview," 86.
68. Bell, "*Playboy* interview," 86.
69. Carlos, letter to Bell, May 1979.
70. Carlos, letter to Bell, May 1979.
71. Mrs. N. J. Perrygo, letter to *Playboy*, Arthur Bell papers, Billy Rose Theatre Division, New York Public Library.
72. Dolly Gelsleichter, letter to *Playboy*, Arthur Bell papers, Billy Rose Theatre Division, New York Public Library.
73. Linda Lee, letter to *Playboy*, Arthur Bell papers, Billy Rose Theatre Division, New York Public Library.
74. Carlos, letter to Bell, May 1979.
75. Carlos, letter to Bell, May 1979.
76. Carlos, letter to Bell, May 1979.
77. Carlos, letter to Bell, May 1979.
78. Carlos, letter to Bell, May 1979.
79. Carlos, letter to Bell, May 1979.
80. Bell, unpublished article draft.
81. Bell, unpublished article draft.
82. Carlos, unpublished interview notes, Arthur Bell papers, Billy Rose Theatre Division, New York Public Library.
83. Carlos, unpublished interview.
84. Carlos, unpublished interview notes.
85. Bell, unpublished article draft.
86. Carlos, letter to Bell, May 1979.
87. Bell, "*Playboy* interview," 76–77.
88. Bell, "*Playboy* interview," 77.
89. Carlos, letter to Bell, May 1979.
90. Carlos, letter to Bell, May 1979.

6

Transformations (1979–1984)

The time surrounding the publication of the *Playboy* interview was one of many changes in Wendy Carlos's life. The period included her last collaborations with Rachel Elkind, the eventual dissolution of their friendship and artistic partnership, her second and final attempt to collaborate with Stanley Kubrick, and the start of her romantic and professional relationship with Annemarie Franklin, the woman with whom she would remain for the rest of her life. Once the 1980s arrived, Carlos would make several other substantial transformations in her music, perhaps most notably by shifting from analog to digital synthesis.

For Carlos, disclosing her gender identity meant that she would finally be able to speak freely and publicly about her work, and the first project in the pipeline was the album *Switched-On Brandenburgs*. Released on Columbia as part of the multi-album deal she had signed with Columbia a decade earlier, *Switched-On Brandenburgs* was the first album released under the name Wendy Carlos. She also posed for a number of publicity photos taken by Leonard DeLessio (see Figure 6.1). Taken in her home studio, DeLessio's photos show Carlos working at the piano, at her Moog synthesizer, and with her homemade mixing board.

In October 1979, Carlos and Elkind gave a series of interviews with music critic Allan Kozinn. Kozinn would write the liner notes for *Switched-On Brandenburgs*. Kozinn also wrote features on Carlos that the *New York Times* and *Fugue* published in early 1980. This interview was only the second time that Carlos would speak on the record with a reporter about her gender, but it would also be the last. She told Kozinn that new acquaintances, upon learning she was the person who had created the music attributed to Walter Carlos, would then begin to gender her with male pronouns when discussing the music: "Suddenly it becomes, 'Oh that Wendy, he's a genius,'" Carlos told Kozinn. "The creativity is automatically credited to the male brain."[1]

Kozinn's interview notes reveal that this is one of the few times Carlos spoke on the topic of her gender in their conversation. Kozinn didn't grill her about her gender identity and about the process of her transition in the

Figure 6.1 Wendy Carlos in her home studio in October 1979. The Moog synthesizer is over her left shoulder, and copies of the masters for *Switched-On Brandenburgs* are over her right shoulder. Photo by Leonard M. DeLessio/Corbis Historical. Getty Images. Used by permission.

way that Arthur Bell had; instead, Kozinn posed issues about gender more broadly, such as mentioning a column Harold Schonberg had written in the *New York Times* about a hypothetical scenario in which blindfolded listeners had to identify performances by male or female pianists.[2] Most of Carlos's responses to Kozinn's inquiries about gender were cagey. Indeed, the most concrete statement she gave about her gender was the statement Kozinn quoted in the piece published in the *New York Times*. Kozinn censored it for the *Times*, however: Carlos actually said, "Oh that Wendy, he's a fucking genius" in the interview.[3]

There is no evidence to suggest that Carlos was upset with Kozinn or the *New York Times* following the publication of the interview. The passage about her gender was only about 5 percent of the total text of the article, and the rest of Kozinn's article was respectful and thorough. It seems Carlos may have already learned from her interview with Bell that anything she said in earshot of a journalist about her gender was likely to be featured prominently in the printed article. She and Kozinn remained on friendly terms until early 1985, when he gave her newest album a less than favorable review.

Kozinn's *New York Times* piece was not the first published interview with Carlos following the *Playboy* article—a lengthy interview with Dominic Milano appeared in the December 1979 issue of *Contemporary Keyboard*. *Contemporary Keyboard*'s editors and readers had been clamoring for interviews with Carlos since the magazine's inception in 1975, and once she was finally available, they jumped at the opportunity. Milano flew to New York and spent two days with Carlos at her home studio conducting the interview. He gushed that he felt as if he had spent those two days with a musical guru, nothing that Carlos was able to articulate ideas about the synthesizer that were thought-provoking and unique.[4] It seems she was just as eager to talk to them as they were to talk to her: the magazine's publisher Jim Crockett noted that the interview with Carlos was the longest that *Contemporary Keyboard* had ever published.[5]

Carlos would become an integral part of *Contemporary Keyboard* (later changed to just *Keyboard*) well into the 1990s. She was featured on at least three of the magazine's covers, gave extensive interviews to accompany those covers, was regularly featured in Bob Moog's column about synthesizers, was invited to contribute guest editorials on multiple occasions, and served on the magazine's advisory board beginning in January 1980. She and eleven other advisory board members were invited to contribute to a gift presented to American composer Aaron Copland on his eightieth birthday. One of Copland's best-known works is a set of variations on the Shaker tune "Simple Gifts" that he used in the ballet *Appalachian Spring* in the 1940s, so the twelve board members each wrote their own version of "Simple Gifts." These twelve versions by Carlos and fellow advisory board members including Keith Emerson, Virgil Fox, Marian McPartland, and Anthony Newman were published in the magazine's November 1980 issue. Incidentally, Carlos and Copland were both born on November 14; his eightieth birthday was her forty-first.

The interview with Milano (conducted in October 1979 and printed in the magazine's December 1979 issue) is, like most interviews with Carlos that *Keyboard* would publish over the next two decades, extensive. In the article, Carlos spoke about her youthful music and technology experiments and inventions, her music education at Brown and Columbia, her work with Bob Moog in the 1960s, and many other topics that she had not had been interviewed about before then. It was the first time she had spoken on the record at length about all of the music she had been making for her entire life. As the publisher explained, it was time for *Contemporary Keyboard* to conduct an interview with Carlos that would finally give the magazine's readers what they wanted with regard to her views on synthesizers and music.[6] Milano's interview also included score excerpts from four of Carlos's original works: the "Piper Pomp" and "Fantasy" sections of "Pompous Circumstances" (from *By Request*), *Timesteps* (from the soundtrack of *A Clockwork Orange*), and J. S. Bach's Fifth Brandenburg Concerto (from *Switched-On Bach II*).[7]

In his publisher's note, Crockett offered a short statement mentioning Carlos's recent disclosure of her gender identity in the *Playboy* interview, noting that the creator of *Switched-On Bach* had not been available for interviews during the past decade because "Carlos was living through one of the most monumental changes a person can undergo."[8] This brief mention of her "complex and difficult physical and emotional transformation" received a single paragraph and was the only mention made of her gender.[9] It was quick, it was respectful, and it made clear that *Contemporary Keyboard* had no interest in discussing the topic that the *Playboy* interview had already covered. Crockett, Milano, and the rest of the magazine's staff seemed delighted that at long last, one of the world's leading experts on synthesizers was finally available to them and their readers. In the interview itself, Carlos was discreet about her gender, mentioning it obliquely and only in the context of why she had not been giving interviews. As she told Milano, she was unprepared for the success of *Switched-On Bach* because the last thing she wanted was for anyone to know who she was: "I was trying to hide off from society and undergo my transformation."[10]

Contemporary Keyboard seems to have been thrilled to have Carlos available at long last: the magazine printed yet another interview with her in the very next issue. In the January 1980 issue, Bob Moog's regular column, "On Synthesizers," was entirely devoted to an interview he conducted with Carlos about her thoughts on control devices for synthesizers.[11] That January 1980 issue of *Contemporary Keyboard* was also the first in which Carlos was listed in the masthead as a member of the magazine's advisory board. The next year, she was voted the second-favorite studio synthesizer musician in a poll of *Keyboard*'s readers (the magazine had changed its name by this time)—she lost out the number-one spot by just a few votes to Brian Eno.[12] Soon after, she would regularly be quoted in advertisements for *Keyboard* subscriptions.

The interviews Carlos conducted with Kozinn and with Milano in October 1979 are striking not only because Carlos is almost completely silent regarding her transition but also because so much of both interviews concern Rachel Elkind. Carlos told both interviewers that she needed to clarify how important Elkind had been to her work during the past decade. Being in hiding, she was unable to talk about the fact that Elkind was, in her eyes, more than just a producer but really more of a co-creator.[13] In both the *New York Times* and *Contemporary Keyboard* interviews, some of the first quotes from Carlos concern the crucial role that Elkind had played in the music she had released since the late 1960s. Further, Milano included a two-page interview conducted exclusively with Elkind, in which she spoke about her contributions as Carlos's friend and producer throughout the 1960s and 1970s.

Yet by 1979, when those interviews were conducted and published, the relationship between Carlos and Elkind was falling apart. To Milano, Carlos said, "I hope Rachel and I get more of a chance to collaborate as soon as we get our life arrangements worked out."[14] By "life arrangements," Carlos was likely referring to major shifts that had happened in both women's personal and professional lives. They had each met new partners, and Elkind's marriage and Carlos's new relationship would forever change their personal and professional relationship with each other.

Elkind has said she figured she and Carlos would continue to live together as two "old maids" if neither of them ever met anyone.[15] Arthur Bell had asked Carlos what she would do if Elkind were to get married, and she responded that she tried not to think about it.[16] Carlos told Bell that the idea frightened her because she and Elkind had lived together and been so close for so many years, and if Elkind were to get married and move away, then their present relationship would come to an end.[17]

By late 1978 when Carlos had begun the series of interviews with Bell, the idea that Elkind might meet someone and get married was not hypothetical. In 1973, Elkind and Carlos had traveled to Africa to chase the total solar eclipse that occurred on June 30 of that year. On this trip, Elkind met Yves Tourré, a French-born physicist and fellow eclipse chaser. The two dated for a long time, not marrying until early 1979.[18] Elkind has said she delayed getting married for several reasons. First, she was in her mid-30s by the time she and Tourré met, and she had already resigned herself to the fact that she probably wasn't going to get married at all.[19] Second, dating was a challenge for her because she was spending so much time trying to protect Carlos's identity and reputation. Elkind has spoken about having a "shield" up with people during this time in her life because she was so afraid about accidentally revealing Carlos's secret to the rest of the world.[20] Finally, she was concerned about her dear friend and what might happen to Carlos if Elkind were to get married and move out.[21]

There was also conflict between Elkind and Arthur Bell during Bell's interviews with Carlos for the *Playboy* article. Bell was furious with what he perceived as Elkind's interference in his conversations with Carlos. In an early unpublished draft of his article for *Playboy*, Bell complained at some length about Elkind's presence:

> Wendy was articulate, albeit verbose. Every now and then, Rachel would interrupt and correct with something like, "That isn't right, Wendy. You didn't see a psychiatrist. You saw a psychologist." Although I kept the thought to myself, I dreaded having Rachel in the room. She was inhibiting Wendy, and she was inhibiting me . . . Thirty minutes into the first taping, Rachel blew her stack . . . She screamed when Wendy told me where her parents live. Rachel flew into her, took my Sony [recorder], erased the section, said she didn't want any part of the interview, and fled from the room. After that, Rachel kept away.[22]

Bell wrote Elkind a note, calling her behavior "neurotic" and "abominable." He even appears to have threatened her, writing, "You should be sending me roses, considering what I could have done to you. And I would have, if it weren't for the fact that both Elly [Stone] and Wendy think the world of you. Remember, you called me into this."[23] It isn't clear what information Bell was referring to, or whether that information had to do with Elkind herself or with Carlos. Regardless, tensions between Carlos and Elkind were clearly building.

With regard to the two women's mutual concerns about how Carlos would be able to cope if Elkind ever married and moved out of their shared home, it turns out that neither of them needed to have been worried. Just as Elkind was forming a new partnership, Carlos met someone new as well. In April of 1979, right about the same time that Rachel Elkind and Yves Tourré were wed and the *Playboy* interview was published, a mutual friend introduced Carlos to a woman named Annemarie Franklin.[24] By the end of that same calendar year, Franklin had moved in with Carlos.[25]

Elkind has said that, in addition to serving as Carlos's producer and artistic partner, she also functioned as a sort of "lawyer-negotiator" for Carlos during the decade of the 1970s.[26] Elkind handled all of the legal and business aspects of Carlos's music.[27] Further, Elkind was not only juggling these various professional dimensions of Carlos's life but also working to hide her friend's gender identity from public knowledge in order to protect Carlos's career and well-being.[28] As Elkind's presence faded from Carlos's life and Annemarie Franklin came in, Franklin began assuming many of the roles for Carlos that Elkind had previously held.[29] Indeed, Franklin would even become Carlos's literal lawyer in the coming years, passing the bar in the early 1990s.[30] Franklin would also become a prolific advocate for Carlos's music, copyright, and artistic status, doing everything from filing copyright infringement complaints to writing letters to the editors of various publications on Carlos's behalf.[31] For a period of time in 1979, it seems that both Elkind and Franklin were an active part of Carlos's life, but ultimately there wouldn't be room for all three of them in the long term.[32]

Franklin's presence was a major source of tension during the final months of Elkind and Carlos's friendship. Elkind recalled thinking that it seemed as if Carlos expected Franklin to step into Elkind's shoes, both personally and professionally.[33] Elkind has said any conversation she and Carlos tried to have about any music during this period also had to involve Franklin, but Franklin didn't have the same kind of musical training or background that Elkind did.[34] Elkind recalled thinking, "I just don't have the strength for two people," and she eventually bowed out of the professional collaborations entirely.[35]

They were also growing apart professionally. By 1979, Elkind was itching to get back to producing acoustic music. She told an interviewer that although she'd had a lot of fun producing electronic music with Carlos over the past decade, she felt they had proved that electronic music could be used to communicate effectively.[36] Now she was ready to move on to a different kind of musical communication. For Elkind, the synthesizer had lost a lot of its appeal for her because it had been so popular so quickly.[37] To her, their early, overwhelming success had been a Faustian bargain, robbing them of a beginner's innocence and leaving them always trying to recreate the feelings they had when they were first starting out.[38] Carlos and Elkind would work together on one last project before things completely fell apart between them.

The final project Elkind and Carlos collaborated on was the soundtrack to Stanley Kubrick's film *The Shining*, an adaptation of the Stephen King novel of the same name. Kubrick had only directed one other film since *A Clockwork Orange*, which was the 1975 period film *Barry Lyndon*. For the film score of *Barry Lyndon*, Kubrick had drawn almost entirely on classical and folk music appropriate to the film's setting in the middle of the eighteenth century. *The Shining*, however, would be a completely different setting and require an entirely different kind of score.

Kubrick seems to have made the initial contact with Carlos about working together again. He sent her a letter in September 1977 in which he explained that he was currently working on the screenplay for the film and that the film might have some "exciting possibilities" for her "past, present, or future" work.[39] He also noted that King's book featured "a very interesting use of distorted voice montages," which he thought might appeal to her.[40] He encouraged Carlos to read the book and then call him to discuss her ideas.[41] By June 1978, Carlos had not only read *The Shining* but also had created some prospective music for Kubrick's film.[42] He wrote to thank her for sending the music and then put her off for nine months, explaining that he would be shooting for the next three months and then editing for the next six months.[43] He told her he was very interested in talking with her about working on the soundtrack and promised to call her "as soon as I can."[44] Things between Carlos and Kubrick began to get messy by the following summer.

The issues related to the soundtrack to *The Shining* seem to have been unconnected to Carlos's gender transition. Both the September 1977 and June 1978 letters from Kubrick were addressed to "Walter Carlos," so despite Carlos's suspicions during their concerns during the *Clockwork Orange* collaboration that Kubrick might have been on to her secret, he seems to have still thought that she was the male Walter Carlos when he initially made contact about working on *The Shining*.[45] Carlos's interview with Arthur Bell was published in the March 1979 issue of *Playboy*; if Kubrick hadn't known already that she was a woman, he would certainly have found out then. Kubrick himself had been the *Playboy* interview subject in 1968, soon after the release of *2001: A Space Odyssey*.

Lucy Kroll, the same agent who had initially connected Carlos and Kubrick, kept extensive notes in her client file about the negotiations between the two with regard to *The Shining*. Kubrick and Carlos had met at some point between June 1978 and September 1979 to discuss his ideas and to listen to her demo tape, but he had still not given Carlos and Elkind any specific instructions about music that he wanted them to produce for the film.[46] In September 1979, Kubrick, through a representative, said he still needed another three or four months to finish working on *The Shining*, which meant the film would likely be released in theaters in the winter of 1980.[47]

Kubrick also said he hoped a teaser trailer for *The Shining* would be ready for Christmas 1979, and did Carlos and Elkind want to create the music for the trailer?[48] They did. The ninety-second cue, called "Clockworks: Bloody Elevators," featured synthesized sounds of percussion and brass mixed with Elkind's voice.[49] The music accompanied the film's iconic trailer, in which the camera holds on a pair of elevator doors while the film's credits scroll across the screen. Then the elevator doors open, flooding the room with blood.

Kroll's notes suggest that Kubrick had flown Carlos to the studio early in 1980 to watch a preliminary cut of the entire film and to listen to recordings of the kinds of music that he wanted to have them create.[50] True to his aesthetic, Kubrick had already selected several pieces of classical music that he wanted to use in *The Shining*, and he was likely using recordings of those pieces as temp tracks while he continued to edit the film.[51] It seems as if Carlos and Elkind kept scrambling to keep up with Kubrick's ideas, constantly producing new cues as quickly as he came up with new ideas. (Carlos did give herself permission to sneak away for a few days in February 1980 to photograph a total solar eclipse in Malindi, Kenya.)[52] When Kubrick said he didn't want any electronic music in the film, for example, Carlos and Elkind created "Colorado," a cue for three flutes, three horns, three cellos, and bass.[53] They jammed ten musicians into Carlos's home studio to record the music, which then they augmented with percussion sounds from the Moog synthesizer.[54]

By the time Carlos spoke with Kozinn in the fall of 1979 about the *Switched-On Brandenburgs* release, she seems to have known that things with Kubrick and *The Shining* were likely not going to end well. She said she sent music to Kubrick for his consideration but had not yet signed a contract to provide music for the film. She also told Kozinn that she and Elkind were thinking about releasing an album called "Music Stanley Kubrick Didn't Use in *The Shining*."[55] Her premonition was spot-on, because ultimately Kubrick hardly used any of their music in the final version of the film. Carlos would, a quarter of a century later, release the complete score she had created for *The Shining*, but with the slightly less combative title *Rediscovering Lost Scores*.

In the end, Kubrick only included two cues that Elkind and Carlos had created: the opening theme, which was a synthesized rendition of the *Dies irae* (the medieval chant for the dead), and a short cue called "The Rocky Mountains," which is heard as the Torrance family drives through the mountains on the way to the Overlook Hotel. According to Carlos, Kubrick didn't use their final version of "The Rocky Mountains" but rather extracted portions of it from a much earlier demo they had sent.[56] For the rest of the soundtrack of *The Shining*, Kubrick used existing records of classical pieces, including music by twentieth-century composers Béla Bartók, Krzysztof Penderecki, and György Ligeti.

Much in the way that Alex North had created an entire score for Kubrick's *2001: A Space Odyssey* that Kubrick chose not to use, the entire score that they had created for *The Shining* was also almost entirely ignored. It seems that Carlos and Elkind didn't know exactly how little of their music would appear in the film until they were invited to a screening of the film in May 1980, an experience very similar to North's when seeing the final cut of *2001: A Space Odyssey*.[57] Elkind and Carlos were furious: Kroll's notes suggest that Elkind and Kroll had discussed suing Kubrick for breach of contract, but there is a key note from this conversation in Kroll's hand: "no signed contract."[58] Kubrick couldn't have breached a contract if a contract hadn't ever been signed.

The music for *The Shining* was the last time Carlos and Elkind would collaborate professionally. After that experience, Elkind has said she no longer wanted to work on film or television at all; she told an interviewer that she had no interest in creating fictional horror when the world was full of too many real horrors.[59] Trying to impress Kubrick had been maddening for the two of them, and no matter what music they produced, Kubrick ultimately kept most of the temp tracks he had been using throughout the production process.

But Carlos's and Elkind's separation was about more than just a professional collaboration with a difficult director. It seems as if the events surrounding *The Shining* were the straw that broke the camel's back. Elkind was married. Carlos had moved out of Elkind's brownstone and into a new place in Greenwich Village with Franklin.[60] Elkind no longer needed to run interference between Carlos and the rest of the world to protect Carlos's identity. Carlos, to Elkind's chagrin, now wanted Franklin's input on her music. Both women were ready to move away from the Moog synthesizer versions of existing music. Elkind and Carlos seem to have reached a point where they decided they no longer needed each other in any capacity.

For the first time in their relationship, they created a contract to formalize their separation. Until this point, they never had any kind of legally binding agreement about their professional and financial relationship.[61] The experience with Kubrick likely taught them that they needed a contract regardless of what kind of personal or professional assurances they had verbally. Elkind has said she took the publishing royalties and Carlos took the production royalties for the albums they had already produced together as well as for the two albums they had remaining in their current contract with Columbia.[62]

By 1980, Carlos's life had changed drastically. The entire world knew that she was a woman. She no longer had to hide, and she could now speak publicly about her music. Her relationship with her longtime producer and collaborator had formally come to an end. She had ended a friendship that had seen her through some of the darkest and most isolated times of her life. She had entered a new relationship with a woman who would in certain respects adopt many of Elkind's roles in Carlos's life. And, with the release of the *Switched-On Brandenburgs* album, she felt freed from having to produce more synthesizer renditions of Johann Sebastian Bach's music. New music production technology was entering the market, enabling her to create sounds she had been dreaming about since childhood.

Several themes permeate the first interviews Carlos gave during the late 1970s and early 1980s. She talked at length about how much work she had done, how little recognition that work had received, and how too many people were claiming to be experts of her caliber without having the proper experience or qualifications. In these initial interviews, Carlos stressed over and over how much work she put into her music. To Bell, she compared her compositional process to the animation process used in Walt Disney studios. In the same way that a Disney animator created a film one frame at a time, one drawing at a time, Carlos explained, she created a piece of music one note at a time, one color at a time.[63] Further, just as Disney studios gave depth and perspective to their images with unique optical processes, Carlos said she layered foreground and background elements to create depth in her sounds.[64]

She also frequently noted that her music had not received proper acknowledgment or recognition. She complained to Kozinn that American music critics pretended that she didn't exist. Carlos insinuated the existence of a type of "New York musical mafia," and she suggested that this "mafia" was ignoring both her and her music.[65] To Carlos, she was being ignored for any number of reasons, many of which were contradictory: she didn't make enough money, she made too much money, she was too successful, she wasn't successful enough, critics were angry with her, critics were disappointed with her, critics thought she should have been out in public more promoting her music, and so on.[66]

She felt slighted in part because she had worked so hard and had created so much music with such limited means, but so few people seemed to recognize how much she had really accomplished. Carlos told Kozinn that her skills had become so much more refined and artistic since the late 1960s and yet nobody seemed to have noticed.[67] On the flip side, Carlos railed against those who, from her perspective, thought electronic music was easy to create, or perhaps even worse, those who didn't try to push the boundaries of electronic music at all. She regularly complained about how many unqualified people were calling themselves "synthesists" without truly understanding the synthesizer in the way that she did.[68] Nobody who started to learn to play the violin would be making recordings on the instrument after only a year, she argued, so why did people seem to think they were qualified to make music with the synthesizer after having only used it for a short time?[69] In a jab likely directed at Keith Emerson and others who played the Moog onstage and in real time, Carlos claimed that too many people had used the Moog as a type of organ or other keyboard instrument.[70] She complained that the synthesizer had either stayed the same or perhaps had even gone backward since she began using it more than a decade earlier.[71]

These themes of her unacknowledged hard work, her shunning by "the establishment," and other people's frustratingly bad electronic music creations would pervade interviews that Carlos gave over the next several decades. Over and over, she would claim that electronic music was stunted or had gone in the wrong direction entirely, that nobody (except her) could or would put in all the necessary work to be a true artist with the synthesizer, and that nobody recognized the value of her work and how technologically advanced and artistically valuable it was.

In the late 1970s, Carlos was exploring a new kind of music technology: digital synthesis. Since the earliest days of the Moog synthesizer in the 1960s, Carlos had been endlessly frustrated with the limits of analog synthesis and with the synthesizers themselves. She purchased a Hewlett-Packard 9825 personal computer in the late 1970s, and she worked with an engineer named Harvie Branscomb to try to develop their own digital synthesizer.[72] She wanted an instrument that would be able to imitate or create any sound that human beings could conceive of.[73] To her, digital synthesis was a new frontier: the technology would enable her and other composers to go places and to accomplish things that would never have been possible with analog synthesis.[74]

At the same time, she wasn't quite ready to leave behind analog synthesis entirely. She liked digital synthesis and saw that it had a lot of potential, but she also remained fond of some of her earlier equipment. In a 1982 interview with Bob Moog published in *Keyboard* magazine, Carlos reported that she was still using the same Moog modular synthesizer that she had built in the late 1960s.[75] She told Moog that although some of her older machines might be dated in some ways, most new equipment wasn't much better—it just looked complicated and intimidating to fool the buyer into thinking it was better than it was.[76] To her, recording equipment was something that should last a lifetime, much like a piano.[77] It shouldn't be updated and replaced constantly with the newest and shiniest thing, both for artistic and for financial reasons; as she told Moog, "We're not made of gold bars."[78]

Although Carlos and Branscomb worked together trying to create their own digital synthesizer, eventually they put the project aside. Carlos began using commercially available digital synthesizers instead. The General Development System (GDS) was introduced in 1980 by Crumar. It had two eight-inch floppy disk drives, a Z80 microprocessor, a computer terminal, and a keyboard controller.[79] Carlos wasn't kidding with her gold bars comment, though: a new GDS sold for $27,500 in 1980 (well over $80,000 today). Carlos liked the GDS and found that she was beginning to use it more often than her trusty Moog modular.[80] As much as she liked the GDS, she still found it lacking. She still wanted to develop her own digital synthesizer eventually, one that would be state-of-the-art and that could create accurate renditions of xylophone and glockenspiel sounds.[81]

Despite all of the challenges she had faced when trying to work with Stanley Kubrick again on *The Shining*, Carlos does not seem to have been fazed about the possibility of scoring other films. At the same time Carlos was working on music for *The Shining*, Lucy Kroll was trying to secure other film music projects for Carlos and Elkind. At one point, Carlos had been recommended to score Ken Russell's 1980 science fiction film *Altered States*, but she apparently rejected the offer so that she could remain completely available for Kubrick; the film's score was ultimately composed by John Corigliano.[82]

Another project Kroll had pursued was a film produced by Donald Langdon that was set to shoot in Greece in the summer of 1980. The name of the film is not given in any of Kroll's notes, but in all likelihood, it was the horror film *Blood Tide*, directed by Richard Jeffries and starring James Earl Jones. Kroll wrote to Elkind that she had recommended her and Carlos to Langdon because the director didn't want "a conventional sound" for the music.[83] Further, Kroll wrote to Elkind, they shouldn't worry about another Kubrick-like disaster for this new project because "the producer and director are human beings and great to work for—it won't be a nightmare."[84]

Carlos and Elkind did not end up scoring *Blood Tide* or any other film to-gether after *The Shining*. It's not clear if they were simply not invited to create the score or if they chose not to pursue the project together. Kroll's last file notes about Carlos and Elkind were written in May 1980, and there are no other mentions of Carlos in Kroll's files after that point.[85] Carlos and Elkind had largely dissolved their partnership by the time the scoring for *Blood Tide* would have taken place, so even if they had been invited to compose the score, they might have been past the point of wanting to work together on it anyway.

The first major project Carlos undertook following her separation from Elkind—film score or otherwise—was the soundtrack to the Disney film *TRON*. Michael Fremer, the film's music supervisor, contacted Carlos in June 1981 to discuss the project, and she had formally signed on by the end of the summer.[86] Much in the way that *TRON* combines the live action "real world" and video graphics for the ENCOM mainframe system, Carlos wanted to combine the sounds of the acoustic symphony orchestra with those of both analog and digital synthesis. In fact, she was initially asked only to provide electronic music for the world inside the video game. When she told Fremer she wanted to write the orchestral music as well as the electronic music, he seemed surprised that she actually knew how to write for an orchestra. Carlos recalled being a bit insulted by the insinuation: "I bristled slightly and said, what do you think my training is?"[87] She told Fremer if she was going to do the score, she was going to do the entire score.[88]

TRON was supposed to have been completely edited by November 1981, after which she could start to score it. In anticipation, Carlos spent the late summer and early fall of that year sketching out a number of motives, themes, and gestures that she could eventually work into the final cut.[89] She was given a rough cut of the film in September 1981 and also created a ten-minute-long demo for the producers to review.[90] The result was problematic because her music didn't stylistically match the onscreen action: Carlos had written long, sweeping melodic lines that were totally incompatible with the film's rapid-fire edits and scene changes.[91] She said that once she saw the film, she real-ized it was like a thirty-second television commercial that lasted for almost two hours.[92] She had to scrap most of her ideas and write new material that was shorter and faster to fit the film's pacing; her revised score pages were "terribly black" because they were filled with notes.[93]

The London Philharmonic Orchestra and conductor Douglas Gamley had been contracted for the third week of March 1982 in London's Royal Albert Hall.[94] Carlos had planned to create the synthesizer tracks first and then have the orchestra play along with the synthesized music during the recording session.[95] There were significant delays in getting the edited film to her in late 1981 and early 1982, which meant that she didn't have enough time to have the synthesizer tracks ready for the recording session with the orchestra.[96]

Carlos had no choice but to record the orchestra first and then add the synthesizer later.[97] This was the opposite of her initial plan, but she received the final cut of the film only five weeks before the recording session was scheduled to begin.[98] The cost of rescheduling the orchestra made that option a nonstarter. Five weeks gave them barely enough time to get the orchestra's parts copied and ready for the musicians to read and record. Carlos worked almost around the clock with music editor Jeffry Gussman and orchestrator Jorge Calendrelli; Gussman set up the page, Carlos wrote in the lines of music and sketched out the desired orchestration (such as which instrument would play which line), and Caldendrelli filled in the orchestra parts.[99] Carlos recalled not only being exhausted but also suffering badly from allergies, forcing herself to work beyond her breaking point; she later said she felt like she was dying during the whole process.[100]

The version of the London Philharmonic Orchestra that appeared in the recording session had a total of 105 musicians, although not all of them played on every track.[101] Carlos had written music with complicated rhythms and a lot of nuance, and she was concerned that such a huge orchestra with many people playing on each part could swallow up the subtle gestures she had composed.[102] The orchestra recorded for a total twelve hours: four three-hour sessions in just two days. The first day was the entire orchestra, including an organist, and the second day was a smaller subgroup of musicians.[103] The recording sessions yielded about forty minutes of music and fifteen minutes of musical textures that could then be edited into the film.[104]

This was the largest group of live musicians Carlos had ever worked with in her career. Until this point, she had worked only with ad hoc chamber groups of her own vetting, such as in the music she composed for *The Shining* or in pieces for solo instruments and electronics that she had composed in graduate school. She was also working alongside recording engineers and other music professionals whose goals and ideas would potentially conflict with her own during the recording sessions. She was dissatisfied with many parts of the process and the contributions of many of the participants, and she didn't hesitate to speak up.

Carlos argued with John Moseley, one of the sound engineers, about microphone placement.[105] Fremer recalled that Carlos wanted to have the microphones as close to the musicians as possible so that she could separate the individual sections of the orchestra during the post-processing, while Moseley wanted to put the microphones far from the musicians to achieve a sense of ambience.[106] According to Fremer, "There were a hundred musicians, a conductor, and two BBC remote trucks sitting there while Moseley argued with Wendy. Of course it turned out that Wendy was right."[107] Carlos was less kind in her recollection of events: she had reseated the members of the orchestra to achieve an antiphonal effect in the sound, but that antiphonal effect was ruined when an "ignorant engineer" collapsed the entire stereo recording down to mono.[108] It's not clear whether Carlos was referring to Moseley or to someone else, but she was extremely unhappy with the entire *TRON* recording session as well as much of what happened during post-processing of the soundtrack.

Carlos was dismayed at how little time the orchestra was able to spend rehearsing and then recording her music, noting that the two allotted days with the orchestra weren't enough because the music she had written was lengthy and complicated.[109] She said good musicians could certainly play her music—if they were given adequate time to rehearse, which she did not think had happened with the London Philharmonic Orchestra during the sessions.[110] As a point of reference, she noted that the orchestra that had played John Williams's score for *Star Wars* had spent two weeks in the recording studio, compared with the two days scheduled for *TRON*.[111] Further, since the orchestra was playing on its own, rather than playing along with her synthesizer recording as she had originally played, there were quite a few more mistakes since the musicians were not hearing and following along with her error-free synthesizer rendition of the score.[112]

A second recording session in April 1982 took place in Los Angeles and featured the members of the UCLA chorus, conducted by Don Weiss. Carlos did not attend that recording session herself and sent Franklin in her place.[113] Carlos was disgusted with the outcome of the choir's recording session. Some of the problems were from the musicians themselves: Carlos complained that the choir sang wrong notes, entered at the wrong time, and even omitted entire parts of the score that she had written because they couldn't or wouldn't sing it.[114] The recording was problematic, too. She wanted the sound in stereo, but it was recorded in mono.[115] She also thought that a bad microphone power supply had led to sound distortion in a number of tracks.[116]

After the recording sessions, Carlos turned to creating the synthesizer parts and marrying the recorded instrumental performances with the synthesizer. She spliced multiple tracks from different takes together to get a single cue that was acceptable to her, she adjusted out-of-tune passages by re-recording passages at faster or slower speeds, and she ultimately discarded some sections that the orchestra had recorded and replaced the passages with synthesizer tracks.[117] She used both her modular Moog and a newer PolyMoog for the analog synthesis along with her new Crumar GDS for the digital synthesis.[118] She has said she used the synthesizers three different ways during the postproduction. First, she used it to augment and complement the orchestra's sounds, which was her original plan for the entire soundtrack. Her other two uses of the synthesizer were the result of her dissatisfaction with the recording sessions. Second, because she wasn't satisfied with the recordings of the orchestra, she doubled the orchestra's lines with the synthesizer to improve the sound. Third, she replaced entire sections of the orchestra when she wasn't happy with the recording, sometimes because the musicians had made a mistake and sometimes because the recording engineer had made a mistake.[119]

As soon as she completed sections of music, she sent them off to be mixed into the final film. Because she was still working on the synthesizer-orchestra-chorus postproduction, she did not attend any of the mixing sessions for the film.[120] Her participation may also have been limited by the fact that she had broken her hip in a car accident in 1982 and could only sit or recline for months.[121] Both she and Fremer were disappointed with the final outcome. According to Fremer, a lack of a spokesperson during the mixing session was a recipe for disaster because the sound effects were given priority over the music.[122] He claimed that the film could have been stronger if the music had been used more prominently.[123] Similarly, Carlos made it clear that the final mix heard in the film was not consistent with her vision for the soundtrack.[124]

The consolation prize for Carlos was that CBS Records released the entire *TRON* soundtrack on LP and cassette tape. Even though the version of her music heard in the film fell far below her expectations, she was satisfied that the complete soundtrack was available for interested listeners.[125] She was less pleased about the fact that the *TRON* video game released later the same year included musical cues that she had been told would be used only in the film and not for any other purpose.[126]

Carlos's work on *TRON* earned her a second cover and feature interview for *Keyboard* magazine. The cover photo is the first publicity photo of her that includes her pets. In the early 1980s, the Carlos-Franklin household had two Siamese cats, a chocolate point named Piccala (whose nicknames included "Peekie," "Peek," and "Pica") and a blue point named Subito (nicknamed "Subi"), as well as a wheaten terrier named Heather (whose full name was "Heather Dog").[127] In the *Keyboard* cover photo, one of the cats snoozes on top of Carlos's monitor while a second sits in her lap, looking apprehensive about the photo shoot. From this point forward, Carlos would rarely pose for publicity photos in her home studio that did not include at least one of her pets.

Despite all of the frustrations during the creation of the *TRON* soundtrack, Carlos tried again to work with an orchestra. Although she claimed that the musical establishment had largely ignored her, Carlos connected in the early 1980s with the Kronos Quartet.[128] Based in San Francisco and founded in 1973, the Kronos Quartet has commissioned hundreds of pieces from living composers. They were, and continue to be, some of the strongest advocates of new classical music in the United States, if not in the world. At some point in 1983, the Kronos Quartet asked Carlos to compose a piece for them.[129]

The result was unlike anything Carlos had ever written or would ever write again. Carlos ended up composing a miniature concerto for string quartet and orchestra.[130] The Kronos Quartet was already performing a piece by Thea Musgrave called *Memento Vitae: Concerto in Homage to Beethoven* on a concert with the Berkeley Symphony Orchestra (BSO), so Carlos opted to write a piece for the same instrumental configuration.[131] She only had about three weeks before the concert, so she knew that anything she wrote had to be relatively short.[132] The result was a ten-minute composition called *Variations on a Yearly Theme*. Since the work was scheduled to be performed on a concert on New Year's Eve or New Year's Day 1984, the "yearly theme" in question was "Auld Lang Syne."[133]

The concert ended up getting delayed until January 11, 1984, which took a little bit of the fun out of the concept, but the piece seems to have been received extremely well.[134] Carlos didn't write a traditional set of variations, where a theme is stated at the beginning of the piece and then repeated and varied several times throughout the piece. Instead, she presented multiple asynchronous parts that blurred the melodies and added effects of ticking clocks and chiming bells.[135] In her program notes for the piece, Carlos explained that there were about a dozen total variations, but the melody wasn't played clearly until the last couple of variations. She wanted to achieve the effect that all of the musicians were not together but were somehow held together by something—that something being the "Auld Lang Syne" melody that only emerged clearly near the end of the piece.[136]

Local critics praised the work, calling it "entertaining," "accessible," "fresh," and "gem-like."[137] One critic even wrote that the piece ended far too quickly and that she longed to hear more.[138] The experience with Kronos and the Berkeley Symphony Orchestra appears to have been positive for Carlos. She didn't have much negative to say after the event, and she particularly praised Kent Nagano, then the conductor of the BSO. In fact, she and Franklin acquired their third Siamese cat soon after this performance, a seal point they named Nagus in honor of Nagano.[139]

Variations on a Yearly Theme was never performed again, nor does it appear that Carlos published the score or make it more widely available. This seems a bit strange, given Carlos's desire to be known not only as a composer of electronic music but also as someone with a traditional background who could write for orchestras as well as for synthesizers. When she was approached about the *TRON* soundtrack, she was insulted that the music director didn't know she was classically trained and could write music for orchestra. Now, just a couple of years later, she had written a work for orchestra and string quartet—a string quartet well known for its promotion of living composers and new works—that received rave reviews from critics. Despite her claims that she wanted to be known as more than a composer of electronic music, she does not seem to have used this successful nonelectronic piece more than once.

1984 was also an exciting year for Carlos in terms of her eclipse photography. There were two solar eclipses that year, an annular one in May and a total one in November. A photo Carlos took of the May 1984 annular eclipse was not only featured in *Sky and Telescope* magazine but was also reprinted in two other specialist magazines.[140] To her amusement, she also received a request to use her photo on the cover of a book called *Divine Love and Wisdom*, a book about spiritual experiences authored by the scientist Emanuel Swedenborg. Carlos granted them permission to use the photo but declined their offer of a complimentary copy, claiming it didn't accord with her own beliefs. Much to her chagrin, the photo was printed on the book's cover upside down.[141]

Following her recent successful collaboration with Nagano and the Berkeley Symphony Orchestra, Carlos set out to work with them again. The second collaboration would go much less well, and it would be the last time Carlos would ever work with an orchestra. The impetus for this second collaboration with the BSO was Carlos's new album *Digital Moonscapes*. Released in 1984, *Digital Moonscapes* was created entirely with the new technology of digital synthesis. Carlos digitally synthesized the sounds of an orchestra using the GDS—she would refer to her digital orchestra as the "LSI Philharmonic" because she used large-scale integration (LSI) circuits.[142] She spent well over two thousand hours over a period of at least eighteen months just creating the sounds (she called them "replicas") that she wanted to use for the recordings.[143] According to Carlos, each sound that she created digitally required between eight and ten hours, compared with the three minutes it took her to create an analog sound.[144] The actual production and recording of the album came later and required hundreds more hours.[145]

Carlos was delighted that the album did not include any acoustic sounds. As she explained in the album's extensive liner notes, the synthesized sounds on *Digital Moonscapes* weren't perfect.[146] She conceded that her digital sounds were, in her estimation, somewhere between 75 and 99 percent successful in terms of how close they were to the sounds of the "real" instruments.[147] But, as she pointed out, the album offered the sounds of the very first digitally synthesized orchestra in history. She was quick to explain that her LSI Philharmonic wasn't exactly "an orchestra in a box," though.[148] Returning to a common theme about how long and hard she had to work, she pointed out in the liner notes that it took her so long to create the album that it wasn't exactly the kind of tool just anyone could pick up and use without mastery. Carlos also noted that she had no interest in replacing the orchestra as a medium. Instead, she viewed her album as an encomium to the ensemble, pointing out that imitation was the sincerest form of flattery and that even she—in most cases—still preferred the traditional acoustic orchestra.[149]

According to Annemarie Franklin, Carlos saw *Digital Moonscapes* and the LSI Philharmonic in particular as the next major steps in the development of electronic music.[150] To Carlos, this project was the inevitable next phase of electronic music. In a letter to the editor of *Opus* magazine, Franklin wrote that Carlos had spent the thousands of hours developing the technology behind the LSI Philharmonic for the simple reason that it needed to be done and nobody else was doing it.[151] Franklin pointed out that major electronic music research institutions such as Stanford University and the Institut de Recherche Coordination Acoustique et Musique (IRCAM) were not working with digital synthesis yet, but Carlos had taken it upon herself (and her limited funds and gear) to take electronic music where she thought it needed to go.[152]

The music that Carlos composed for *Digital Moonscapes* was written with each individual instrument in the orchestra in mind.[153] In *Switched-On Bach* and her other Moog projects, Carlos had used the analog synthesizer to play the musical lines that someone else had composed. In *Digital Moonscapes*, however, she composed the orchestral parts and then rendered them using the digital synthesizer. The twelve individual tracks on *Digital Moonscapes* can be divided into two different multi-movement suites. The first three tracks, "Genesis," "Eden," and "Intergalactic Communications," are called "Cosmological Impressions." Tracks four through twelve are called "Moonscapes" and are named for various moons, including Ganymede, Calisto, Io, and Titan.

Compared with the Moog synthesizer, the LSI Philharmonic's instrumental sounds are far closer to those of acoustic instruments. Despite Carlos's claim that the digital sounds were 75 to 99 percent accurate in their replication of instruments, though, no listener is likely to mistake the LSI Philharmonic for an acoustic orchestra. Some instruments, those of the percussion section in particular, are easy to identify. But the colors of the treble instruments are nearly impossible to differentiate at times; the listener can't always tell if a digitally synthesized clarinet or violin is playing the melody. Further, the warmth and human touch that pervaded Carlos's Moog synthesizer music is far less apparent in the music of *Digital Moonscapes*. The digitally synthesized snare drum rolls near the beginning of the "Io" movement, for example, sound rigid compared with the analog Moog synthesizer snare drum rolls heard throughout her rendition of Rossini's overture to *La gazza ladra*, from the soundtrack of *A Clockwork Orange*.

Carlos scored the music of *Digital Moonscapes* not just for her digital LSI Philharmonic but also for any orchestra that might want to play it; *Keyboard* magazine even printed excerpts from the scores of the "Ganymede" and "Io" movements.[154] This is what brought her to the second collaboration with Nagano and the Berkeley Symphony Orchestra. A printed program for a June 19, 1985, concert by the Berkeley Symphony Orchestra lists pieces by Carl Philip Emmanuel Bach, Leos Janacek, and Wendy Carlos. The program states that the concert will include the world premiere of *Moonscapes* by Wendy Carlos. It appears that Carlos and Nagano had planned for the BSO to perform all nine movements of *Moonscapes* on the concert, with "digital" having been dropped from the piece's title since the music would be played live and not by the LSI Philharmonic.

Something seems happened between the time that the program was printed and when the concert took place, though.[155] The orchestra actually performed "Genesis," a movement from the "Cosmological Impressions" suite. The other two movements of "Cosmological Impressions" were played from their *Digital Moonscapes* album recordings as the intermission music ("Eden") and exit music after the concert ("Intergalactic Communications"). "Moonscapes" was not performed as listed, either. The majority of the piece's nine movements were played from the *Digital Moonscapes* album, with the orchestra only performing one or two movements live from the score. A note accompanying the program indicates that the recordings from *Digital Moonscapes* were played because the orchestra parts had not been copied and distributed in time for the concert.

Carlos does not appear to have spoken about this particular performance of *Moonscapes* with the Berkeley Symphony Orchestra. When Carlos found that someone else was at fault, she usually didn't hesitate to identify them and rail against them. Her relative silence in this case suggests that perhaps she was the one at fault for not having the parts ready in time for sufficient rehearsals. At the same time, she was quick to place the blame on the orchestras themselves, suggesting that their limited budgets prevented sufficient rehearsal time for new pieces of music.[156] In an interview published a couple of years after the *Moonscapes* concert in Berkeley, Carlos complained that performances of her music suffered if an orchestra lacked enough time to rehearse it properly.[157] She grumbled that improperly prepared performances of new works were little more than "half-assed rehearsals."[158] The *Moonscapes* performance with the Berkeley Symphony Orchestra in 1985 appears to the last time she wrote music for a (nonsynthesizer) orchestra.

In the early 1980s, Carlos began likening herself to the actor Leonard Nimoy. Like Nimoy, she became inextricably linked with a particular dimension of popular culture in the late 1960s. For Carlos, it was the Moog synthesizer and *Switched-On Bach*, for Nimoy, it was the character he had played on *Star Trek*. As Carlos told multiple interviewers, Nimoy's fans only wanted to see him in the role of Mr. Spock and had little interest in anything else that he might have working on. Similarly, she felt that people only wanted to see or hear her in the context of electronic music despite her efforts to branch out from her Moog days.[159]

In all likelihood, Carlos was also frustrated by media's focus on her gender, wanting to ask her questions about a topic that she considered closed for discussion. Further, she was unable to leave some parts of the past behind because the majority of her music still had her birth name on it. Despite the fact that she had disclosed her transition quite publicly in 1979, some were slow to catch on or catch up. This issue is particularly notable in the context of record labels not acknowledging her name. It would take more than two decades and a change of record label before she would finally get her name on her entire recorded catalogue.

Of the items in her back catalogue, *Switched-On Bach* was the only item that Columbia Masterworks would reissue under her name, which it did in 1981. Her remaining albums on Columbia—including *The Well-Tempered Synthesizer, Sonic Seasonings, Switched-On Bach II*—were not reissued and would remain listed as having been produced by "Walter Carlos." Columbia chose not to re-issue any of those albums on CD in the 1980s, either, which may explain in part why Carlos's music was not available under the correct name until the late 1990s, when she took her entire catalogue to a different record label and remastered reissued everything on CD for the first time. In addition to having her name not listed as the artist, at least two of the albums' titles included a name that was no longer part of her identity: *Walter Carlos's A Clockwork Orange* and *Walter Carlos: By Request*.

Another album that did not update her name was *Stanley Kubrick's A Clockwork Orange*, the soundtrack for the film that had been issued by Warner Brothers in 1971. Even when this version of the soundtrack was first released on CD in 1984, Warner Brothers did not change Carlos's name in the liner notes or accompanying material. Subsequent CD issues of this album in 1990 and 2001 also did not include the correct name. To this day, more than forty years after Carlos disclosed her transition and legally changed her name, Warner Brothers still has not corrected her name in the printed material for *Stanley Kubrick's A Clockwork Orange*.[160]

Notes

1. Kozinn, " 'Switched-On Bach' Creator Returns," D22.
2. Kozinn, unpublished interview with Carlos, 32.
3. Kozinn, unpublished interview with Carlos, 34.

4. Crockett, "From the Publisher," 3.

5. Crockett, "From the Publisher," 3.

6. Crockett, "From the Publisher," 3.

7. Milano, "Wendy Carlos" (1979), 38–39.

8. Crockett, "From the Publisher," 3.

9. Crockett, "From the Publisher," 3.

10. Milano, "Wendy Carlos" (1979), 68.

11. Moog, "On Synthesizers: Wendy Carlos on Control Devices," *Contemporary Keyboard* (January 1980), 67.

12. *Keyboard* (December 1981), 27.

13. Kozinn, " 'Switched-On Bach' Creator Returns," D22.

14. Milano, "Wendy Carlos" (1979), 69.

15. Pinch, "Rachel Elkind," n.p.

16. Bell, "*Playboy* interview," 101.

17. Bell, "*Playboy* interview," 101.

18. Carlos, "The Wendy Carlos Total Solar Eclipse Page" available at http://www.wendycarlos.com/eclipse.html.

19. Pinch, "Rachel Elkind," n.p.

20. Pinch, "Rachel Elkind," n.p.

21. Pinch, "Rachel Elkind," n.p.

22. Bell, unpublished article draft.

23. Bell, undated letter to Elkind, Arthur Bell papers, Billy Rose Theatre Division, New York Public Library. The letter was likely written in 1979 following the publication of the *Playboy* interview.

24. Carlos and Franklin, letter to Harry Benjamin, 31 December 1979. Harry Benjamin papers, Box 27, Folder 8, Kinsey Institute and Library, Indiana University.

25. Carlos and Franklin, letter to Harry Benjamin, 31 December 1979.

26. Pinch, "Rachel Elkind," n.p.

27. Pinch, "Rachel Elkind," n.p.

28. Pinch, "Rachel Elkind," n.p.

29. Pinch, "Rachel Elkind," n.p.

30. Carlos, letter to Bob Moog, 18 December 1991. Robert Moog papers, #8629. Box 60, folder 15. Division of Rare and Manuscript Collections, Cornell University Library.

31. See, for example, Serendip LLC v. Hugh Murray Atkin, 16 CV 08790 (New York, 2016).

32. Pinch, "Rachel Elkind," n.p.

33. Pinch, "Rachel Elkind," n.p.

34. Pinch, "Rachel Elkind," n.p.

35. Pinch, "Rachel Elkind," n.p.

36. Milano, "Rachel Elkind," 36.

37. Milano, "Rachel Elkind," 36.

38. Milano, "Rachel Elkind," 36.

39. Kubrick, letter to Carlos, September 5, 1977.

40. Kubrick, letter to Carlos, September 5, 1977.

41. Kubrick, letter to Carlos, September 5, 1977.

42. Kubrick, letter to Carlos, June 26, 1978.

43. Kubrick, letter to Carlos, June 26, 1978.
44. Kubrick, letter to Carlos, June 26, 1978.
45. Bell, "*Playboy* interview," 100.
46. Kroll, notes from meeting with Elkind, Carlos, and Larry Marks. September 14, 1979.
47. Kroll, notes from meeting with Elkind, December 5, 1979.
48. Kroll, notes from meeting with Elkind, October 18, 1979.
49. Carlos, liner notes from *Rediscovering Lost Scores: Volume 1* (East Side Digital, 2005), 7.
50. Kroll, notes from meeting with Elkind, January 20, 1980.
51. Kroll, notes from meeting with Elkind, January 20, 1980.
52. Carlos, "The Wendy Carlos Total Solar Eclipse Page," available at http://www. wendycarlos.com/eclipse.html.
53. Kroll, notes from meeting with Elkind, September 13, 1979.
54. Carlos, liner notes from *Rediscovering Lost Scores: Volume 1*, 3.
55. Kozinn, unpublished interview with Carlos, 26.
56. Carlos, liner notes from *Rediscovering Lost Scores: Volume 1*, 3.
57. Kroll, invitation to film screening of *The Shining*, May 13, 1980.
58. Kroll, notes from meeting with Elkind, May 19, 1980.
59. Bozung, "Rachel Elkind."
60. Robert Moog, "Wendy Carlos: New Directions for a Synthesizer Pioneer," *Keyboard* (November 1982), 51.
61. Pinch, "Rachel Elkind," n.p.
62. Pinch, "Rachel Elkind," n.p.
63. Bell, "*Playboy* interview," 102.
64. Bell, "*Playboy* interview," 102.
65. Kozinn, unpublished interview with Carlos, 29.
66. Kozinn, unpublished interview with Carlos, 29.
67. Kozinn, unpublished interview with Carlos, 29.
68. Milano, "Wendy Carlos" (1979), 72.
69. Milano, "Wendy Carlos" (1979), 72.
70. Milano, "Wendy Carlos" (1979), 72.
71. Kozinn, unpublished interview with Carlos, 15; George Estrada, "Synthesizer Pioneer Wants to Go Further," *Oakland Tribune* (January 10, 1984), D1.
72. Robert Moog, "On Synthesizers: Wendy Carlos on Computers," *Keyboard* (December 1982), 64.
73. Bell, "*Playboy* interview," 102.
74. Kozinn, unpublished interview with Carlos, 30.
75. Moog, "Wendy Carlos," 58.
76. Moog, "Wendy Carlos," 58.
77. Moog, "Wendy Carlos," 58.
78. Moog, "Wendy Carlos," 58.
79. Unless otherwise noted, all information about the GDS is drawn from Holmes, *Electronic and Experimental Music*, 505,
80. Moog, "Wendy Carlos," 58.

81. Moog, "Wendy Carlos," 58.
82. Kroll, notes from meeting with Elkind, Carlos, and Marks, September 9, 1979.
83. Kroll, letter to Elkind, April 30, 1980.
84. Kroll, letter to Elkind, May 7, 1980.
85. Kroll, letter to Elkind, May 7, 1980.
86. Moog, "Wendy Carlos," 54.
87. Bond, "Wendy Carlos," 21.
88. Larson, "The Sound of *TRON*," *CinemaScore* 11/12 (1983), 34.
89. Moog, "Wendy Carlos," 54.
90. Moog, "Wendy Carlos," 54.
91. Moog, "Wendy Carlos," 54.
92. Larson, "The Sound of *TRON*," 35.
93. Larson, "The Sound of *TRON*," 35.
94. Moog, "Wendy Carlos," 55.
95. Moog, "Wendy Carlos," 55.
96. Moog, "Wendy Carlos," 55.
97. Larson, "The Sound of *TRON*," 34.
98. Moog, "Wendy Carlos," 55.
99. Moog, "Wendy Carlos," 55.
100. Moog, "Wendy Carlos," 55.
101. Larson, "The Sound of *TRON*," 34.
102. Moog, "Wendy Carlos," 55.
103. Moog, "Wendy Carlos," 56.
104. Moog, "Wendy Carlos," 55.
105. Moog, "Wendy Carlos," 56.
106. Moog, "Wendy Carlos," 56.
107. Moog, "Wendy Carlos," 56.
108. Diliberto, "Wendy Carlos," 12.
109. Moog, "Wendy Carlos," 56.
110. Moog, "Wendy Carlos," 56.
111. Moog, "Wendy Carlos," 56.
112. Moog, "Wendy Carlos," 56.
113. Moog, "Wendy Carlos," 56.
114. Moog, "Wendy Carlos," 56.
115. Moog, "Wendy Carlos," 56.
116. Moog, "Wendy Carlos," 56.
117. Moog, "Wendy Carlos," 56.
118. Carlos, liner notes to *TRON* soundtrack (CBS, 1982), 2.
119. Moog, "Wendy Carlos," 56.
120. Moog, "Wendy Carlos," 57.
121. Carlos, "Wendy's Artwork," available at http://www.wendycarlos.com/artwork. html. She has only mentioned the car accident and the broken hip in the context of her artwork, because she spent the period of her rehabilitation following the accident drawing extensively.

122. Moog, "Wendy Carlos," 57.
123. Moog, "Wendy Carlos," 57.
124. Moog, "Wendy Carlos," 57.
125. Moog, "Wendy Carlos," 57.
126. Bond, "Wendy Carlos," 22.
127. Carlos, "The 'Critters' Pose," available at http://www.wendycarlos.com/photos2. html#critters.
128. Oteri, "Wendy's World," 3.
129. Oteri, "Wendy's World," 3.
130. Oteri, "Wendy's World," 3.
131. Oteri, "Wendy's World," 3.
132. Oteri, "Wendy's World," 3.
133. Marilyn Tucker, "A Heady Experience at the Berkeley Symphony," *San Francisco Chronicle* (January 13, 1984): 64.
134. Oteri, "Wendy's World," 3.
135. Carlos, untitled program note to *Variations on a Yearly Theme*; Berkeley Symphony Orchestra concert program (January 11, 1984). Many thanks to Grant, BSO intern extraordinaire, for finding, scanning, and sharing this document with me from the BSO's archives.
136. Carlos, program note to *Variations on a Yearly Theme*.
137. Tucker, "A Heady Experience"; Janet Livingstone, "Mixing the old and the recent to ring in the new: Kent Nagano and Berkeley Symphony joined by Kronos Quartet in a winning concert," *Berkeley Gazette* (January 14, 1984).
138. Livingstone, "Kent Nagano and Berkeley Symphony joined by Kronos Quartet in a winning concert."
139. Liane Hansen, "'Switched-On Bach' Back after 25 Years," (includes interview with Wendy Carlos), *Weekend All Things Considered*, National Public Radio (August 23, 1992) (hereafter Hansen, "Wendy Carlos").
140. Carlos, "The Wendy Carlos Total Solar Eclipse Page."
141. Carlos, "The Wendy Carlos Total Solar Eclipse Page."
142. Carlos, liner notes to *Digital Moonscapes* (Columbia, 1984; East Side Digital, 2000), 3 (citations are to the 2000 reissue).
143. Dominic Milano, "Wendy Carlos and the LSI Philharmonic Orchestra: Excerpts from 'Ganymede' and 'Io,'" *Keyboard* (December 1984), 29–30, quote on 26 (hereafter Milano, "Wendy Carlos" (1984)).
144. Milano, "Wendy Carlos" (1984), 26.
145. Milano, "Wendy Carlos" (1984), 26.
146. Carlos, liner notes to *Digital Moonscapes*, 3.
147. Carlos, liner notes to *Digital Moonscapes*, 3.
148. Carlos, liner notes to *Digital Moonscapes*, 4.
149. Carlos, liner notes to *Digital Moonscapes*, 3.
150. Franklin, letter to *Opus*, March 11, 1985. Allan Kozinn personal collection.
151. Franklin, letter to *Opus*, March 11, 1985.
152. Franklin, letter to *Opus*, March 11, 1985.

153. Oteri, "Wendy's World," 5.
154. Milano, "Wendy Carlos" (1984).
155. All information about changes in the concert are from an undated handwritten insert accompanying the concert program in the BSO's archives.
156. Peter Kobel, "Wendy Carlos Synthesizes the Sciences and Humanities," *Chicago Tribune* (April 5, 1987), K16.
157. Dave DiMartino, "Wendy Carlos Invents New Sounds," *Billboard* (February 21, 1987), 23,
158. DiMartino, "Wendy Carlos Invents New Sounds," 23.
159. See, for example, Estrada, "Synthesizer Pioneer Wants to Go Further," D3.
160. A list of all known releases and their respective dates and countries can be found at https://www.discogs.com/master/view/76290.

7

The Last of the New (1985–1997)

The late 1980s and first part of the 1990s were the last period when Carlos created new music. By the early 1990s, she had already gone back to old formulas, creating more renditions of Johann Sebastian Bach's music using the newest digital synthesizers. During this period, Carlos also seems to have become increasingly distrustful of journalists and other musicians. After the difficult concert with the Berkeley Symphony Orchestra in 1985, Carlos would never again collaborate with an orchestra. That same year, two different journalists presented her and her music in ways that she probably found pretty problematic.

According to Annemarie Franklin, Carlos saw her album *Digital Moonscapes* as the next chapter in the history of electronic music.[1] It seems, though, that *Digital Moonscapes* barely even registered for music critics. Even though it was released on the CBS (formerly Columbia) label, it received minimal fanfare or promotion, at least according to Carlos. Very few reviews of it appeared in print. Andrea Houtkin gave it a rave review in *Computer Music Journal*, but her review appeared in the spring 1986 issue of the scholarly journal and likely didn't reach readers until at least two years after the initial 1984 release of *Digital Moonscapes*. Further, *Computer Music Journal* was a highly specialized periodical with limited circulation; even if all of its readers ran out and purchased Carlos's album, it probably wouldn't have made a huge sales bump.

One person Carlos may have thought she could count on ended up letting her down. Carlos had worked closely with music critic Allan Kozinn a few years earlier. He wrote the liner notes for *Switched-On Brandenburgs* and also published an interview with her in the *New York Times* soon after she had disclosed her transition. Carlos seems to have come away from those conversations feeling warmly toward Kozinn. A letter to Kozinn from Carlos dated February 1980 invited him over to dinner sometime in the next month, reminded him about how many things they had in common, and included inside jokes that they had made up during the interviews.[2]

Carlos and Kozinn didn't work together again and didn't have much contact in the early part of the 1980s. In September 1984, Annemarie Franklin sent Kozinn a copy of *Digital Moonscapes* and asked him to reach out if he wanted more information about how Carlos had made the "extraordinary sounds" on the album.[3] In the letter that accompanied the copy of the album, Franklin used "we" (instead of "I" or "she") throughout the text, which likely meant her and Carlos. She told Kozinn that "we" believed *Digital Moonscapes* was the "first giant step" in the progress of electronic music since *Switched-On Bach*.[4]

Kozinn did write a review of *Digital Moonscapes* for the short-lived classical music magazine *Opus*.[5] In the review, Kozinn gave Carlos a lot of credit for all the work she had put in creating the LSI Philharmonic and its digital sounds, but he wrote that the album didn't really work.[6] He suggested that using a synthesizer to mimic orchestral instrument sounds was wasteful and a poor use of the synthesizer as a medium. He noted that a listener would struggle to differentiate the quality of "the sounds" from the quality of "the music."[7] Ultimately, Kozinn wrote, "The aggregate is so unquestionably electronic-sounding that the attempt to create a credible orchestral sound must be deemed a failure."[8] To Kozinn, Carlos's LSI Philharmonic Orchestra had failed.

He wrote favorably about particular tracks but noted that there was little cohesion among the individual lunar portraits presented in the *Moonscapes* suite. Kozinn also remarked that parts of the album felt forced and eventually became tiresome: some movements would "lapse into mundane noodling" and others sounded "popsy."[9] He wrote that although he found some of the individual movements attractive, he couldn't shake the sense that he was listening to a demonstration disc. He praised Carlos's skill, acknowledged her earlier album *Sonic Seasonings* as "evocative" and "beautifully sculpted," and wrote that he looked forward to her next album.[10]

Carlos and Franklin were unhappy with Kozinn's review. A March 1985 letter from Franklin suggested that Kozinn had been to their house for a visit recently and that they had expressed concern about what he had written in *Opus*.[11] Kozinn had suggested that Carlos write a letter to *Opus* and respond to the review herself.[12] Franklin explained that since Carlos was reluctant to write such a rebuttal letter, Franklin had taken it upon herself to draft one.[13] She included a copy of her rebuttal with the note to Kozinn, asking whether he found it offensive or too harsh.[14] It's not clear how he responded, if he responded at all.

Franklin's letter to the editor of *Opus* is nearly as long as Kozinn's original review. According to Franklin, Kozinn had failed to understand what Carlos was trying to accomplish in *Digital Moonscapes*.[15] Franklin then attempted to rebut several items from his review. She wrote that Kozinn was flat-out wrong in his assumption that the album's success should be judged on how closely it replicated orchestral sounds; if Kozinn had read the liner notes thoroughly, Franklin argued, he would have known that Carlos wasn't trying for perfect accuracy but rather for taking the sounds of digital synthesis further than anyone had taken them before.[16] Franklin also took him to task for judging the album's digital orchestra sounds to be a failure, citing anecdotes in which other listeners thought they were listening to an actual orchestra instead of to synthesized sounds.[17] Franklin claimed that the movements Kozinn called "tiresome" were among the favorites of other listeners.[18] She also jabbed at Kozinn's assessment of the album's inconsistency, mentioning Gustav Holst's multi-movement orchestral work *The Planets* as an example of a similar composition whose individual celestial movements were not unified but whose overall experience was one of cohesion.[19]

Yet again, Carlos was writing a letter to the journalist or to the publication in which the journalist's article appeared to protest how she was depicted. Much as Carlos had felt that Bell had misrepresented her in the *Playboy* interview by focusing excessively on her gender, Carlos and Franklin felt that Kozinn had missed the point of *Digital Moonscapes*. In both cases, Carlos had no control over what had been printed and how what the journalists had written would affect the public's reception of her music and perception of her. In this case, *Opus* wasn't a major publication, but it was one of the very few reviews of *Digital Moonscapes* that had been published relatively soon after the album's release. And it said that Carlos's music was a failure, an assessment that likely didn't inspire many people to purchase the album.

At the same time that Carlos and Franklin were addressing what they saw as inaccuracies in Allan Kozinn's review of *Digital Moonscapes*, an interview with Carlos appeared in the June 1, 1985, issue of *People* magazine. The article's headline was provocative, announcing, "After a Sex Change and Several Eclipses, Wendy Carlos Treads a New Digital Moonscape."[20] The article opens with the story of Carlos's suicidal ideations at her 1970 St. Louis Symphony engagement and her subsequent move out of the public eye. Carlos is quoted at length talking about her childhood, her time spent in hiding, and her regrets about having been in hiding all that time.

Much like Arthur Bell had done in the *Playboy* interview with Carlos in 1979, author Susan Reed focused the *People* article on Carlos's gender but did mention a few other accomplishments. *Digital Moonscapes* received an entire paragraph that included effusive praise from Bob Moog about the album. Carlos's eclipse photography also earned a mention. But the vast majority of the article (more than 700 of the 1,100 words) is about her transition. Reed framed *Digital Moonscapes* as "the creative resolution of years of personal misery," suggesting that the album symbolized Carlos making peace with herself after years of difficulty. In the article, Reed mixed female and male names and pronouns, using the moment of surgery as the point at which Carlos "became" female. The result is some interesting and convoluted sentences such as, "In the fall of 1972 Walter Carlos had a sex change operation but did not reveal her new identity."

It is not clear who interviewed Carlos for this article. Neither Susan Reed, the author, nor her editorial assistant at the time, Barbara Rowes, could recall when or under what circumstances they had spoken with Carlos.[21] Reed suggested that Rowes had probably created the file on Carlos and done the background research and interview, which Reed then used to write the article. Reed said she recalled that Carlos was "straightforward" and a great subject, but she wasn't sure if she had interviewed Carlos or if Rowes had. Rowes could not remember whether she had interviewed Carlos or any other specifics pertaining to this particular piece.

This *People* magazine article and interview seems bizarre given Carlos's prior bad experience talking with a journalist about her gender. Carlos hadn't spoken with any journalists about her transition since Arthur Bell in 1979. Why would she suddenly go on the record about her transition again? She had been so badly hurt by what happened with Bell and *Playboy* that it seems strange that she would try again to talk with another journalist about her gender.[22] There is no documentation currently available to reconstruct what might have happened. It seems plausible that she might have offered to talk on record because she was being interviewed by a woman (possibly Susan Reed but more likely Barbara Rowes). No woman had ever interviewed Carlos before this point in time. She had trusted Bell with the *Playboy* interview in part because he identified himself as a writer who was gay as opposed to a gay writer, so perhaps she felt she could trust a journalist who was also a woman.[23]

The pairing of the *People* interview and Kozinn's review of *Digital Moonscapes* seem to have effected a shift in how Carlos began relating to journalists and the media. To her, Kozinn hadn't understood her music, and he hadn't even tried to understand her music. Plus, his review in *Opus* would likely have discouraged others from buying *Digital Moonscapes* and trying to understand it themselves. Reed's *People* article would have given Carlos wide exposure to the general public, but that exposure wasn't exactly focused on Carlos's music. Reed had framed Carlos as a person who spent most of her time being transgender but who occasionally made music and took photos of eclipses. In one paragraph, for example, Reed notes that at Brown, Carlos was "trying to act like a college Joe when he really wanted to be a Betty coed," and electronic music was a means of distracting herself from that identity.[24] In fact, Reed quoted Bob Moog talking about Carlos's music more than she quoted Carlos herself talking about her own music.

After the *People* interview was published, Carlos seems to have stopped talking about her gender on the record with journalists entirely. Her experiences with *Playboy* and *People* had built a strong case that if she spoke with a journalist about her gender, then that information would dominate the printed interview. Carlos was never quoted again in any publication speaking about her gender or her transition again after 1985. Further, it appears that she only gave interviews to music or music technology journals, magazines, and (eventually) websites. Apart from one interview she would eventually give with National Public Radio's *All Things Considered* in 1992, interviews with her would only appear in music-focused publications.

The articles by Kozinn and Reed, as well as the disastrous attempt to work with the Berkeley Symphony Orchestra again, all took place in 1985. Further, Carlos missed seeing the total solar eclipse in November of that year.[25] Perhaps a salve the next year was an interview she gave to Connor "Freff" Cochran for the monthly magazine *Electronic Musician*.[26] Published in the November 1986 issue of the magazine, Freff's introduction interview reads like it was written a star-struck fan meeting his idol. He uses superlatives including "brilliant," "fascinating," and "diverse," and he offers a lengthy explanation about why Carlos is one of the few people he feels comfortable calling a genius.[27] Yet this interview also contains more of what Carlos would call "real" information about herself and her interests than any other printed interview before.[28] The reader learns that Carlos loves garlic, reads hard science fiction by authors such as Arthur C. Clarke, enjoys the work comic book artist Carl Banks, and adores puns, *Monty Python* references, and theater organs. She once received a marriage proposal from a sheriff in Texas by mail. Any or all of the three Siamese cats in her home could usually be found lounging on top of Carlos's equipment in the studio, Freff noted.

Freff not only gushed about Carlos's accomplishments and listed many biographical items, but he also read CBS the riot act. He argued that CBS had mistakenly believed that the secret to success was the Moog synthesizer and the music of Bach as opposed to the synthesist herself. He called her post-*Switched-On Bach* releases "a case study in artist mismanagement," lamenting that he desperately needed to replace his worn-out copies of *Sonic Seasonings, A Clockwork Orange, By Request*, and *TRON* but could not because the record company had let them go out of print.[29] Further, he railed against CBS Masterworks for how it had handled the release of *Digital Moonscapes* the previous year. He called the album a "marvel" and implored designers and collectors of DX7 patches to listen to the album as a model of "how it should be done."[30]

The interview with Freff was one of a few given in advance of the release of Carlos's next album. Carlos was already planning this next album when *Digital Moonscapes* was released—she wrote about it in the earlier album's liner notes, mentioned it in the People magazine interview, and noted it in the letter Franklin sent to the editor of *Opus*. *Digital Moonscapes* was the showpiece for the LSI Philharmonic, the orchestra she had created using digital synthesis. Her next project was to develop alternate tuning systems and use digital sounds to showcase the music created with these tuning systems.

To create this newest album, called *Beauty in the Beast*, she used two Synergy digital synthesizers, the GDS, and a Sony PCM 701 that she had modified to go between 1610, 1630, and PCM F-1 formats.[31] For pitch changing, delay, and ambience, she used AMS dmx 15-80s and a Lexicon PCM-42, and for one piece on the album, "C'est Afrique," she even used her old Moog vocoder (a Synton 216).[32] She was still using a 3M 56 16-track tape to record her music.[33] The Synergy digital synthesizer was released in 1982 by Crumar, the same company that had created the GDS. This digital synthesizer was far less expensive than its predecessor—it retailed for about $6,000, less than a quarter of the price of the GDS.[34] Stoney Stockell, one of the inventors of the Synergy, worked with Carlos to retrofit her two synthesizers; she could then develop and design different tunings and scales on her desktop computer and load them into her synthesizers in real time.[35]

Carlos had been interested in alternate tuning systems since her childhood. Recall from chapter 1 that she would retune her parents' piano into different temperaments so that she could hear what they sounded like. When she acquired her first computer in the late 1970s, one of the first things she did with it was calculate ratios for nontempered scales and equal-tempered scales with more than twelve parts per octave.[36] She visited Bali in 1983 to photograph a total solar eclipse, and she was also moved by the sounds of the Balinese gamelan and its instruments, which use two different equal tempered scales.[37] This trip to Bali prompted her to reach out to Stockell to find out how she could use her Synergy to render the sounds of the scales she had heard in Bali as well as scales of her own invention.[38] She had used words ranging from "bored" to "disgusted" to describe how she felt about equal temperament in interviews, and she told Dominic Milano of *Keyboard* magazine that she found alternate tunings inspirational and saw them as a cause that she wanted to champion.[39]

For *Beauty in the Beast*, Carlos used the available technology and equipment to create new scales and also to render scales that already existed.[40] Drawing on music she had heard during her trip to Bali, Carlos used the Balinese slendro and Balinese pelog tuning systems. Each has five notes in the scale. The slendro scale has five notes in equal temperament, meaning that the notes are equidistant from each other. The pelog scale has seven notes in equal temperament, but only five of those notes are played. Carlos also developed a just-intonation scale, which had 144 pitches per octave, and each pitch was the exact same distance from the next. She also developed what she called her alpha and beta scales: the alpha scale had 15.3 notes per octave and 78 cents per note, and the beta scale had 18.8 notes per octave and 63.8 cents per note.

In much the same way that Carlos had criticized other electronic musicians for taking the easy way out, not using the available technology to its fullest extent, and using the Moog and other synthesizers as glorified keyboards, she criticized those who were unwilling (in her perception) to use alternate tunings in their music or to listen to music composed with alternate tunings. She told Freff she believed many people were interested in alternate tunings but few would adopt them because they were too lazy. She explained that she had spent more than twelve hours writing just six chords for the piece "Just Imaginings," and she couldn't imagine that many other people would be willing to spend that much time or energy working on something so tedious.[41] She wrote elsewhere that the electronic music mainstream was "rut-bound" despite the fact that so many better options (at least in her opinion) were available.[42]

Carlos didn't just create new tunings and scales for *Beauty in the Beast*. She also created completely new instrument sounds and effects. Using digital synthesis, she went beyond replicating the instruments of the orchestra as she had in *Digital Moonscapes*. Now, she created sounds that would not be physically or acoustically possible in real life: percussive violins, sustained timpanis, woodwind glockenspiels, metal marimbas, and bowed pianos, to name a few.[43] Synthesis allowed Carlos to create sounds that had never existed before, and she didn't use digital sampling to do it.[44] She told one interviewer that the sound of a sample is always the same, and it doesn't change when it gets louder or softer, unlike a real physical instrument would.[45] Curiously, the only sound that she did sample from a physical instrument was the sound of her own voice.[46]

Digital synthesis allowed Carlos to put instruments and sounds from different musical traditions together in ways that were otherwise not possible. One section of "Poem for Bali" is a concerto featuring a symphony orchestra and a Balinese gamelan; Carlos adjusted the digital symphony orchestra into the appropriate tuning system to avoid clashing with the gamelan.[47] The final pieces on the album, "A Woman's Song," blended instruments from many different traditions and regions, including a Bulgarian shepherdess song, Indian tambura and dilruba, horns and crotales from the symphony orchestra, and a number of Carlos's hybrid instrument sounds.[48]

Carlos has written that *Beauty in the Beast* is her most important album because it most successfully demonstrated that electronic music was a new medium as opposed to a new kind of music.[49] *Keyboard* magazine ran a sizeable feature on it in the November 1986 issue, including not only Dominic Milano's lengthy interview with Carlos about the album and the tuning systems but also a two-page feature in which Carlos guided the listener through the sounds and technology of every track on *Beauty in the Beast*.[50] The feature included a section of Carlos's handwritten score for the gabor dance section of "Poem for Bali" and a photo of her in her studio.[51]

Keyboard wasn't the only specialist periodical that gave Carlos substantial air time for her new album and the technology and tuning it featured. She also provided an article that was printed in the spring 1987 issue of *Computer Music Journal* but that had been written the previous year. The *Computer Music Journal* article is about fifteen pages in length, and it is the longest first-person account Carlos had ever published up to this point. She spent the first third of the article critiquing past writings about alternate tuning systems, the middle third theorizing about alternate tuning systems, and the final third talking about how she created the tuning systems used in *Beauty in the Beast*.[52] The article has several graphs and graphics that she used to visualize the frequencies of the various tuning systems under discussion.

The following issue of *Computer Music Journal* contained an apology from the journal's editor, Curtis Roads. The deadlines for the issue had been tight, Roads explained, and due to errors on the parts of the authors, himself, and the publisher, MIT Press, an unusual number of errors were printed in the issue.[53] He noted that they had received all five articles from their authors only a week before they had to go to print, and the short turnaround time meant that they missed a number of errors. In this instance, Carlos and her fellow authors were each given space to correct the errors in their articles. An entire page of Douglas Leedy's bibliography was omitted from the publication, and an omitted left parenthesis from an equation in James Dashow's article could have resulted in what he called "a potentially computer-blasting error."[54]

Carlos, too, had written a short letter correcting the errors in her article. It was nothing like other corrections she had tried to make in the past twenty years, such as the letter from Franklin to *Opus* about Allan Kozinn's misunderstanding of *Digital Moonscapes* or the letter she had written to Arthur Bell after she felt he had misrepresented her. It was simply a correction of the record with regard to misspelled words, inverted "<" and ">" symbols, and abbreviations that misconstrued her meaning: for instance, she had used a single letter "c" to indicate a specific pitch, which the journal's copy editor had turned into the word "circa."[55]

She also expressed her surprise at how small her illustrations had been, but she acknowledged that their smallness had to be due to space considerations and in fact praised the journal's reproduction of them that allowed all details to be visible—with a magnifying glass.[56] She didn't seem upset or act as if she had been misrepresented, though, which was a stark change from other letters to the editor she had written over the years. Instead, she again thanked the journal for the excellent job it did on the article and for giving her the opportunity to connect with people who had written to her since its publication.[57]

In addition to her article in *CMJ* and her interview in *Keyboard*, Carlos contributed the foreword to *Tuning In: Microtonality in Electronic Music*. Written by Scott R. Wilkinson and published by Hal Leonard in 1988, *Tuning In* offered readers a guide to using synthesizers to create alternate scales, temperaments, and tuning systems. In her foreword to the text, which was dated April 1988, Carlos reiterated her point that microtonality was vastly underappreciated and overlooked. Only stubborn people who were stuck in their ways would refuse to explore the wealth of interest and color available in the world of microtonality, she suggested.[58] Further, she argued, Bach himself would probably use synthesizers if he was alive in the late twentieth century because they would allow him to overcome the "limitations" of equal temperament.[59]

At the end of the original *CMJ* article about her tuning systems, Carlos thanked the journal for inspiring her over the years. She expressed delight that she had been able to contribute information to the readership, and she wrote that "the real work now can begin."[60] If by "real work," she meant that composers of electronic and acoustic music would begin exploring alternate tuning systems in droves, then she was to be sorely disappointed. At the beginning of the article, she explained that her love of alternate tuning systems was not unlike her preference of a Dvorak keyboard as opposed to a QWERTY keyboard. It had taken her a long time to unlearn her QWERTY habits, she explained, but she knew that the "unloved but demonstrably better" Dvorak keyboard was far superior.[61] Similarly, in her foreword to *Tuning In*, she likened microtonality to a mountain that had to be scaled because it was there.[62] She hoped many more musicians would follow her lead into the challenging and new world of microtonal music.

Carlos told one interviewer that *Beauty in the Beast* was her most important album, followed closely by *Digital Moonscapes*.[63] But neither of these later albums registered in popular culture in the way *Switched-On Bach* had. These albums made only the smallest of inroads with electronic music specialists; her "Poem for Bali" from *Beauty in the Beast* appears as an example in a couple of electronic music production textbooks, for example.[64] Her initial early success with the Moog synthesizer may have given her unrealistic expectations about how each of her subsequent innovations would be received. If she had hoped that microtonality would become even half as popular in the 1980s as the Moog synthesizer had become in the late 1960s, she was to be sorely disappointed.

The digitally synthesized instrumental sounds of *Beauty in the Beast* have about the same veracity and warmth as they did on *Digital Moonscapes*, which is to say not very much, at least not when compared with Carlos's earlier analog Moog music. Indeed, the most expressive and human-sounding musical moments on *Beauty in the Beast* are heard during "C'est Afrique," the piece in which Carlos processed her own voice through her Moog vocoder.

The passages of synthesized gamelan music in "Poem for Bali" are more convincing replicas of the acoustic originals than are the orchestral instruments. The most successful passages are those in which melodies and harmonies in different temperaments are held in place by a musical drone, such as in "Yusae-Aisae."

The challenging aspect of the music on *Beauty in the Beast* is the fact that the listener does not have anything familiar to use as an anchor point in many of the pieces. In the various *Switched-On* albums of the 1970s, Carlos introduced people to the sounds of the Moog synthesizer by using it to render music that people already knew. Even though the sounds of the Moog were new, the piece of music were familiar, which allowed a listener to focus on just exactly what kinds of sounds were being used to perform those familiar pieces. But in *Beauty in the Beast*, the pieces of music are unfamiliar, the instrumental sounds are unfamiliar, and the tuning systems are unfamiliar. Carlos took this unfamiliarity a step further with the hybrid instrumental sounds of her own invention. The combination of so many new sounds is more than likely to overwhelm the listener. Further, even the most openminded listener will probably be startled by how "out of tune" music rendered in alternate tuning systems sounds. A lifetime of auditory expectations from equal tempered listening cannot be undone quickly, and, as Carlos learned, many listeners just weren't interested in dedicating themselves to these kinds of sounds the way that she had.

Carlos's next album, *Secrets of Synthesis*, was released in 1987. It was an instructional record on which Carlos narrated various techniques and provided clips of her own music as examples of those particular techniques. Music from each of her previous CBS albums was included, perhaps as a condition of the contract. Techniques included "Examples of Analog Timbres," "Simple Orchestration," "Imitative Synthesis," and "Ensemble Performance via Click Tracks." Of the sixteen bands on the album, Carlos primarily focused on music that she had made using the Moog during the 1960s and 1970s, including several Bach and Scarlatti examples. The final five bands included music she had created with digital synthesis during the 1980s, including excerpts from *TRON* and *Digital Moonscapes*.

The spoken parts of the album were a compilation of content from lectures and keynote addresses that Carlos had given at various conferences and meetings of Ars Electronica, the Audio Engineering Society, and others.[65] Carlos explained in an interview that *Secrets of Synthesis* was supposed to be entertaining first and foremost and then instructive.[66] She hoped that every lay person would find something in it to enjoy but noted that specialists might need to listen to it dozens of times before they gleaned all possible information out of it.[67] Carlos saw the album as a fitting summary of the music she had produced for CBS over the past nearly two decades and as the right album to complete the long contract she had with the company.[68]

Soon after Carlos had released *Secrets of Synthesis*, she entered a brief period that she has called a "divertimento" or diversion.[69] She has said that this brief period gave her a chance to step back from her current projects that involved tuning and digital synthesis and instead to explore some new techniques and work with some new people.[70] She began working another new mode of electronic music production: Musical Instrument Digital Interface, or MIDI. MIDI is a standard interface language for personal computers and synthesizers.

Much as Bob Moog had worked closely with Carlos on his modular synthesizers and Stoney Stockell had customized Synergys for Carlos, Jim Cooper collaborated with Carlos as she began using MIDI.[71] Cooper created for her a custom version of his Expression Plus (also stylized Expression+) that gave her the expressive quality she wanted. Before Cooper's intervention, she said, MIDI music sounded "inexpressive" and "wooden," none of which suited her.[72] Cooper also customized a Mix-Mate for Carlos that gave her the ability to decode eight simultaneous MIDI voices that she had originally played with the Expression Plus.[73]

During this so-called divertimento period, Carlos began collaborating with another musician in one of the most unlikely pairings one could imagine. The head of CBS Masterworks asked Carlos whether she'd be interested in working with none other than "Weird Al" Yankovic.[74] Yankovic was already a household name by this time, having released five studio albums and three compilation albums (including a Greatest Hits) by 1988. Yankovic is best known for his humorous parodies of top 40 songs, such as "I Love Rocky Road" (1983, a parody of Joan Jett and the Blackhearts' "I Love Rock and Roll"), "My Bologna" (1983, a parody of the Knack's "My Sharona"), "Another One Rides the Bus" (1983, a parody of Queen's "Another One Bites the Dust"), and "Eat It" (1984, a parody of Michael Jackson's "Beat It"). A skilled accordion player, Yankovic often includes polka renditions of pop songs on his albums as well. He was featured on the cover of the December 1987 issue of *Keyboard* magazine and interviewed about his accordion playing.

Although it might seem like a strange pairing (indeed, *Keyboard* magazine published an interview in the January 1989 issue about the pair and their album entitled, "What's the Strangest Artistic Collaboration You Can Think Of?"), the project at hand was well suited to the two artists. Carlos and Yankovic would produce a new rendition of Sergei Prokofiev's *Peter and the Wolf*, and on the album's B-side, they created a sequel of sorts to Camille Saint-Saëns's *The Carnival of the Animals*.

Carlos created most of the sounds using two Synergy synthesizers, the Kurzweil K150, and three Mulogix Slave 32s.[75] Her keyboards were a Kurzweil MIDIboard and her customized Synergy unit. Percussion sounds were created using a Yamaha RX5. She controlled volume and timbre with MIDI through a JL Cooper Expression+ and Mix Mate unit, which were connected through an MSB+ box. She played all of the music into a Macintosh Plus/Levco Prodigy computer that was running the most recent versions of Performer (later called Digital Performer) software, one of the first MIDI sequencing programs available for a Macintosh. The computer also had a Southworth Jambox 4+ and an Apple MIDI Interface, which allowed her to have thirty-two channels of in and out. She used a direct SMPTE lockup for sound effects and Yankovic's narration.

Sergei Prokofiev completed the music and the text of *Peter and the Wolf* in 1936. The narrator tells the story of young Peter, who interacts with a variety of animals and who disregards his grandfather's warning about wolves. Each character in the tale is represented by a specific instrument or group of instruments in the orchestra, such as the bassoon representing Peter's grandfather and a group of horns representing the wolf. For the new album, Carlos reimagined the sounds of the orchestra using digital synthesis, and Yankovic provided the narration. Carlos returned to the Moog to create the duck's quack and the cat's meow in *Peter and the Wolf*, connecting her modular Moog 904A to a control output on the Expression+, which she told an interviewer was a way of including something old and something new on the album.[76]

Carlos and Yankovic did make a few lighthearted additions to the original story, such as a new character named Bob the Janitor who was represented by the sound of the accordion. They also gave names to a few characters who had been unnamed in the original text, such as Seymour the Wolf and Bruce the Duck. In his narration, Yankovic informed the listener that actor Don Ameche had been slated to play the role of the grandfather, but since Ameche couldn't make it, the grandfather would have to be played by the bassoon. At the end of the tale, Yankovic assured listeners that although Bruce the Duck had died a horrific death after having been eaten by Seymour the Wolf, one needn't worry because the duck would later be reincarnated as actress Shirley MacLaine. Carlos also augmented Prokofiev's original score with various musical quotations, such as a snippet of the iconic shrieking violins that Bernard Hermann had composed for the "shower scene" in Alfred Hitchcock's film *Psycho*—heard when Seymour the Wolf eats Bruce the Duck.

Their *Carnival of the Animals: Part Two* was a completely original work. Camille Saint-Saëns wrote the lighthearted suite of fourteen animal-inspired movements in the middle of the 1880s:

1. Introduction and Royal March of the Lion
2. Hens and Roosters
3. Wild Asses
4. Tortoise
5. The Elephant
6. Kangaroos
7. Aquarium
8. Personages with Long Ears [Donkeys]
9. The Cuckoo in the Depths of the Woods
10. Aviary
11. Pianists
12. Fossils
13. The Swan
14. Finale (includes musical fragments from almost all of the previous movements)

Saint-Saëns didn't take this piece too seriously, including "pianists" and "fossils" among the animals, for example. In 1949, Ogden Nash wrote poems to accompany each movement, and these were first recorded in a performance by conductor Andre Kostelanetz and his orchestra and read by Noel Coward.

Originally, Carlos and Yankovic had planned to render *The Carnival of the Animals* the same way that they had approached *Peter and the Wolf*, with Carlos's music production and Yankovic's reading of Nash's poems—with plenty of artistic license from both. Carlos asked Yankovic to write a couple of poems in the style of Ogden Nash that would allow them to add a couple of extra animals to the musical menagerie.[77] Carlos fell in love with the three poems Yankovic had written, so she asked him for a couple more. Soon, they decided to completely scrap the Saint-Saëns and Nash originals and instead do only their new music and poetry.[78]

As Yankovic cautioned in the first poem of their collection, "You'll find that it's not quite exactly the same / as the one by Camille Saint what's-his-name." Together, Carlos and Yankovic created the following movements:

1. Introduction
2. Aardvark
3. Hummingbirds
4. Snails
5. Alligator
6. Amoeba
7. Pigeons
8. Shark
9. Cockroaches
10. Iguana
11. Vulture
12. Unicorn
13. Poodle
14. Finale

Like Saint-Saëns, Carlos wrote between ninety seconds and three minutes of music for each animal, and each movement is in a completely different style and with contrasting instrumentation. She also wove in numerous musical quotations from other pieces. The "Snails" movement features Rossini's *William Tell Overture* slowed to a crawl, and the "Shark" movement weaves together the two-note motif John Williams composed for the film *Jaws* with the *Dies irae*, the chant from the medieval mass for the dead.

Together, Carlos and Yankovic were nominated for a Grammy Award for the Best Recording for Children in 1989. It was Carlos's first Grammy nomination since *The Well-Tempered Synthesizer* twenty years earlier. It was also the last time she would be nominated for a Grammy. Carlos and Yankovic ended up losing out to an album of the tale of Pecos Bill with music by Ry Cooder and narration by Robin Williams. As a solo artist, Yankovic was nominated for two additional Grammys that year, winning one of them: Best Concept Music Video for "I'm Fat."

Since the early 1970s, Carlos had regularly criticized other musicians for taking what she thought was the easy road and for being too motivated by profit to challenge themselves in their music. She seemed to become increasingly angry at what she saw as other musicians' limited mindsets in the late 1980s. In an editorial from 1988, she said—dripping with sarcasm—that since the "good old American Equal-Tempered Scale" had been good enough for Mom and Dad, there was no reason to bother doing anything different now.[79] Plus, she wrote, those "dumb foreign instruments" that could produce microtonal music were probably sent to the United States as some kind of Communist conspiracy plot.[80] She was particularly vitriolic toward digital sampling, which she has called everything from "trivial" to "audio clip art."[81]

Carlos has also complained that other musicians were not taking advantage of the musical tools at their disposal; instead, it seemed to her like they were just creating the same content over and over again.[82] To her, musicians were wasting the new tools that were available by creating the same kinds of music using the same kinds of scales that had been used for decades before.[83] Why, she wondered, would anyone stick with the same meter, tempo, timbre, and tuning when they could create any sounds they could possibly imagine, sounds that didn't exist anywhere except within one's own imagination?[84] She chalked some of this up to profit motives: fame and fortune, she wrote, were likely to come from conformity and from aiming for the lowest common denominator.[85] She also attributed some of the lack of interest to sheer laziness, although she connected laziness to profit motive because, to her, anyone who spent hundreds or thousands of hours working on new systems wasn't looking to make a quick buck.[86] Some of these critiques may have been an act of subterfuge, because Carlos appears to have been running into financial trouble herself by the late 1980s.

By the time *Peter and the Wolf* was released in October 1988, Carlos was turning her attention back to Johann Sebastian Bach. She would spend the next few years creating yet another *Switched-On Bach* album. In the extensive liner notes to this newest album, she identified several factors that had led her back to the music of Bach: a desire in middle age (she turned fifty in November 1989) to rework music from her youth, encouragement from her fans, and a desire to use her knowledge of tuning systems in Bach's music.[87] She only acknowledged privately that she also needed to sell some albums to keep herself afloat financially.

She returned to the same repertoire that had appeared on the original 1968 *Switched-On Bach* album, but she reworked all of it using the most cutting-edge digital technology she had at her disposal. Carlos noted that nobody criticized conductor Herbert von Karajan for recording Beethoven's Symphony no. 9 several times over his career or pianist Glenn Gould for recording Bach's Goldberg Variations multiple times.[88] Carlos argued that an artist in middle age would have a very different perspective than they would have had as a young adult; she noted that an older artist might not have the same "spark" as a younger artist, but an older artist was likely to bring more balance and a solidified technique to their interpretation.[89]

She also acknowledged that many people had been asking her for years to create more electronic renditions of Bach's music.[90] At this point, it had been about a decade since her last Bach album—*Switched-On Brandenburgs* had been released in 1979. Further, she noted that her fans frequently wondered out loud to or in writing her what it would be like to hear Bach's music produced using the latest technology, such as digital synthesis and MIDI sequencing.[91] Carlos joked that she had been strong, holding her own and not succumbing to the requests for more Bach until she realized that the new technology meant she could use Bach's original tunings as opposed to equal temperament.[92]

Carlos was also struggling financially and knew from experience that Bach's music rendered on the synthesizer would probably sell well. In late 1991, she wrote to Bob Moog that she and Franklin had experienced their second "grim" financial year in a row.[93] Franklin had just passed the bar and was trying to start her own law practice without much luck.[94] Carlos had been invited to score the Tony Maylam-directed film *Split Second*, but after spending fifteen hours a day for twelve weeks working on the project, the plug was pulled and she was left with nothing except debt for the new equipment she had purchased to work on the music for the film.[95] Some of the music she composed for *Split Second* would be released in 2005 on the album *Rediscovering Lost Scores*, but for the time being, she had nothing commercial to show for the work she had done on that film score.

In fact, Carlos confided to Moog, she needed a new lucrative album deal if she and Franklin were going to be able to continue living in New York.[96] She then bragged to Moog that the president of a major record label (she didn't name the label in her letter, but the new album would be released on Telarc the following year) had visited her multiple times in an attempt to sign her for a new album, which suggests that at least one label also had faith that a new Bach album by Carlos would be a worthwhile financial investment.[97]

The new album would be called *Switched-On Bach 2000*, despite the fact that it would be released in 1992, almost a decade before the start of the new millennium. She provided a complete list of the equipment that she had used, taking up nearly an entire page of the album's liner notes. In addition to the two Synergy synthesizers, the Kurzweil K150, and the three Mulogix Slave 32s that she had used for *Peter and the Wolf*, Carlos added a second K150, four Kurzweil K1000s, and two Yamaha synthesizers, the TX 802 and SY77. She had upgraded to a Macintosh IIfx computer for the bulk of the project, augmenting with a Hewlett-Packard 9825 for the Synergy and Slave 32 tuning tables.[98] Digidesign released Sound Tools and Pro Tools in 1990, as she was in the thick of the project, and she switched over to them and away from the previous editors that she called "horrible little devices."[99] Her equipment also included an Akai ADAM DR1200 digital multitrack with a custom audio interface, a Panasonic SV3700 DAT recorder, and two Sony EDV9500 ED Beta recorders.[100] For software, Carlos was still using Performer, as well as MIDI Time Pieces, Opcode's DX/TX librarian, and Boss BL1.[101]

All in all, Carlos would claim that the work on *Switched-On Bach 2000* took anywhere between ten months and a year and a half (she gave both of these numbers in a single interview), amounting to something like three thousand hours in her studio.[102] Not surprisingly, she wrote extensively about how much work it had taken and how much time she had spent. In the liner notes, she explained that any claims that new technology made things easier and faster were bunk: the original *Switched-On Bach* had "only" taken a thousand hours to create, but *Switched-On Bach 2000* had taken three times as long.[103] Despite her decades of complaining about all of the problems she had with her Moog modular synthesizer, she seemed nostalgic for that time and technology; she even wrote to Moog that MIDI wasn't nearly as intuitive as his system had been, and she longed for the ability to create spontaneous color changes again.[104]

She included all of the music that had appeared on the first *Switched-On Bach* album, plus two new tracks: Bach's iconic Toccata and Fugue in D Minor and a short original ditty called "Happy 25th, S-OB." Carlos also reworked the middle movement of the third Brandenburg concerto to reflect Bach's musical style and expression as closely as she could.[105] She explained to one interviewer that a melody came into her mind that she simply couldn't shake, and even though she thought it was silly at first, she ended up using it as the basis for the new second movement. She called it "heartfelt," "honest," and "exactly right."[106]

Some of the sounds on *Switched-On Bach 2000* are far more accurate than were their Moog predecessors. The harpsichord jangles convincingly, and the flutes—at least when they hold sustained pitches, such as in the Air on the G String—have a humanistic vibrato. Carlos noted that none of the music was created using a Moog synthesizer, save for a single note placed somewhere on the album.[107] She gleefully challenged listeners to identify its location and write to her; a few years later, when she began her website, she named all of those who had identified the Moog note correctly and awarded them a "Gold Leaf."[108] She stopped updating the list in 2009, after naming twenty-eight separate winners.[109]

Switched-On Bach 2000 was released on the Telarc label, and Carlos gave a brief interview in the 1992 Telarc newsletter about it. She explained that she always thought the newest thing was the best, which was why she considered the Toccata and Fugue her favorite piece on the new album.[110] She also asserted that regardless of what anyone else might say, she knew she had made the album as well as she was capable of having made it.[111]

Carlos was briefly back in the spotlight when *Switched-On Bach 2000* was released in 1992, in part because it was a new album and in part because the twenty-fifth anniversary of the release of the original *Switched-On Bach* was fast approaching. But her moment was very short: she gave only a handful of interviews, although those interviews were with major national outlets such as *Billboard* magazine and National Public Radio's *All Things Considered*. It is likely that she didn't give very many interviews because she didn't talk about her gender.

Julia Serano has written about the complicated web of positive and negative issues that can arise when a person comes out as transgender in a high-profile way. Serano points out that public disclosures can normalize transgender identity for those who might otherwise not see or interact with transgender people on a daily basis. For example, Serano's mother called her, thrilled, when writer Jenny Boylan appeared on Oprah Winfrey's TV show; before that, Serano was the only transgender woman that her mother knew. Then, there was not only at least one more transgender woman out there, but she was important enough to be on *Oprah*! These high-profile disclosures can also be problematic. Serano explains that coverage can be sensationalistic, focusing far too much on physical aspects of a person's transition.[112]

Media coverage of transgender people can often be reductive, minimizing a person's accomplishments in favor of a discussion about their bodies. Parker Molloy wrote an op-ed in *The Advocate* in 2014 whose title made her point clear: "Can Media Please Stop Focusing on Trans People's Bodies?" Using a recent episode of the short-lived talk show *Katie*, hosted by Katie Couric, as an example, Molloy criticized Couric for her treatment of model Carmen Carrera and actress Laverne Cox. On the show, Couric explained that Carrera and Cox were each "born a man" (to which Molloy responded: "Carmen Carrera wasn't 'born a man,' she was born a baby") and had undergone "shocking transformations." Couric then asked each woman pointed questions about their genitals, explaining that she wanted them to educate her as well as other people who were "curious" about the women's bodies. Carrera responded that the topic was personal and that she would not discuss it. Cox explained to Couric that it was a topic that was potentially dangerous for transgender people, wondering why hers or anyone else's genitals were acceptable to discuss in any context simply in the name of "curiosity." Molloy argued that such questions ignored the women's work, philanthropy, and other accomplishments, reducing them to a collection of body parts.[113]

Neither the interview in *Billboard* or *All Things Considered* mentioned Wendy Carlos's birth name or gender, but that didn't stop people from asking. For example, one listener wrote to *All Things Considered*, wanting to know why Liane Hansen had not asked Carlos in the interview about her gender or how her gender affected her art. Hansen replied in a subsequent episode that although she and Carlos had gone back and forth about discussing her gender identity, they ultimately "decided that the story we wanted to convey was about music and not about sexual identity." Hansen did ask Carlos a broad question how she felt the many changes in her life over the past quarter-century affected how listeners might hear the music on *Switched-On Bach 2000*. Carlos replied that one should not "try to perceive art as autobiography."[114] Hansen's question and Carlos's answer were not broadcast.

"Curious" listeners didn't get to hear Carlos discuss her gender or her anatomy on *All Things Considered*, but they did learn about the animal menagerie in her home. She told Hansen about her three Siamese cats, all of whom appeared in recent publicity photos with her (see Figure 7.1). The cats were Nagus (who had been named for conductor Kent Nagano), his mother, Piccala, and Subito, who was lounging on top of a computer monitor in the photo. During the interview, Hansen asked Carlos whether she let the cats in the studio as a rule.

Figure 7.1 Wendy Carlos in her studio in October 1988. The cat in her lap is Nagus, and the cat on top of the monitor is Subito. Piccala is not pictured here. Photo by Ebet Roberts. Getty Images. Used by permission.

CARLOS: Are you joking? Have you ever had a Siamese cat? Even regular kitty cats, they have their own way, their own mind and they come in and they're on top of you and on top of the equipment.

HANSEN: Well, we had a very technical question from some of the people on our staff about how do you keep the cat hair off of the equipment?

CARLOS: We don't.[115]

Following the release of *Switched-On Bach 2000*, Carlos worked on several major projects that were largely new for her. She wrote one final piece for a live musician to play on an acoustic instrument, she played her own music live in public for the first time in almost three decades, and she started her website, wendycarlos.com.

In the fall of 1995, Carlos learned that a fan of hers was trying to create a website about her.[116] A mutual friend helped her make contact with the fan, Matthew Davidson. She was suspicious but very interested: a website about herself seemed a bit narcissistic (recall that this is 1995!), but would also give her the opportunity to present her work and to connect with those who were interested in her work. She was also concerned that a website would allow people to drag her into "prurient-interest muck," her way of saying that she didn't want people trying to hurt her or exploit her. She and Davidson connected quickly and on many levels: according to Carlos, Davidson was also a composer, a lover of Photoshop, and a fan of whimsy. It took several weeks for them to build sufficient rapport to the point that she trusted him to create the site for her. She particularly appreciated his empathy and his ability to anticipate her concerns and questions about the website itself and the process of creating it.

Davidson built the original site, which launched in early 1996. He was responsible for most of the content that went on the site, including audio files. He then taught Carlos how to update and maintain it; she was relieved to learn that this work was not so much difficult as it was tedious. According to a post dated April 2001, Davidson was still the one answering email addressed to the site's webmaster. Another friend of Davidson's, John Romkey, purchased the domain name wendycarlos.com and gave it to Carlos as a Christmas present in 1997.

At the same time that she and Davidson were building her website, Carlos began working with live musicians for the first time since the Berkeley Symphony in 1985. In April 1997, Carlos appeared on stage with a group of musicians to perform some of her music. It was the first time she had appeared on stage with a synthesizer since her disastrous attempt in St. Louis more than a quarter of a century earlier. Carlos and an ensemble performed as part of the Bach at the Beacon concert, a venture headed up by Ettore Stratta. Rachel Elkind had worked with Stratta at Columbia, and he helped Elkind and Carlos bring *Switched-On Bach* to the label's attention. The two-day festival included the music of Bach performed by many different kinds of musicians, including Anthony Newman and the Brandenburg Collegium, clarinetist Richard Stoltzman, and jazz musician Jacques Loussier.[117] According to James Oestreich of the *New York Times*, Carlos was the first person Stratta had approached when putting together the initial roster for the festival.[118]

The performance took place at the Beacon Theatre in New York. Eight people in addition to Carlos performed: Gloria Cheng, Clare Cooper, Matthew Davidson, Larry Fast, Chris Martirano, Mayumi Reinhard, and Jordan Rudess.[119] Stratta himself conducted the ensemble in the larger pieces. They called themselves the Kurzweil Baroque Ensemble because they played on contemporary Kurzweil synthesizers that could produce sound in real time.[120] They performed music from Carlos's earlier Moog synthesizer albums as well as from her recent *Switched-On Bach 2000*.[121]

The live performance of Carlos's music seems not to have gone particularly well, at least according to her assessment. She complained on her website that she had not received a contract by March for the April concert, so she had not begun any preparations until she had the contract in hand.[122] Given her past experiences with Stanley Kubrick and other film projects, it's not surprising that she wanted to wait until she had a signed contract for the project. With less than a month to go before the performance, she tried to postpone until the next year; she was apparently "persuaded" to continue with the original April 5 commitment.[123] Much to her chagrin, this meant that she had to miss an opportunity to see a total solar eclipse in March 1997 that would have taken her to northern China.[124] She was too busy getting ready for the performance.

The day after the Bach at the Beacon performance, Carlos wrote a lengthy essay on her website. She was thrilled with the musicians and their performance. Otherwise, she was infuriated. She wrote that the group had been promised forty-five minutes on stage and could even run over their allotted time a bit if necessary.[125] By the time their portion of the concert arrived, Carlos wrote, the schedule was so far behind that her ensemble was given thirty-one minutes total because there was a strict 11 p.m. end time for the event.[126] They had to cut two entire pieces and play others at breakneck speeds in order to fit everything into their time slot.[127] She was particularly disappointed that the two pieces that were cut were both new, so the group only played her "old" music.[128] She assured her readers that if they hadn't been able to come, they needn't fret because it wasn't that great of an event.[129]

Others aspects that disappointed her may have just been a result of her lack of familiarity with performance conventions, particularly since it had been nearly thirty years since she had appeared onstage. (She did acknowledge that she might have been overreacting since she was new at such events.)[130] She complained that their friends could not come visit them in the dressing room.[131] Further, she was enraged that a friend of hers was stopped while trying to take a video of the event. Carlos wanted the video for her parents, both of whom were in their nineties and not well enough to travel to New York for the event.[132] Despite all of her anger and disappointment, Carlos said, she would be interested in doing more live events if there was a way to do them without losing "scads" of money.[133]

Carlos had one other live music performance event in 1997. Pianist Gloria Cheng, who had played first synthesizer in the Kurzweil Baroque Ensemble in April, played an original composition by Carlos in a recital she gave in November. Carlos seemed to adore Cheng, calling her a "brilliant young concert pianist who's [sic] star is in ascent."[134] Part of a series called "Piano Spheres," Cheng's recital featured music by other living composers including John Adams, William Kraft, Chinary Ung, and Andrew Waggoner. Cheng performed "Ravelled Threads," an homage to Maurice Ravel that Carlos had composed over a period of about two decades.[135]

Of the piece, Carlos wrote that she greatly admired Ravel for his masterful orchestration and understanding of color and timbre.[136] She had spoken about her admiration of Ravel in several earlier interviews, even comparing her approach with the synthesizer to Ravel's approach to orchestration.[137] Because Ravel wrote most of his orchestral works (such as *Le tombeau de Couperin* and *Vales Nobles et Sentimentales*) for the piano first and then orchestrated them later, Carlos wrote for the piano because she wanted to follow Ravel's example.[138] She also noted that she wanted to orchestrate "Ravelled Threads" one day, although she wasn't sure whether she would do so for an acoustic or digital orchestra—or perhaps both.[139] Much like what had happened with the Berkeley Symphony Orchestra more than a decade earlier, Cheng's performance of Carlos's music was apparently a one-time occurrence. The score has not yet been published or otherwise distributed, and there does not seem to be any record of other musicians performing it, either.

In the liner notes of *Switched-On Bach 2000*, Carlos stated: "For every parameter that you CAN control, you MUST control."[140] She wrote that she had learned this valuable lesson years earlier and, likely as a nod to her physics background, decided to call it her "First Law."[141] This phrase suggests how Carlos thought about both her music and her biography. From asking Columbia to withdraw the quadraphonic version of *Switched-On Bach* in the early 1970s to her experiences with human musicians from London, Los Angeles, New York, and Berkeley, she tried to control exactly how her music was played, recorded, and heard.

Human orchestras, choirs, recording engineers, conductors, orchestrators, copyists, producers, and event planners had made a lot of mistakes, in her estimation. It seemed as if her personal studio was the only place she could create music that was exactly what she wanted, without any unwanted or uninvited human interference. In the studio, there was no room for misinterpretation, a lack of practicing, a shortened performance time slot, or a copyist's hand. Carlos even tried to create a computer music notation program so that she wouldn't have to hire orchestrators or copyists for her film and other orchestral scores—even the best orchestrators and copyists still made mistakes, after all.[142] After 1997, Carlos seems to have stopped working with human musicians in any capacity. There does not appear to be any record of any of her music being played live or by acoustic instruments since that time.

Notes

1. Franklin, letter to *Opus*, March 11, 1985.
2. Carlos, letter to Kozinn, February 28, 1980. Allan Kozinn personal collection.
3. Franklin, letter to Kozinn, September 27, 1984. Allan Kozinn personal collection.
4. Franklin, letter to Kozinn, September 27, 1984.
5. *Opus* ran bimonthly from 1984 to 1988, after which it was absorbed by *Musical America*.
6. Allan Kozinn, "Review: *Cosmological Impressions; Moonscapes*," *Opus* (April 1985), 25.
7. Kozinn, "Review: *Cosmological Impressions; Moonscapes*," 25.
8. Kozinn, "Review: *Cosmological Impressions; Moonscapes*," 25.
9. Kozinn, "Review: *Cosmological Impressions; Moonscapes*," 25.
10. Kozinn, "Review: *Cosmological Impressions; Moonscapes*," 25.
11. Franklin, letter to Kozinn, March 4, 1985.
12. Franklin, letter to Kozinn, March 4, 1985.
13. Franklin, letter to Kozinn, March 4, 1985.
14. Franklin, letter to Kozinn, March 4, 1985.
15. Franklin, letter to the editor of *Opus*, March 11, 1985.
16. Franklin, letter to the editor of *Opus*, March 11, 1985.
17. Franklin, letter to the editor of *Opus*, March 11, 1985.
18. Franklin, letter to the editor of *Opus*, March 11, 1985.
19. Franklin, letter to the editor of *Opus*, March 11, 1985.
20. All quotations are from Susan Reed, "After a Sex Change and Several Eclipses, Wendy Carlos Treads a New Digital Landscape," *People* 24, no. 1 (1 July 1985).
21. Susan Reed, personal correspondence, July 23, 2015; Barbara Rowes, personal correspondence, July 23, 2015.
22. Carlos, letter to Bell, May 1979.
23. Bell, unpublished article draft.
24. Reed, "Wendy Carlos Treads a New Digital Landscape."
25. Wendy Carlos, "Wendy Carlos Total Solar Eclipse Page."
26. Freff, "Tuning in to Wendy Carlos."
27. Freff, "Tuning in to Wendy Carlos."

28. Carlos, letter to Bell, May 1979. In the letter, Carlos repeatedly criticized Bell for omitting the "real me" from what was printed in the *Playboy* interview.
29. Freff, "Tuning in to Wendy Carlos."
30. Freff, "Tuning in to Wendy Carlos."
31. Dominic Milano, "Wendy Carlos: Defying Conventions, Discovering New Worlds," *Keyboard* (November 1986), 78 (hereafter Milano, "Wendy Carlos" (1986)).
32. Milano, "Wendy Carlos" (1986), 78.
33. Carol Wright, "The Digital Phases of Wendy Carlos" (December 2000), available at http://www.wendycarlos.com/intvw01.html.
34. Holmes, *Electronic and Experimental Music*, 506.
35. Vail, *The Synthesizer*, 44.
36. Moog, "Wendy Carlos on Computers," 64.
37. Carlos, liner notes to *Beauty in the Beast* (CBS, 1986; East Side Digital, 2000), 2. (Citations are to the 2000 edition.)
38. Vail, *The Synthesizer*, 44.
39. Milano, "Wendy Carlos" (1986), 82.
40. The information in this paragraph is drawn from Carlos's own liner notes to *Beauty in the Beast* and from Vail, *The Synthesizer*, 44–45.
41. Freff, "Tuning in to Wendy Carlos."
42. Carlos, "Tuning: At the Crossroads," *Computer Music Journal* 11, no. 1 (Spring 1987): 29.
43. Carlos, liner notes to *Beauty in the Beast*, 2.
44. Carlos, liner notes to *Beauty in the Beast*, 4.
45. DiMartino, "Wendy Carlos Invents New Sounds," 23.
46. Milano, "Wendy Carlos" (1986), 63.
47. Carlos, liner notes to *Beauty in the Beast*, 2–3.
48. Carlos, liner notes to *Beauty in the Beast*, 3.
49. Carlos, liner notes to *Beauty in the Beast* reissue, 3.
50. Milano, "Wendy Carlos" (1986), 50–56, 61, 70–82.
51. Milano, "Wendy Carlos" (1986), 62–63.
52. Carlos, "Tuning: At the Crossroads," 29–43.
53. Milano, "Wendy Carlos" (1986), 63.
54. Curtis Roads, "Editor's Reply," *Computer Music Journal* 11, no. 4 (Winter 1984):11.
55. Carlos, "Errors in Wendy Carlos Article," *Computer Music Journal* 11, no. 4 (Winter 1984): 10–11.
56. Carlos, "Errors in Wendy Carlos Article," 10–11.
57. Carlos, "Errors in Wendy Carlos Article," 11.
58. Carlos, "Prelude," foreword to Scott R. Wilkinson, *Tuning In: Microtonality in Electronic Music* (Milwaukee: Hal Leonard, 1988), 3.
59. Carlos, "Prelude," 3.
60. Carlos, "Tuning: At the Crossroads," 43.
61. Carlos, "Tuning: At the Crossroads," 29.
62. Carlos, "Prelude," 3.

63. Kurt B. Reighley, "Vocoder Questions" (interview with Wendy Carlos), available on http://www.wendycarlos.com/vocoders.html.

64. See, for example, Andrew Hugill, *The Digital Musician*, second edition (New York: Routledge, 2012), 198–199.

65. Carlos, liner notes to *Secrets of Synthesis* (CBS, 1987; East Side Digital, 2003), 4. (Citations are to the 2003 edition.)

66. Milano, "Wendy Carlos" (1986), 63.

67. Milano, "Wendy Carlos" (1986), 63.

68. Carlos, liner notes to *Secrets of Synthesis*, 1.

69. "What's the Strangest Artistic Collaboration You Can Think of?" *Keyboard* (January 1989): 64. The editors of *Keyboard* noted that the interviewer's name and questions had been lost due to a tape malfunction, so only Carlos's responses were recorded and printed.

70. "What's the Strangest Artistic Collaboration You Can Think of?" 64.

71. "What's the Strangest Artistic Collaboration You Can Think of?" 63.

72. "What's the Strangest Artistic Collaboration You Can Think of?" 63.

73. "What's the Strangest Artistic Collaboration You Can Think of?" 63.

74. "What's the Strangest Artistic Collaboration You Can Think of?" 58.

75. All information about the equipment used on the album is drawn from Carlos, "The LSI Philharmonic," available at http://www.wendycarlos.com/+pwca2.html, and "What's the Strangest Artistic Collaboration You Can Think of?" 59.

76. "What's the Strangest Artistic Collaboration You Can Think of?" 63.

77. "What's the Strangest Artistic Collaboration You Can Think of?" 62.

78. "What's the Strangest Artistic Collaboration You Can Think of?" 62.

79. Carlos, "The Psychology of Copyright Protection," *Keyboard* (January 1988), 12.

80. Carlos, "The Psychology of Copyright Protection," 12.

81. Milano, "Wendy Carlos" (1986), 74; Oteri, "Wendy's World," 5.

82. Carlos, "Wasted Tools," *Keyboard* (October 1990), 12.

83. Freff, "Tuning in to Wendy Carlos."

84. Carlos, "Wasted Tools," 12.

85. Carlos, "Wasted Tools," 12.

86. Freff, "Tuning in to Wendy Carlos."

87. Carlos, liner notes to *SOB2K*, 2–3.

88. Carlos, liner notes to *SOB2K*, 2–3.

89. Carlos, liner notes to *SOB2K*, 3.

90. Carlos, liner notes to *SOB2K*, 2.

91. Carlos, liner notes to *SOB2K*, 3.

92. Carlos, liner notes to *SOB2K*, 3.

93. Carlos, letter to Bob Moog, December 18, 1991. Robert Moog papers, #8629. Box 60, folder 15. Division of Rare and Manuscript Collections, Cornell University Library.

94. Carlos, letter to Bob Moog, December 18, 1991.

95. Carlos, letter to Bob Moog, December 18 1991.

96. Carlos, letter to Bob Moog, December 18, 1991.

97. Carlos, letter to Bob Moog, December 18, 1991.

98. Carlos, liner notes to *SOB2K*, 26–27.

99. Susan Nunziata, "Wendy Carlos Goes 'Bach' and Forward All at Once with New Reading of Old Set," *Billboard* (August 15, 1992), 67.

100. Carlos, liner notes to *SOB2K*, 26–27.

101. Nunziata, "Wendy Carlos," 67.

102. Nunziata, "Wendy Carlos," 67.

103. Carlos, liner notes to *SOB2K*, 5.

104. Carlos, letter to Bob Moog, December 18, 1991.

105. Carlos, liner notes to *SOB2K*, 20.

106. Hansen, "Wendy Carlos."

107. Carlos, liner notes to *SOB2K*, 26.

108. Carlos, "=Ye Olde Gold Leaf Awards!=" available at http://www.wendycarlos.com/open7.html.

109. Carlos, "What's New," available at http://www.wendycarlos.com/new.html.

110. No author, "Wendy Carlos: *Switched-On Bach 2000*," *Quarter Notes: The Telarc International Newsletter* (Spring/Summer 1992): 11.

111. Telarc newsletter, "Wendy Carlos."

112. Julia Serano, "Laura Jane Grace and Coming Out as Trans in the Public Eye," (May 30, 2012), available at http://juliaserano.blogspot.com/2012/05/laura-jane-grace-and-coming-out-as.html.

113. Parker Molloy, "Op-ed: Can Media Please Stop Focusing on Trans People's Bodies?" *Advocate* (January 9, 2014), available at https://www.advocate.com/commentary/2014/01/09/op-ed-can-media-please-stop-focusing-trans-peoples-bodies.

114. Hansen, "Listener responses" (1992).

115. Hansen, "Wendy Carlos."

116. Unless otherwise noted, all information about the origins of Carlos's website is from "A Brief History of this HomePage," available at http://www.wendycarlos.com/metanotes.html.

117. James Oestreich, "Play it Jazzy, Switched On or Straight, It's Bach," *New York Times* (April 2, 1997), C9.

118. Oestreich, "Play it Jazzy, Switched On or Straight, It's Bach," C9.

119. Carlos, "Wendy Carlos in Live Synthesizer Concert," March 14, 1997, available at http://www.wendycarlos.com/newsold.html#BatB%201

120. Carlos, "Wendy Carlos in Live Synthesizer Concert," March 14, 1997.

121. Carlos, "Wendy Carlos in Live Synthesizer Concert," March 14, 1997.

122. Carlos, "Wendy Carlos in Live Synthesizer Concert," March 14, 1997.

123. Carlos, "Wendy Carlos in Live Synthesizer Concert," March 14, 1997.

124. Wendy Carlos, "Wendy Carlos Total Solar Eclipse Page."

125. Carlos, "Wendy Carlos in Live Synthesizer Concert," April 6, 1997.

126. Carlos, "Wendy Carlos in Live Synthesizer Concert," April 16, 1997.

127. Carlos, "Wendy Carlos in Live Synthesizer Concert," April 6, 1997.

128. Carlos, "Wendy Carlos in Live Synthesizer Concert," April 6, 1997.

129. Carlos, "Wendy Carlos in Live Synthesizer Concert," April 6, 1997.

130. Carlos, "Wendy Carlos in Live Synthesizer Concert," April 6, 1997.

131. Carlos, "Wendy Carlos in Live Synthesizer Concert," April 6, 1997.

132. Carlos, "Wendy Carlos in Live Synthesizer Concert," April 6, 1997.

133. Carlos, "Wendy Carlos in Live Synthesizer Concert," April 6, 1997.

134. Carlos, "Wendy Carlos in Live Synthesizer Concert," April 6, 1997.

135. Carlos, "Piano Performance Premiere," available at http://www.wendycarlos.com/ newsold.html#piano%20premiere.

136. Carlos, "Piano Performance Premiere."

137. See, for example, Milano, "Wendy Carlos" (1979), 33.

138. Carlos, "Piano Performance Premiere."

139. Carlos, "Piano Performance Premiere."

140. See, for example, Carlos, liner notes to *SOB2K*, 5, note 2. In some places, she has written "can" and "must" in all capital letters, and in other places she italicizes them.

141. Carlos, liner notes to *SOB2K*, 5, note 2.

142. Moog, "Wendy Carlos on Computers," 64.

8

Reissuing the Past (1998–2005)

The year 1998 marked thirty years since the initial release of *Switched-On Bach*. Carlos would turn sixty in November of the following year. This period of her life is marked by a combination of trying to revisit the past on her own terms (sometimes with substantial revisions) and of starting to fight against anyone who tried to talk about her in any way other than what she wanted. Carlos began filing lawsuits against individuals and organizations that she thought had harmed her. Carlos also used her website to blast those whom she couldn't stop from talking about her. Further, she remastered and reissued all of her music on a new label, and some of the changes that she thought were improvements were met with disappointment by listeners.

In 1998, she took her entire catalogue to a new record label, East Side Digital (ESD). Carlos had been shopping around for a small label on which she could release new albums as well as older albums that had recently reverted to her. She lamented that large labels cared more about money than about making music.[1] Distribution, she grumbled, was a "dicey business" primarily run by "flakes."[2] After meeting with Rob Simonds, then the president of East Side Digital, in July 1998, Carlos made the move.[3] She was thrilled to work with a smaller label that could give her the time and attention she felt her music warranted.[4] She praised the staff at East Side Digital for being bright, nice, and honest, something she said was notably lacking in her previous experiences with record labels.[5] The staff at ESD seemed to share Carlos's dry sense of humor, as well: a postcard inserted into a CD tells the reader, "Congratulations! We're certain you'll find this recording to be not unlistenable. There's more where this came from," and the reader can then sign up for the label's mailing list. Between 1998 and 2004, East Side Digital re-released almost all of Carlos's albums on CD. The exceptions were the *TRON* soundtrack and the *Peter and the Wolf* album with "Weird Al" Yankovic, both of which were owned by CBS/Sony and did not make the leap to East Side Digital with the rest of Carlos's catalogue.

Many items in her catalogue were released under the name "Wendy Carlos" for the first time only when she made the move to East Side Digital.

Columbia had not reissued *The Well-Tempered Synthesizer*, her music for *A Clockwork Orange*, *Sonic Seasonings*, *Switched-On Bach II*, and *By Request* when Carlos had disclosed her transition and name change in 1979. Only now, more than two decades after her public disclosure in the *Playboy* interview and her legal name change, were these albums available under her name. Prior to this point, her back catalogue had been available only under the name "Walter Carlos." In addition, this was the first time that any of her earlier albums (with the exception of *Switched-On Bach*) would be released on CD. CDs had been commercially available since the early 1980s, and they were outselling vinyl records by 1988 and cassette tapes by 1991.[6]

Carlos would only release one more album of new material once she moved to East Side Digital. Released in the fall of 1998, *Tales of Heaven and Hell* was touted as a return to the dark world of *A Clockwork Orange*. The album's cover contains a caution not to listen alone to it alone or in the dark.[7] Carlos wrote that there weren't very many pieces of scary classical music—apart from the final movement of the *Symphonie fantastique* by Hector Berlioz or *A Night on Bald Mountain* by Modest Mussorgsky—and she hoped that the music on *Tales of Heaven and Hell* would join their sparse ranks.[8] The album included seven new works that engaged Carlos's past and present music in a variety of ways.

The longest cut on the album is "Clockwork Black," which Carlos said she spent more than a year composing.[9] She explained that the work was a return to the music she had created for *A Clockwork Orange* more than a quarter of a century earlier.[10] Indeed, the cover art of *Tales of Heaven and Hell*, created by Carlos herself, is a play on the images from the film posters of *A Clockwork Orange*.[11] In "Clockwork Black," she created an eighteen-minute fantasia based on the major musical themes from the film, including Beethoven's "Ode to Joy," Purcell's *Funeral Music for Queen Mary*, and the overture to Rossini's *La gazza ladra*.[12] "Clockwork Black" also includes ticking clocks, human voices weeping and screaming in agony, and chorale-like passages of phrases such as "We are all in hell," "we are the damned," and "let us prey on those who are weak/let us pray that we may be strong."[13] One imagines this is the soundtrack that played in Alex's mind as he was undergoing the Ludovico technique during *A Clockwork Orange*.

The music on *Tales of Heaven and Hell* contains some odd stylistic juxtapositions. Some tracks, like "Clockwork Black" and "Afterlife," would not be out of place as the atmospheric music played during a Halloween party. Others, like "Heavenscent" and "Memories," are ballad-like. "City of

Temptation" features a full synthesizer orchestra along with what Carlos called a "heartbeat" motif that sounds like half timpani, half thunderclap.[14] As opposed to the literal ticking of a clock heard in "Clockwork Black," however, Carlos uses the digitally synthesized orchestra to create jagged, jumpy ticks and tocks in the various instrument groups.

Although she used the newest synthesizers throughout the album, including the Kurzweil K150 and K2000, Carlos also went back to an instrument she had built in the 1970s.[15] The Circon (a portmanteau of "circular" and "controller"), as Carlos explained, is not an instrument but rather a continuous controller.[16] She had first built the Circon when she was working on music for Stanley Kubrick's *The Shining*.[17] Unhappy with the colors produced by her Moog synthesizer's keyboard controller, she began looking for an oscillator that would allow her to create melodies; when she couldn't find one that suited her, she designed it herself.[18] Combining aspects of HP and Heathkit oscillators, Carlos called on her old friend Bob Moog to build her a circuit that would improve the stability and accuracy of the controller.[19] She likened the resulting sound to that produced by a Theremin, although she claimed that the Circon was far easier to use than the Theremin.[20] She particularly liked that the Circon could create human-sounding vibrato, which made a striking contrast to the sounds produced using MIDI.[21]

Carlos used the sounds of the Circon prominently on *Tales of Heaven and Hell*. The album's first track, "Transitional," was meant to transport the listener from their daily musical world into the realm of the album, and fragments of the Circon's sounds are audible.[22] The album's second track, "HeavenScent," was an etude written specifically to showcase the possibilities of Circon.[23] Carlos even made the MIDI file of the piece available on her website.[24] She introduced thematic material on a piano and then used the Circon for the rest of the track.

Once again, Carlos had released a new sound and concept into the world, optimistic that others would be as excited about it as she was. On her website, she mentioned that she and Bob Moog had discussed the possibility of building more Circons for other people to purchase.[25] Moog was skeptical, leading Carlos to suggest that interested readers should write Moog directly to prove that they could make his investment in Circon manufacturing worthwhile.[26] Moog must not have received too many letters—he doesn't appear to have built any others except what he had done for Carlos.

Tales of Heaven and Hell, *Digital Moonscapes*, and *Beauty in the Beast* all sound incredibly dated to a twenty-first-century listener. Digital synthesis has improved in accuracy so much since the late 1990s that earlier digital works like Carlos's sound crude and cartoonish now. It's a troubling assessment, because these albums are so artful and required hundreds of hours of work and creative innovation. The knowledge that they were cutting-edge at the time of their releases can only do so much to mitigate how dated they sound now.

The phrase "Tales of heaven and hell" might be an accurate descriptor for the year 1998 in Carlos's life. She was not only creating what she considered some of her most beautiful music, but she was also fighting a legal battle against a musician for writing and recording a song about her that caused her a lot of anguish.[27] Scottish singer-songwriter Momus (b. Nick Currie) chose his artist name after the Greek god of mockery and satire. His songs are quirky and bizarre ("I Was a Maoist Intellectual," "The Angels are Voyeurs"), and many have explicit and unusual takes on sexual behavior ("Sex for the Disabled," "My Pervert Doppelganger"). Momus had been sued for his music once already in 1991, after the Michelin Company took issue with his song "Michelin Man," in which he compared the company's iconic mascot to a blow-up doll and touted the sexual prowess of said doll.[28]

On his 1998 album *The Little Red Songbook*, Momus included songs such as "Lucretia Borgia" (which included graphic depictions of incest), "How to Spot an Invert" (a list of stereotypes of gay men), and "Coming in a Girl's Mouth." He also included a song that he claimed was written as a tribute to Carlos, titled "Walter Carlos." In the song's lyrics, Momus explained that Walter Carlos, "international transsexual composer of that glorious epoch," no longer existed because "he had a gender operation done / just after making *Switched-On Bach*, volume one."[29] Momus then envisioned an alternate universe in which Wendy Carlos could travel back in time through a wormhole and marry Walter Carlos. Alas, Momus explained near the end of the song, Albert Einstein has said traveling back in time will not be possible, and Carlos's time travel could only occur in musical contexts.

Like many of Momus's songs, "Walter Carlos" depicts fictional encounters between historical figures that involve unorthodox sex acts. In the song, Momus also attributes the musical accomplishments that he so admires to Walter Carlos, despite the fact that the song's opening line informs the listener that Walter Carlos no longer exists. The character of "Wendy Carlos" in the song is a post-surgical figure whose only goal is to go back in time and marry the person who no longer exists.

When Momus released *The Little Red Songbook*, he was touring in the United States. One of the venues where he was performing in New York was near where Carlos lived, so he, through a promoter, invited her to attend the show and possibly give some interviews together.[30] Carlos was horrified by the song and by the request. She wrote a raw response on her website soon after hearing about it.[31] Carlos repeatedly referred to the song as a "rape," and she likened it to being pushed down a flight of stairs and to being stabbed in front of an audience for entertainment purposes.[32] She called the song a "Trojan tribute," a vicious personal attack that Momus had wrapped up to look like a generous gift.[33] She canceled a vacation, unable to eat or sleep for days knowing that he was about to perform the song not far from her home.[34] Writing that she felt like she was the butt of a joke and a twisted sexual fantasy, she decided she wasn't going to take it, and she filed a lawsuit.[35]

Carlos wrote that she was troubled by the notion that she was suing another musician over their art, but she wrote that she didn't feel one person had the right to attack, slander, or inflict pain on an innocent person for the sake of art.[36] To her, she had to defend her rights as a human being or risk losing those rights entirely.[37] Carlos implored her readers not to use or abuse living people.[38] As she wrote, true empathy requires respect for how a person actually feels, not what someone else thinks that person should feel.[39]

Momus seemed relatively unconcerned about Carlos's response to his song. He seemed to shrug off her concerns, attributing them to her own insecurities: "I guess she's not very comfortable with the fact that she's a transsexual."[40] He told one interviewer that he'd invited Carlos to the show that he was playing in New York because he hoped they could give some joint interviews to promote their new albums together, since *The Little Red Songbook* was released at about the same time as *Tales of Heaven and Hell*.[41] He claimed that his song and album could have drawn more attention to her new album, and that she should have been grateful for his tribute because she hadn't sold very many albums in the past decade.[42] Despite his claims of tremendous respect for Carlos, Momus didn't offer much of it in interviews he gave at this time. He called her a "drama queen" in one interview, and in another, he claimed that since he had recently received a corneal transplant from a female donor, he was "more of a transsexual" than Carlos was.[43]

Although Carlos initially filed a $22 million lawsuit, the case was settled out of court relatively promptly. Momus agreed to remove the song from the CD and to not include it on any future releases. Momus and his record label, Le Grand Magistery, had to pay somewhere between $30,000 and $50,000 in legal fees.[44] Le Grand Magistery was on the verge of bankruptcy as a result of the suit, so Momus came up with the idea for his next album *Stars Forever*. On his website, Momus told fans that for a donation of $1,000 dollars, he would write a song for the person who had donated the money. Although the notion of a crowd-funded album on sites such as Patreon is common in the twenty-first century, this approach was relatively unheard of in the 1990s. Thirty people took Momus up on the offer, including cartoonist Adam Green and artist Jeff Koons. *Stars Forever* was released in 1999, saving Le Grand Magistery from bankruptcy.[45]

In the press, Carlos was not treated particularly kindly in the fallout. She was treated as a humorless, money-grubbing freak in a number of cases. David Sprague of the *Village Voice* wrote that Carlos had forced Momus into his latest project because she didn't understand his song, while Douglas Wolk of *Spin* asked his readers, "You've got an angry transsexual on your tail and legal bills threatening to shut down your label. What's a pop star to do?"[46] Another journalist praised Momus for his "triumph over adversity."[47] A few critics were unimpressed with the new Momus album but framed it as being Carlos's fault. Brent DiCrescenzo of *Pitchfork* eviscerated both parties in his review of *Stars Forever*:

> A cloud of irrelevance and judicial waste hovers over the entire [lawsuit and new Momus album]—two quirky pop artists bickering on the fringe of cultural significance. After all, isn't it a bit sad that a perverted keyboard bard who writes toe-tappers about "cumming in a girl's mouth" is being sued by a trans-gendered, avant-new-age synthesizer freak who sauces vocoded bits like "We are in hell" over Moog belches?[48]

One can only imagine Carlos's reaction to this review and to others that similarly framed her as a relic of a bygone pop culture era, a freak (at least Momus was a "bard" in DiCrescenzo's assessment), and, perhaps worst of all, a creator of bad music.

Legal measures weren't the only way that Carlos started to fight back against those she felt were misrepresenting or slandering her. During the late 1990s, she began to use her website, too. She started writing lengthy letters, editorials, and other types of posts to explain her point of view on various issues. For example, Carlos had written at length about her disappointment following the Bach at the Beacon festival in April of 1997. That same year, she wrote a letter to the editor of the *New York Times* that wasn't published in the newspaper, only on her website.

The topic of the letter was one that Carlos had touched upon in the past but that was becoming more and more a part of her conversations in the 1990s. She was speaking out against the advent of serial (or twelve-tone, or dodecaphonic) music in academic music composition circles. This compositional approach, originated by Arnold Schoenberg in the 1920s, treated all twelve notes of the chromatic scale equally. Unlike tonal harmony, in which one pitch is the tonic or home key, serial composition systematized all of the pitches in a chromatic scale in a way that none was more important than another.

In a few interviews given earlier in the 1990s, Carlos had mentioned the prevalence of serialism during her studies at the Columbia-Princeton Electronic Music Center and offered unsparing critiques of the twelve-tone approach and the music that was composed using it. In her 1992 interview with Liane Hansen of *All Things Considered*, for example, Carlos called serialism "arbitrary," "nasty," and "deliberately ugly."[49] She likened composing serial music to taking castor oil: a person who did either was told to be brave and strong while ultimately producing a rather unpleasant result.[50]

Carlos's letter to the *New York Times*, dated August 1997, expands a number of the thoughts she had already presented in some earlier interviews. She explained that during her time as a music composition student in the late 1950s and early 1960s, most composers in academic institutions seemed to treat serialism as a holy grail; students who wanted to use any other approaches were condescended to or even alienated.[51] She likened the experience to that of women being excluded from leadership roles in large corporations and to white neighborhoods pushing out black residents; she noted that there was no explicit rule or statement forbidding such people or behaviors but that those in power worked to maintain their power by excluding those who were different.[52] Carlos explained that she did not want to write serial music when she was a student, so she began to pour her efforts into electronic music instead.[53]

She went on to critique serial composers for their lack of interest in alternate tuning systems, pointing out that a twelve-note scale is made up of uneven intervals and therefore does not offer the "democratic" balance that is claimed of it.[54] To her, an eleven-note or thirteen-note scale would have offered true democracy and balance because those scales were "intervallically neutral."[55] Carlos suggested that twelve--tone composers' reluctance and ignorance to embrace different kinds of scales resulted in a body of music that all sounded the same: ugly, astringent, and forgettable.[56] She noted that her efforts to point out these issues during her time as a graduate student were met with "snotty" and derisive responses, so she wrote her obligatory twelve-tone compositions for her teachers to get the credit she needed to be able to go on and compose the kind of music that she actually wanted to compose.[57] Ultimately, she noted, she should probably thank those who pushed her away from serial music and toward electronic music, since that was where she had flourished and made a name for herself.[58]

Throughout the letter, Carlos returns to themes that had permeated her interviews and writings for almost twenty years. She felt she was still under-appreciated and not getting the recognition she deserved.[59] She lamented the fact that she was not recognized as a real composer, both aesthetically and financially. She pointed out that orchestras didn't typically commission new works from synthesizer virtuosos such as herself.[60] Further, she hinted that electronic music was finally (in 1997) starting to get the recognition it de-served because of the diligent work she (and perhaps a few others) had been putting in for decades.[61] She was the one who had worked countless hours to help get electronic music to where it was in the present day, but nobody seemed to recognize that fact.[62]

Carlos also used her website to issue a multipart essay entitled "On Prurient Matters."[63] Dated December 1998, this section was likely written in response to the lawsuit against Momus and the trauma Carlos was experiencing as a result. The essay is headed by Carlos's own drawing of an eyeball with a blue iris and the word "SEX" scratched across the iris in red capital letters. The essay explains—albeit obliquely—that she did not want her gender to be a topic of conversation and that those who insisted on talking about it were "near-sadists," "creeps," "villains," "bastards," "brain-dead," "asses," and "bigots."[64] The essay does not contain any explicit references to her transition or to her gender; she claimed this obliqueness was to avoid visitors who had typed "prurient terms" into their search engines.[65] Her page was for those visiting her site, she wrote, not for those looking for a sexual thrill.

She wrote that that Internet was, in its early days, much like her adopted city of New York: welcoming, civilized and open, full of people who accepted others exactly as they were and didn't tell others how to live their lives. By the end of 1998, she wrote, the Internet had been more or less ruined by those with what she called "BIC Syndrome" ("brain-in-crotch," a term she repeatedly uses to refer to those who talked about her transition).[66] Those with said syndrome weren't interested in any of her real accomplishments. She said those who did happen to acknowledge her accomplishments as a musician did so as if she was a talking dog—Brian DiCrecenzo called her a "trans-gendered, avant-new-age synthesizer freak" and Douglas Wolk called her a "transgendered synth pioneer." She lamented that the perpetrators didn't have the common decency to wait until she was dead to talk about her.[67] Plus, she added, once she did die, she'd likely only be described with clichés about her gender that would dismiss anything else she'd done during her life.[68]

Carlos wrote that she had long ago let go of particular aspects of her past and that they played no active role in her present life unless other people dragged them out yet again.[69] She asked why people insisted on talking about aspects of her past that had nearly killed her but that she had survived and put behind her.[70] She compared her situation to that of a cancer survivor, a former stutterer, and a car crash victim whose face had been reconstructed, pointing out how painful it was to those individuals to refer to their past maladies.[71] She practically begged readers to show respect and empathy: she might be the victim this time, she wrote, but anybody out there could be next.[72]

The essay "On Prurient Matters" culminates in a link to "The Ouch List: A Shortlist of the Cruel."[73] Here, Carlos names by name the "real shits," those individuals and organizations she deemed to be cruelly indifferent, arrogant, self-righteous, and willing to abuse her and make her the object of ridicule.[74] She wrote that she was using this list as a way to fight back since she didn't have any connections in the press that she could use instead.[75] Carlos implored her readers to be wary of anything else said by the people on the list, invoking the computer science term GIGO (garbage in, garbage out) to suggest that the named individuals were likely untrustworthy.[76] Those on the list Carlos "awarded" anywhere from zero to three black leaves. Those with zero she said were probably just insensitive or sexually insecure, one leaf meant the perpetrator had sexual hang-ups and no empathy, two leaves indicated an axe to grind and a need for sensitivity training, and three leaves were reserved for those whom she deemed to be arrogant, selfish sadists.[77]

The Ouch List is populated with both individual names and names of specific publications. *Playboy*'s editors, the *New York Observer*, *All Music Guide*, and *Grande Royal Magazine* (a short-lived magazine published in the mid-1990s by hip-hop group the Beastie Boys) are among the popular culture publications listed. Reference publications include *The Grove Dictionary of Music and Musicians, Baker's Biographical Dictionary of Musicians*, and the *Virgin Encyclopedia of Popular Music*. Specific individuals include Colin Larkin (author of entries on Carlos in the *Oxford Encyclopedia of Popular Music* and on Robert Moog in the *Virgin Encyclopedia of Popular Music*), Trevor Pinch and Frank Trocco (co-authors of *Analog Days: The Invention and Impact of the Moog Synthesizer*, published by Harvard University Press), Ira Glass (host and producer of *This American Life*), and Sarah Vowell (the only woman on the list and a regular contributor to *This American Life*).

Most of the recipients of zero or one black leaf are clumsy about their handling of Carlos's gender and name and attribute her success to a male persona. *Amazing's Amazing Sounds*, an online periodical with articles written in Spanish and English and published irregularly since the 1990s, frequently refers to "Walter Carlos." Wendy Carlos is typically only mentioned in parentheses or as if the names are interchangeable (i.e., "Walter/Wendy Carlos"). A short article by Monste Andreu entitled "Innovative Women Composers," for example, offers the following assessment: "Wendy/Walter Carlos, having triumphed as a man, continues to harvest unending success as a woman . . . One may wonder whether her success would have been the same, should she had begun as a woman in the music field."[78]

Another recipient of zero leaves is *Obsolete's 120 Years of Electronic Music*, a compendium of electronic musical instruments that had been created between 1870 and 1990. The entry on the Moog synthesizer, authored by Simon Crab, refers to "Walter (later Wendy) Carlos." Crab also seems to misunderstand how *Switched-On Bach* was produced, suggesting the album was "entirely recorded using Moog synthesisers."[79] A recent photo of Wendy Carlos was included, likely without her permission.

Although she had appeared on the cover of an issue of *Grand Royal Magazine*, Carlos gave the magazine one black leaf and called it "glitzy" and "mediocre."[80] A two-page interview with her in the magazine uses her name and gender correctly, but an interview elsewhere in the issue with Bob Moog repeatedly misgenders her.[81] In fact, in the interview, Moog corrected interviewer Jamie Frasier and instructed him to use Carlos's correct name and pronouns.

The two-leaf recipients are those that not only handle Carlos's gender with little care (most mention surgery) but also those that don't necessarily present her music in the most favorable terms. Colin Larkin, who received two black leaves, was the editor of both the *Oxford Encyclopedia of Popular Music* and the *Virgin Encyclopedia of Popular Music*.[82] Both publications contain entries claiming that the male Walter Carlos had created *Switched-On Bach* with the assistance of Benjamin Folkman. No mention was made of Rachel Elkind, despite the fact that Carlos had repeatedly discussed Elkind's contribution to the album in print since 1979. Similarly, only "Walter Carlos" is named in the entry on Robert Moog in the *Virgin Encyclopedia of Popular Music*.

All Music, including its guidebook and website, was also given two black leaves; Carlos accused it of fabricating information.[83] Her artist biography by Joseph Stevenson uses her name and female pronouns throughout (there is no mention of any other name), including high praise for her music as well as for her eclipse photography.[84] Elsewhere on the site, however, "Walter Carlos" was credited for older albums, even those that had long since been reissued under the correct name. Since about 2014, almost all of the albums on *AllMusic* that were once credited to "Walter Carlos" have now been corrected, suggesting that Carlos or an advocate for her has been making the changes or advocating to have those changes made.

Another recipient of two leaves was a person who made Carlos the butt of a joke in front of a national audience. In a piece that first aired on *This American Life* in 1998, Sarah Vowell spoke in front of a live audience about her love of electronic music and her fascination with the Moog synthesizer when she was in junior high school. In her efforts to learn more about the music and the people who made it, Vowell tried to research the creator of *Switched-On Bach* but invariably found a different name than what was listed on her copy of the album. She asked a teacher what happened to Walter Carlos and who Wendy Carlos was. The teacher told her, after an embarrassed pause, "Walter had a sex change operation and changed his name to Wendy." Vowell explained to a laughing audience that she was completely shocked by this information:

> I knew absolutely nothing about sex. We didn't talk about sex in my house, and sex ed wasn't scheduled until spring. I was a wholesome, small-town, Christian kid engaged in wholesome, small-town, Christian pursuits. And suddenly, bam, I'm standing at the corner of Sodom and Gomorrah, and where's my street map?[85]

Vowell presented Carlos not only as a freak but also as a symbol of sexual deviancy. Vowell conflated gender identity with sexual behavior, and deviant sexual behavior at that. In the story, Carlos's gender was a topic first for horror and then for hilarity. Yet again, Carlos was treated like a freak and a sexual deviant, and her music was completely lost. It's worth noting that Carlos also gave Ira Glass, host of *This American Life*, one black leaf, likely in response to his role in this episode and piece.

The individuals and organizations Carlos gave three leaves, however, are those that include armchair psychological diagnoses of her and repeated or explicit mentions of surgical procedures or anatomy. Most of the three-leaf recipients also frame Carlos as a conduit for the Moog synthesizer's popularity instead of as an artist in her own right. The editors of *Playboy* were awarded three black leaves, almost certainly in response to what was printed about her in her 1979 interview. The interviewer Arthur Bell himself does not appear on this list, likely because he had died in 1984. Carlos, despite her demands that people wait to talk about her until after she was dead, may not have wanted to speak ill of the dead, so she named the magazine's editors instead. The remaining recipients on the Ouch List were far more recent offenders.

The Grove Dictionary of Music and Musicians was awarded three black leaves and told to "grow up." Carlos may have been responding to the entry written about her by Judith Rosen in the 2001 edition that calls her, in the first complete sentence of the entry, "an early experimenter in electronic music" and "a transsexual."[86] A quick search of dozens of other twentieth-century composers and musicians reveals that their genders were not mentioned in any of their entries, nor were they introduced to the reader as "experimenters." They are, rather, "champions," "innovators," and "influencers." Carlos might also have been upset about a double standard in a 2001 *Grove* entry on electronic instruments, in which author Hugh Davies referred to her as "Walter (later known as Wendy) Carlos." Two sentences later, Davies mentioned the First Moog Quartet, an ensemble founded by Gershon Kingsley, whose birth name Götz Gustav Ksinski was not provided.[87]

Another "award" of three black leaves went to Trevor Pinch and Frank Trocco. Their discussion of Carlos in their 2002 history of the Moog synthesizer refers to her with male pronouns, discusses her physical body and her medical treatments at length, and suggests that Carlos's skills with the synthesizer were somehow attributable to her "unusual transformation."[88] Pinch and Trocco propose that Carlos used the synthesizer to transcend "her former gender identity" and to "find herself" because her identity was "bound up with the machine."[89] Like many other authors, Pinch and Trocco refer to Carlos using male pronouns and her birth name until the moment of her surgery, after which they switched to female pronouns. Further, the male Walter Carlos was called "Carlos" in the text, but Wendy Carlos was referred to as "Wendy" once her name was finally introduced.[90] Referring to women by their first names and men by their last names is a pervasive sexist microaggression that has been well documented in a number of fields, including medicine, politics, and entertainment.[91]

The most explicit document to receive three black leaves was Nicolas Slonimsky's entry on Carlos in *Baker's Biographical Dictionary of Twentieth-Century Classical Musicians*.[92] Slonimsky dedicated approximately half of the entry to a graphic explanation of the surgical procedures that Carlos would likely have undergone. He referred to Carlos's gender identity as a "sexual tergiversation" (*Merriam-Webster*: n., a desertion of a cause, position, party, or faith) and referred to Carlos throughout the entry as "he" with one instance of "he/she." Moreover, Slonimsky implied that Carlos had somehow pulled one over on the American public with *Switched-On Bach*, noting that the album was "unexpectedly successful, especially among the wide-eyed, susceptible American youth." Carlos called the entry "pulp" and "trash" on her website, furious that it would be categorized as "scholarship."[93]

The late 1990s had many moments of great sorrow and joy for Carlos. In February of 1998, she made a whirlwind trip to Aruba to photograph an eclipse. Some of these photos would be filed with NASA and archived in the agency's solar eclipse photo galleries. In 1998, she also had to say goodbye to Nagus, the seal point Siamese cat that she'd had since the middle of the 1980s. Pica had died the previous year. Although sick with cancer, Nagus had remained a constant companion to Carlos until the very end: while she was working, he would bat her on the elbow if he needed attention.[94] The household soon after gained two new Siamese cats: a chocolate point named Pandora (or Pandy for short) and a seal point named Charly-O (the "o" was for the constellation Orion).[95] For good measure, a Border terrier puppy named Brritannia (or Brritty for short, and the two letter "r"s in her name were for the cold climate of Ithaca, NY, where she was born) also joined them in 1998 (Heather, the wheaten terrier, had died in 1995).[96] The three new animals joined Subi the blue point Siamese cat, who was already seventeen at the time but who would live until May 2001.[97]

Around the same time that she was working on *Tales of Heaven and Hell*, Carlos was also composing the score for the 1998 film *Woundings*. Based on a play by Jeff Noon, *Woundings* was written and directed by Roberta Hanley.

The film is set in an unnamed British military base during a fictional civil war. The documentary-like style focuses on the emotional lives of the characters.

Carlos created the music in collaboration with Clare Cooper (one of the musicians from the ill-fated Bach at the Beacon concert the previous year), Matthew Davidson (her friend and originator of her website), and Manya (a musician whom Carlos had known since childhood).[98] Carlos wrote a number of themes for the score that each of the three musicians vocalized. She recorded the vocal sounds on DAT tables. She also used Digital Performer to create MIDI and digital audio events, which she synchronized to video using the latest version of Digital Time Piece.[99]

Carlos explained that the film was full of disenfranchised youth and anti-heroes, and in order to help depict the depressing landscapes of their emotional states, she created "inside-psyche mood paintings."[100] She was pleased with the way that her score could reflect the conflicted emotional lives of the characters and the fact that they had survived the film's events "sadder but wiser."[101] Unfortunately, critics didn't find *Woundings* or its score nearly as emotionally compelling as Carlos did. Leonard Krady, writing for *Variety*, noted that director Roberta Hanley "captures the sense of monotony in subtle visual terms but undercuts it with a lulling pace and a musical score that too often plays the obvious sentimental notes."[102]

She told an interviewer during this time that hoped to take on another film project in the next year or two.[103] But the *Woundings* score and *Tales of Heaven and Hell*, both completed in 1998, were the last two original projects she would create. Indeed, the process of composing *Woundings* took a major physical toll on her. Working seven days a week for twelve to fourteen hours a day, she became so ill by the end of the project that she was bedridden for weeks.[104] At almost sixty, she likely no longer had the same physical stamina that she'd had at thirty for eighty- or ninety-hour workweeks.

From the middle of 1998 forward, all of her releases on East Side Digital would be either compilations or re-releases of past projects. The first of these compilations was the four-CD *Switched-On Boxed Set*. Released in October of 1999, the *Switched-On Boxed Set* came out two weeks before Carlos's sixtieth birthday and thirty-one years after *Switched-On Bach*'s premiere. The *Switched-On Boxed Set* included remastered versions of *Switched-On Bach, The Well-Tempered Synthesizer, Switched-On Bach II,* and *Switched-On Brandenburgs*. The reissues were remastered twenty-bit transfers from the original 1/4-inch and 1/2-inch tapes.[105] Four bonus tracks of music with Carlos's spoken explanations were included. The bonus tracks include early experiments, such as a version of *Jesu, Joy of Man's Desiring* in which the instrumental sounds were created using tuned white noise. As Carlos notes in her commentary, they didn't proceed with this idea because "the tuned noise quickly becomes annoying."[106] This is an understatement: the tuned white noise is the unpleasant marriage of unintentional record scratching and nails on a chalkboard.

The *Switched-On Boxed Set* included a 45-page booklet of notes from the original albums' releases as well as a 141-page booklet of new notes. Also included was an offline version of Carlos's website (captured and archived in the middle of 1999) and eight MIDI files from the 1992 album *Switched-On Bach 2000*. She put some excerpts from the new liner notes on her website as a teaser but instructed interested readers to obtain the new boxed set if they wanted to see and read everything.[107]

Carlos regularly lamented that she and the Moog were like Leonard Nimoy and Mr. Spock.[108] She tried to forge an identity separate from *Switched-On Bach*, but she was inextricably linked to her first album. She complained to an interviewer that those who only talked about the Moog lacked curiosity, were mindless, and seemed intent on denying her "the right as a human being" to continue to grow and mature in her art.[109] One could easily read this passage as being about her gender identity as much as it is about the Moog. Those who refused to stop talking about one aspect of her life, in her estimation, were not only small-minded but also uninterested in artistic advancement.

Carlos's *Switched-On* compilation didn't make as big of a splash as she had probably hoped, and most critics who did mention it opted to talk about her gender instead of about her music. In many cases, the reviews went far beyond just mentioning that Carlos had been known by another name when some of the albums were initially released. In a review for the *Austin Chronicle*, for example, Margaret Moser devoted 175 of her 500-word review to a discussion of Carlos's gender.[110]

Moser, like Montse Andreu, author of an entry in *Amazing's Amazing Sounds* that earned a zero black leaf rating on Carlos's "The Ouch List," speculated about whether Carlos would have had the same success in the late 1960s if listeners and colleagues had known she was a woman. At the same time, Moser seems to suggest that Carlos's female identity isn't valid. For example, Moser expresses regret that Carlos couldn't accept her three Grammy Awards in person because she would have been the first woman to win in those categories, but she then suggests that Carlos's desire to have her name on all of her past albums and awards is "revisionism."[111]

The revisionism in this instance comes not from Carlos herself but from critics who seem unaware of how a transgender woman would likely have been treated three decades earlier. In 1968, Carlos was not only terrified of having physical violence inflicted on her, but she was also afraid of being labeled a freak. Her music would then be freakish by association, because she was concerned that people would be unable to disentangle her music from her identity. Her fears from the late 1960s seem to be just as realistic thirty years later: there are hardly any reviews of the *Switched-On Boxed Set* that do not mention her transition or her former name. Despite the fact that those writing in the late 1990s act as if those times were past, it is clear that they were not. Just in the year 1999, music critics and journalists had done everything from call Carlos a freak to insinuate that her existence was a symbol of sexual deviancy.

This is not to say that Carlos wasn't engaging in her own systematic revision of her own history during this time. She may not have wanted to talk about her gender, but she did begin exercising some control about how her story was being told. In addition to berating those who she felt had slandered her on the Ouch List, Carlos also used her website to curate her professional biography.

In a lengthy interview given with Trevor Pinch in 1999, Rachel Elkind suggested that Carlos was trying to recreate the past, particularly the material from the late 1960s and 1970s during their collaborations together.[112] According to Elkind, Carlos had told her that she was now was working with musicians whom she claimed sounded "just like" Elkind had when the two women were working together.[113] Elkind wondered aloud why Carlos was trying to revisit the past, but she also noted that her one-time friend and collaborator was rapidly approaching the age of sixty and might be feeling pressure to compete with the work she had produced decades earlier.[114]

Despite Elkind's suspicion that Carlos was trying to return to the glory of their collaborations from decades earlier, it appears that Carlos was, consciously or not, writing Elkind out of her own story as it suited her. On her website, for example, Carlos has posted PDFs and transcriptions of a number of interviews that she has given since 1979, but almost all of the posted interviews do not mention Elkind.[115] For example, the extensive interview Carlos and Elkind gave with Allan Kozinn in the *New York Times* in 1980 is not posted on her site, nor is the 1984 interview she gave in *Polyphony* with John Diliberto in which she spoke at length about how much she missed working with Elkind. Perhaps most conspicuously absent from the website is the massive interview Carlos gave with Dominic Milano for *Contemporary Keyboard* in December 1979. It was the longest interview the magazine had ever published and included rich information about Carlos, but it also had a two-page interview with Rachel Elkind.

This lack of Elkind's presence in the interviews Carlos chose to post may also be because the earliest published interviews in which Carlos frequently mentioned Elkind (or in which Elkind was herself a participant) were also those in which Carlos's gender was mentioned. The omissions may be more about the mention of her gender or her time in hiding than they are about Elkind's presence. Elkind is not absent from Carlos's website, but she does not seem to be as prominent as might be warranted given the two women's long partnership. Carlos did include a copy of a 1998 *Exclaim* interview with Chris Twomey that mentions Elkind, but it's only in a professional context: Carlos credited Elkind with the creative impetus behind the introduction of the vocoder into the piece *Timesteps*.[116]

This is not to say that Elkind is entirely absent from Carlos's website. Indeed, she is given an entire page full of praise and acknowledgment. Carlos wrote about Elkind's importance to her music as a producer but says virtually nothing about the women's friendship. She blamed Elkind's marriage and subsequent move to France with her new husband for the dissolution of their working partnership.[117] Reading the page, one does not come away with any sense of the close friendship that they shared for more than a decade. Rather, it sounds like a polite professional collaboration that had come to an end.

Carlos also seems to have avoided posting interviews that may have indicated any weakness or failures on her part. Several interviews she gave to Dominic Milano in *Contemporary Keyboard* and *Keyboard* are posted on her site. Notably absent is her 1984 interview with him, an interview that included copies of scores from *Digital Moonscapes* as well as a discussion of an upcoming performance of the piece by the Berkeley Symphony Orchestra. Since the performance of *Digital Moonscapes* by Berkeley or any other orchestra never came to fruition in the way Carlos had envisioned, it seems plausible that she didn't share this interview on her website because she wanted to keep fans from knowing about a project that didn't exactly go as planned. It may also have been a way to protect her intellectual property since this is one of the few published interviews with her that includes her notated music.

Her website also gave her the opportunity to begin revising her relationship with film music. In 1999, she told an interviewer that she had never pursued a film project herself and only wrote film music if she was approached by someone.[118] This was not the case, though. She and Rachel Elkind had made first contact with Stanley Kubrick in the early 1970s when they heard he was adapting *A Clockwork Orange* for film. Through Lucy Kroll, they sought him out and sent him an early version of *Timesteps*. Kroll had pursued several film projects for Carlos throughout the 1970s, culminating with *The Shining* in 1980.

Carlos began editing her history with film music in the context of her work with Kubrick after Kubrick's death in 1999. In 2000, she told an interviewer that she had loved working with him and regretted the fact that they did not have a chance to "mature together" artistically.[119] She seemed to place the blame for this lack of mutual artistic maturation on Kubrick's well-documented love of using pre-existing music for his scores (what Carlos called "needle drops").[120] Even after Kubrick's death, Carlos claimed that Kubrick became too locked into his temp tracks to consider any other music, even music that she knew was "superior" to what he had chosen.[121] Although she had considered suing him for breach of contract in 1980 after he didn't use most of the music she had written for *The Shining*, by 1999, she had softened, noting that a lack of compensation for unused film music was the fault of the industry and not of Kubrick himself.[122] Her previous criticisms of him for being too exacting were transformed into praise. In a tribute she wrote on her website soon after his death in March 1999, she likened her own working methods to his, noting that she, like Kubrick, wanted to redo scenes or phrases until they were perfect.[123] She also noted the fact that she was one of the very few people who had worked with Kubrick more than once. She praised his brilliance but said that he "often drove me nuts."[124]

By the late 1990s, Carlos was becoming increasingly involved in the process of the interviews that she gave. She gave very few interviews during this period, and the interviews she did give were massive in length and minimally edited. She seems to have pulled away from individuals and institutions with whom she had previously had great working relationships. For example, in 1995, she gave what would be her final interview with *Keyboard* magazine.[125] This interview, like several others Carlos had given to the magazine since 1979, featured extensive discussions of her music and the technology she used to create it, plus photos of her studio. Something happened, though, and this would be the last interview she gave to the magazine.

It's not clear what led Carlos and *Keyboard* to part ways. Her past interviews for the magazine had been with Bob Moog and Dominic Milano, and this one was with Bob Doerschuk, so she may have been unhappy with the questions he asked or what he and the magazine ultimately printed. She was also horrified by the photos that had been taken for the article, later posting them on her website and claiming they were candidates for "the world's ugliest photos."[126] She went on at some length about the mistakes the photographer had made that had yielded such "horrific" photos, calling the end result "a shame." She may also have been upset because the *Keyboard* article included a photo of the cover of *Switched-On Bach*. Not only was she sick of this album being discussed again and again, but the magazine's editors also used the 1968 album cover, not a more recent reissue that said "Wendy Carlos" on the cover.

Between 1999 and 2003, the only published interviews with Carlos were conducted by Carol Wright, a freelance journalist who was the new age music editor for barnesandnoble.com as well as a contributor to the magazine *New Age Voice*. Wright was assigned by barnesandnoble.com to interview Carlos about the *Switched-On Boxed Set*. The interview between Carlos and Wright ended up being the only one Carlos gave at the time of the set's release. According to Wright, Carlos had been scheduled to give more interviews, but a long illness followed by a trip to photograph an eclipse near Bucharest, Romania, in August 1999 meant that she had cancelled several other interviews.[127] As a result, Wright said she ended up with an exclusive interview ahead of the release of the *Switched-On Boxed Set*.[128]

The interview with Wright was published in the November 1999 issue of *New Age Voice*, and Carlos promptly shared the full text on her website as well. It was also posted on the Synth Museum website (touted as "Your Vintage Synth Resource"). If Carlos had planned to give additional interviews to any other journalists or outlets in 1999, she seems to have abandoned the idea. She gave two more interviews to Wright in the next two years, and she didn't give interviews to anyone else.

The second published interview with Wright was a transcription of a multi-hour phone conversation between the two women that took place in December 2000. The resulting text was more than ten thousand words in length (as a point of reference, each chapter of this book is approximately ten thousand words long). It was published both on Carlos's website and on Synth Museum's website. A few months later, in March 2001, Wright conducted a third phone interview with Carlos. Portions of the third interview were used in a July 2001 issue of the magazine *New Age Retailer*, where quotes from Carlos appeared alongside those of new age musicians Constance Demby, Susan Osborn, and Tom Winter. Although not as long as the December 2000 interview, the 2001 interview included Wright pushing Carlos on issues pertaining to her inspiration and spiritual life. Again, the entire transcript of this interview was posted on Carlos's website.

Carlos clearly delighted in the conversations with Wright, claiming that she had never been asked before about most of the topics that Wright raised (or least having never had that portion of an interview printed). For example, Carlos called herself "an old agnostic skeptic" and said the notion that she communicated with a god who channeled music through her was "hogwash."[129] She told Wright that her inspiration came from her past experiences that she had internalized and then turned around in her own voice.[130] She noted that she sought wisdom, claiming that wisdom is what would remain once she had forgotten everything that she had learned.[131] She also praised Wright for asking her about tape splicing, which she said no one had ever asked her about in an interview before.[132] (Carlos had spoken about tape splicing in a number of past interviews, so her comment seems to be about Wright being the one to bring up the topic.)

Because they were transcripts of spoken conversations, the interviews with Wright would have given Carlos the opportunity to present a portrait of herself entirely on her own terms. When Carlos had met with Arthur Bell to conduct the interview for *Playboy* more than twenty years earlier, she brought along pages and pages of questions that she wanted Bell to ask her as well as what answers she planned to give. She learned the hard way that most journalists don't let their subjects dictate the interview questions and that the journalist will select specific parts of the subject's responses to publish. The three interviews Carlos gave to Wright allowed her to have authority over how she came across.

These three interviews set a precedent for nearly all of the interviews Carlos would give during the twenty-first century. Apart from conversations with Thom Holmes and Mark Vail, both of whom were writing histories of electronic music, the only other published interviews Carlos gave in the 2000s were similar in style and scope to those she had conducted with Wright. They were thousands of words long and were minimally edited, appearing in print as transcripts of a conversation with the interviewer. They are not placed within an article where a journalist or scholar might have the opportunity to interject their own conclusions or interpretations—they are presented in her voice and her voice alone.

Two major interviews from this first decade of the twenty-first century also included audio and video. Alan Baker of American Public Media conducted an interview with Carlos that constituted more than twelve thousand words once transcribed. The interview transcript and audio were posted online as part of the *Music Mavericks* series in January 2003. An audio- and videotaped interview with Frank Oteri of *NewMusicBox* in January 2007 took approximately six and a half hours to complete (the interview is timestamped on the site as starting at 8 p.m. and ending at 1:30 a.m.). A final text version of this interview, posted by *NewMusicBox* in April 2007, is almost twenty-thousand words in its entirety.

The shortest published print interview that Carlos gave during this period was with Chuck Miller of *Goldmine*, a record collecting magazine. In the two printed pages of the interview, Carlos explained why her website contained so many "lengthy treatises and essays," and this explanation also sheds light on why she prioritized such extensive and minimally edited interviews during this period.[133] She told Miller that she hoped young people would be inspired to follow her path, and she promised that the information on the website would live on long after she was gone.[134]

Carlos also seemed to equate these types of interviews with respect. Following her 2007 interview with Oteri, he sent her the transcript of the interview to review, edit, and approve before it went online.[135] She worked on it several hours a day for more than a week, turning what she called "ad lib comments" into what she considered to be "a more publishable form."[136] (One wonders if she made additions or deletions to her original comments, as well.) She thanked Oteri and his colleagues for their time, noting that she didn't receive that kind of respect very often.[137] In this context, respect seems to mean that she was allowed to tell her story exactly how she wanted, with minimal input or interference from the person conducting the interview. Indeed, these printed interviews from this period look more like long postings on her website that she had written. There are no interpolations except for the interviewer's questions.

In the twenty-first century, Carlos was relying on her own words to tell her story, likely to prevent misrepresentation and to keep the printed interviews away from topics that she didn't want discussed. Entirely absent from the massive interviews with Wright, Baker, and Oteri is any mention of gender at all. She doesn't discuss being a female composer and musician. She never once speaks about her own gender or even about gender as an abstract concept. It seems very likely that any mention of her gender or even of gender more broadly could have become the focal point for the interviewer or for the reader.

Carlos didn't release any new compositions after 1998's *Tales of Heaven and Hell*. Between 1998 and 2004, she released remastered versions of most of her catalogue on CD with East Side Digital, starting with *A Clockwork Orange* in 1998 and ending with *Switched-On Bach 2000* near the end of 2004. Carlos was directly involved in every step of every process, from preparing all of the audio to overseeing the graphics.[138] Rob Simonds of East Side Digital has suggested that one reason Carlos may not have produced any new material during this period was because she was utterly consumed with the process of reissuing her entire catalogue.[139]

Carlos may also have not had much time or creative energy for new works during this period because both of her parents were nearing the ends of their lives. Her parents had moved into an assisted living facility in the summer of 2000; animal lovers like their daughter, Clarence and Mary Carlos were the only people in the facility with a pet, a gold-colored cat aptly named Honey.[140] Although Carlos had not been close to her parents during the 1970s, by the early 1990s, she was visiting them regularly.[141] In 1991, she wrote to Bob Moog that her father, Clarence, who had recently turned eighty-five, had survived a "small heart attack" and was also receiving radiation therapy for prostate cancer.[142]

Her father died in 2003 at the age of ninety-six, and her mother declined quickly after that. Carlos, grief-stricken after her father's passing, wrote out a tribute to him on her website. She included several photos of her father from various parts of his life, and she also scanned and shared a variety of pencil drawings that her father had made in his spare time.[143] She lamented that both of her parents had been unable to pursue their own artistic gifts— her father as an artist, her mother as a soprano—beyond hobbies pursued in their spare time.[144] Taking care of her parents and grieving their losses likely consumed a lot of her thoughts and energy at the same time that she was remastering her catalogue on East Side Digital.

Every track on the remastered albums was taken from the original mixed master recordings. Some of the remasters were challenging because the original master tapes were fragile or damaged. According to Carlos, tape manufacturer 3M "idiotically" began using polyurethane-based binders on its tapes during the 1970s.[145] This meant that the bindings on the tapes had stuck to each other over time. Each tape from masters she had made between 1980 and 1985, therefore, had to be handled with the greatest of care to avoid physically damaging them.[146]

Carlos worked tirelessly to repair what she heard as defects in the original masters. She removed as many extraneous sounds such as hisses, hums, thumps, and clicks as she could.[147] She also tweaked levels and EQ, delighted that the distortions and "forced squashing" that had been required to fit the master on an LP were no longer necessary for CDs.[148] In fact, Carlos claimed that the CD reissues sounded virtually indistinguishable from the masters.[149] Much to her surprise, many listeners were disappointed that all of the hisses and other sounds were gone on the reissues. She claimed that East Side Digital had been inundated with complains from listeners who were missing their "favorite little technical problems" on the albums.[150] In response, she wrote out an explanation to listeners on her website explaining that removing all of those glitches was meant to improve the sound quality on the reissues.[151]

The only "new" music Carlos would release in the twenty-first century had been composed much earlier but had not been available commercially before. In the spring of 2005, Carlos released the two-volume set *Rediscovering Lost Scores* on East Side Digital, the final release of her recording contract with the company.[152] The album's cover, which she designed, is a clear homage to the *Indiana Jones* movie posters. The album's title, in yellow and red script with prominent shadows, frame a pile of scores, film, and magnetic tape. Hieroglyphics cover what appears to be a temple wall in the background. A figure who is probably supposed to be Carlos holds a magnifying glass in one hand and a flashlight in the other over the pile; the figure's arms are clad in khaki sleeves. (One imagines that a whip is close by.)

The two *Rediscovering Lost Scores* volumes include a total of sixty-one tracks of film music that had never been released before. Volume one had several of the cues for *The Shining* that Carlos had recorded with studio musicians as well as electronic music cues from the film (including the "Bloody Elevators" music from the film's iconic trailer). There were also three previously unreleased cuts from *A Clockwork Orange* and the soundtracks of several short UNICEF films. Volume two had additional studio music from *The Shining*, plus cues she had composed for the films *TRON*, *Split Second*, and *Woundings*. In 1980, Carlos had joked with Allan Kozinn that she might one day release an album called "Music Stanley Kubrick Didn't Use in *The Shining*," and, in a way, that would not have been an inappropriate title for the two volumes of *Rediscovering Lost Scores*.[153] Between the two volumes, she included more than thirty cues that she had written for *The Shining*.

As Carlos noted, *Rediscovering Lost Scores* was an eclectic mix of musical styles and of composition media that spanned more than three decades of her career.[154] There was traditional orchestral and chamber music, music for various types and combinations of voices, the sounds of her trusty Moog modular, and music created with newer digital music synthesis technology. In the liner notes, Carlos said it was a relief to release this collection because she had feared some of the music on it was never going to see the light of day.[155] The two volumes of *Rediscovering Lost Scores* were the last albums Carlos would release.

The release of *Rediscovering Lost Scores* in 2005 was not the only indicator that Carlos's career was reaching its twilight stage. That same year, she received a lifetime achievement award from the Society for Electro-Acoustic Music in the United States (SEAMUS). The first recipient of the society's lifetime achievement award in 1987 had been Carlos's graduate school professor Vladimir Ussachevsky, and Bob Moog had received it in 1991. Although Carlos rarely used Moog's synthesizers in her music after the early 1980s, the two remained on good personal and professional terms. Moog had interviewed Carlos several times for *Keyboard*, both in his own column and in longer features for the magazine. For a period in the 1980s, Moog had served as a consulting engineer and head of new production research at Kurzweil Music Systems.[156] It doesn't seem unlikely that Moog and Carlos might have consulted with each other since she was using Kurzweils during this period.

Carlos did not travel to the conference to receive the award from SEAMUS. Moog was asked to recognize her in her absence. In his speech, Moog recalled playing *Switched-On Bach* for a roomful of audio engineering professionals a few weeks before the album's release in the fall of 1968.[157] Everyone present gave Carlos a standing ovation, which Moog suggested was a harbinger of things to come.[158] (Elsewhere, Moog recalled seeing "a couple of those cynical old bastards starting to cry" when they first heard *Switched-On Bach*, although he left this particular memory out of his SEAMUS address.)[159] He praised her for setting high musical and technical standards and for her "keen aesthetic sense and meticulous attention to detail."[160] Moreover, Moog said, with each new release, Carlos was scaling new heights of technical sophistication and artistic creativity and excellence.[161]

Bob Moog died on August 21, 2005, just a few months after he had honored Carlos at SEAMUS. He had been diagnosed with a brain tumor in April of that year. Carlos was deeply moved by the loss of her friend and colleague. When she learned he was gravely ill, she drew a pencil sketch portrait of Moog for her website, which she frequently did as a means of tribute to those close to her.[162] Carlos, along with many other friends and family members, were invited to a memorial service in Asheville, North Carolina. Many, including Carlos, spoke about Moog informally, sharing stories and fond remembrances (see Figure 8.1). Some people played music on Moog's instruments live, and Carlos played a few recorded examples of her own music made using Moog's synthesizer, including the third movement of the Brandenburg Concerto no. 3 and the Scarlatti Sonata in G (K455).[163] At the suggestion of film director Steve Martin, their mutual friend, Carlos played her Moog version of Henry Purcell's *Funeral Music for Queen Mary* from the soundtrack to *A Clockwork Orange*. She also played a portion of the title

Figure 8.1 Wendy Carlos at Bob Moog's memorial service, August 24, 2005. AP Photo/Alan Marler. Used by permission.

track from *Beauty in the Beast*—a favorite of Moog's even though it had not been created using one of his synthesizers.[164] Carlos noted that the gathering, emceed by Moog's son Matthew, suited her friend's spirit and memory because it was informal and friendly.[165]

The warmth that pervaded the memorial service didn't last. Conflicts between Moog's widow, Ileana Grams-Moog (his second wife, whom he married nine years before his death) and his daughter Michelle Moog-Koussa have complicated researchers' abilities to gain access to Moog's papers. The two women have different goals and priorities, and researchers have had to wait while they make decisions. Grams-Moog retained control of Moog Music, which is still run by Michael Adams. Moog-Koussa founded the Bob Moog Foundation, which is not affiliated with Moog Music. Moog-Koussa reportedly offered to buy her father's archives from her stepmother for $100,000, which Grams-Moog found "offensive."[166] Grams-Moog eventually agreed to give her late husband's papers to the Cornell University archives (the university where Moog had earned his PhD). Only in late 2018—well over a decade after his death—were Bob Moog's papers processed and available for researchers to view.

Moog's death brought a brief resurgence of recognition for Carlos, too. Nearly every Moog obituary not only mentioned Carlos but also mentioned her transition, and usually by referring to her birth name first and putting her name as a parenthetical afterthought (i.e., "Walter [later Wendy]"). The *New York Times* did not mention her birth name in an article about Moog but later issued the following correction: "At the time of the recording, the performer, who later underwent a sex change, was Walter Carlos, not Wendy."[167] A number of obituary authors stated that "Walter Carlos" had created *Switched-On Bach*, treating Wendy Carlos as if she had not really existed until the moment she woke up from surgery in 1972.

As the first decade of the twenty-first century got underway, the technology for sharing music began to change rapidly. By the time Carlos had released her entire catalogue on CD with East Side Digital, consumers were no longer buying CDs or full albums. Instead, they were purchasing MP3s from Amazon, Apple, or other services or using online streaming services such as Pandora, YouTube, and Spotify. People had unprecedented access to music from all time periods, styles, genres, and record labels. As Carlos told Frank Oteri in 2007, "The internet alters everything."[168] But Carlos wasn't willing or able to make the leap to allowing her music to be distributed via

MP3 downloads or streaming services. Instead, she started to fight against anyone who tried to put any of her music online.

Notes

1. Carlos, "ESD," available at http://www.wendycarlos.com/newsold.html.
2. Bond, "A Clockwork Composer," 23.
3. Chris Morris, "Wendy Carlos Takes Her Moog Music to East Side Digital," *Billboard* (3 October 1998), 69.
4. Miller, "Wendy Carlos," 47.
5. Miller, "Wendy Carlos," 47.
6. See, for example, Dorian Lynskey, "How the Compact Disc Lost Its Shine," *Guardian* (UK) (May 28, 2015), available at https://www.theguardian.com/music/2015/may/28/how-the-compact-disc-lost-its-shine.
7. Carlos, *Tales of Heaven and Hell* (East Side Digital, 1998), cover.
8. Carlos, liner notes to *Tales of Heaven and Hell*, 2.
9. Carlos, liner notes to *Tales of Heaven and Hell*, 5.
10. Carlos, liner notes to *Tales of Heaven and Hell*, 5.
11. Carlos, liner notes to *Tales of Heaven and Hell*, 5.
12. Carlos, liner notes to *Tales of Heaven and Hell*, 5.
13. For the complete text, see Carlos, liner notes to *Tales of Heaven and Hell*, 11.
14. Carlos, liner notes to *Tales of Heaven and Hell*, 10.
15. Carlos, liner notes to *Tales of Heaven and Hell*, 4.
16. Carlos, "The Story of The Circon," available at http://www.wendycarlos.com/circon.html.
17. Carlos, "The Story of The Circon."
18. Carlos, "The Story of The Circon."
19. Carlos, "The Story of the Circon."
20. Carlos, liner notes to *Tales of Heaven and Hell*, 4.
21. Carlos, liner notes to *Tales of Heaven and Hell*, 3.
22. Carlos, liner notes to *Tales of Heaven and Hell*, 2.
23. Carlos, liner notes to *Tales of Heaven and Hell*, 3.
24. Wendy Carlos, "The Downloads: 'HeavenScent,'" available at http://www.wendycarlos.com/heavens/heavens.html#download.
25. Carlos, "The Story of The Circon."
26. Carlos, "The Story of The Circon."
27. Carlos, liner notes to *Tales of Heaven and Hell*, 4.
28. Martin Aston, "A Song for You," *Times (London)* (August 28, 1999): 14.
29. "Walter Carlos lyrics," https://genius.com/Momus-walter-carlos-lyrics.
30. Aston, "A Song for You," 14.
31. Carlos, "The Trojan 'Tribute,'" available at http://www.wendycarlos.com/newsold.html.
32. Carlos, "The Trojan 'Tribute.'"

33. Carlos, "The Trojan 'Tribute.'"
34. Carlos, "The Trojan 'Tribute.'"
35. Carlos, "The Trojan 'Tribute.'"
36. Carlos, "The Trojan 'Tribute.'"
37. Carlos, "The Trojan 'Tribute.'"
38. Carlos, "The Trojan 'Tribute.'"
39. Carlos, "The Trojan 'Tribute.'"
40. John DeRosa, "Interview with Momus [Nick Currie] Backstage at Fez, October 17, 1998," Silbermedia.com, available at http://www.silbermedia.com/qrd/thieves/momus.htm.
41. Aston, "A Song for You," 14.
42. DeRosa, "Momus."
43. DeRosa, "Momus"; Aston, "A Song for You," 14.
44. Aston, "A Song for You," 14.
45. Aston, "A Song for You," 14.
46. David Sprague, "Three Minutes of Fame," *Village Voice* (June 29, 1999), 138; Wolk, "Bizarre Publicity Stunt Alert," *Spin* (April 1, 1999), 57.
47. Aston, "A Song for You," 14.
48. Brian DiCrescenzo, "Review: Momus, *Stars Forever*," *Pitchfork* (August 24, 1999), available at https://pitchfork.com/reviews/albums/5383-stars-forever/
49. Hansen, "Wendy Carlos" (1992).
50. Hansen, "Wendy Carlos" (1992).
51. Carlos, "To the Editor," available at http://www.wendycarlos.com/resources/2ed-nyt.html.
52. Carlos, "To the Editor."
53. Carlos, "To the Editor."
54. Carlos, "To the Editor."
55. Carlos, "To the Editor."
56. Carlos, "To the Editor."
57. Carlos, "Resources: Music, MIDI & Text," available at http://www.wendycarlos.com/resources.html.
58. Carlos, "To the Editor."
59. Carlos, "To the Editor."
60. Carlos, "To the Editor."
61. Carlos, "To the Editor."
62. Carlos, "To the Editor."
63. Carlos, "On Prurient Matters," available at http://www.wendycarlos.com/pruri.html.
64. Carlos, "On Prurient Matters."
65. Carlos, "On Prurient Matters."
66. Carlos, "On Prurient Matters."
67. Carlos, "On Prurient Matters."
68. Carlos, "On Prurient Matters."
69. Carlos, "On Prurient Matters."
70. Carlos, "On Prurient Matters."

71. Carlos, "On Prurient Matters."

72. Carlos, "On Prurient Matters."

73. Carlos, "Ouch! A Shortlist of the Cruel," available at http://www.wendycarlos.com/ouch.

74. Carlos, "Ouch! A Shortlist of the Cruel."

75. Carlos, "Ouch! A Shortlist of the Cruel."

76. Carlos, "Ouch! A Shortlist of the Cruel."

77. Carlos, "Ouch! A Shortlist of the Cruel."

78. Montse Andreu, "Innovative Women Composers: A Silent Minority? (9)," available at http://www.amazings.com/articles/article0055.html.

79. Simon Crab, "Robert Moog and Moog Synthesisers," 114, available at https://www.mathieubosi.com/zikprojects/120YearsOfElectronicMusic.pdf.

80. Carlos, "Ouch! A Shortlist of the Cruel."

81. Blinx, "Wendy Carlos"; Jamie Fraser, "Bob Moog: Scientific Method Man," *Grand Royal Magazine* 3 (1995?): 54–57.

82. "Carlos, Wendy (Walter)." *Encyclopedia of Popular Music*, 4th ed., *Oxford Music Online*. Oxford University Press. Accessed November 10, 2014. http://www.oxfordmusiconline.com/subscriber/article/epm/4257; Colin Larkin, ed., "Robert Moog," *Virgin Encyclopedia of Popular Music, Concise Fourth Edition* (London: Virgin, 2002), 878.

83. Carlos, "Ouch! A Shortlist of the Cruel."

84. The earliest version of Joseph Stevenson's artist entry was archived August 15, 2012, by the Internet Archive Wayback Machine. It is likely that earlier entries existed and included different information, but I have not been able to find archived versions of any of those sites. See "Wendy Carlos," http://www.allmusic.com/artist/wendy-carlos-mn0000203175/biography.

85. Sarah Vowell, "Act Two: Toccata and Fugue in Me, a Minor," *This American Life* 104 (June 5, 1998). Transcript and audio available at http://www.thisamericanlife.org/radio-archives/episode/104/transcript.

86. Judith Rosen, "Wendy Carlos," (2001) *Grove Music Online/Oxford Music Online*. Available at https://doi-org.ezproxy.interlochen.org/10.1093/gmo/9781561592630.

87. Hugh Davies, "Electronic Instruments," (2001). *Grove Music Online/Oxford Music Online*. Available at https://doi-org.ezproxy.interlochen.org/10.1093/gmo/7981561259600.

88. Pinch and Trocco, *Analog Days*, 132–154.

89. Pinch and Trocco, *Analog Days*, 138.

90. They refer to "Carlos" from pages 132 to 137. From page 137 to 154, they refer to "Wendy."

91. See, for example, Janice Newman, "Why Are Female Doctors Introduced By First Name While Men Are Called 'Doctor'?" *Washington Post* (June 24, 2017), available at https://www.washingtonpost.com/national/health-science/why-are-female-doctors-introduced-by-first-name-while-men-are-called-doctor/2017/06/23/b790ddf2-4572-11e7-a196-a1bb629f64cb_story.html/; Stav Atir and Melissa J. Ferguson, "Do You Use Somebody's First Name or Last Name? The Answer Speaks Volumes," *Wall Street Journal* (August 12, 2018), available at https://www.wsj.com/

articles/do-you-use-somebodys-first-name-or-last-name-the-answer-speaks-volumes-1534125720.

92. Theodore Baker, *The Concise Edition of Baker's Biographical Dictionary of Musicians*, 8th ed., rev. Nicolas Slonimsky (New York: Schirmer, 1994), 158.

93. Carlos, "Ouch! A Shortlist of the Cruel."

94. Carlos, "The 'Critters' Pose."

95. Carlos, "Newest Critters," available at http://www.wendycarlos.com/photos2.html.

96. Carlos, "Fade to 1999," available at http://www.wendycarlos.com/newsold.html.

97. Carlos, "Newest Critters."

98. Carlos, liner notes to *Rediscovering Lost Scores, Volume 2* (East Side Digital, 2005), 8.

99. Carlos, "Wendy Finishes Soundtrack for 'Woundings,'" available at http://www.wendycarlos.com/newsold.html.

100. Bond, "A Clockwork Composer," 23.

101. Carlos, liner notes to *Rediscovering Lost Scores, Volume 2*, 10–11.

102. Leonard Klady, "*Woundings,*" *Variety* (November 1, 1998), available at https://variety.com/1998/film/reviews/woundings-1200456089/.

103. Bond, "A Clockwork Composer," 23.

104. Carlos, "Wendy Finishes Soundtrack for 'Woundings,'"

105. Carlos, *The Switched-On Boxed Set*, available at http://www.wendycarlos.com/+sobox.html.

106. Carlos, *The Switched-On Boxed Set* (East Side Digital, 1999), disc 1, track 14, "Initial Experiments," 4:00–5:15.

107. Carlos, *The Switched-On Boxed Set*.

108. See, for example, Estrada, "Synthesizer pioneer wants to go further," D3.

109. Baker, "Carlos" (2003).

110. Margaret Moser, "Wendy Carlos *Switched-On Boxed Set* (East Side Digital)," *Austin (TX) Chronicle* (December 17, 1999), available at https://www.austinchronicle.com/music/1999-12-17/75124/.

111. Moser, "Wendy Carlos *Switched-On Boxed Set* (East Side Digital)."

112. Pinch, "Rachel Elkind," n.p.

113. Pinch, "Rachel Elkind," n.p.

114. Pinch, "Rachel Elkind," n.p.

115. Most of the articles mentioned here are posted in Carlos, "Resources: Music, MIDI & Text."

116. Twomey, "Wendy Carlos."

117. Carlos, "Rachel Elkind-Tourre," available at http://www.wendycarlos.com/rachel.html.

118. Bond, "Clockwork Composer," 21.

119. Wright, "The Digital Phases of Wendy Carlos."

120. Wright, "The Digital Phases of Wendy Carlos."

121. Carlos, "Farewell, Stanley," available at http://www.wendycarlos.com/kubrick.html.

122. Carlos, "Farewell, Stanley."

123. Carlos, "Farewell, Stanley."

124. Carlos, "Farewell, Stanley."

125. Bob Doerschuk, "Wendy Carlos: The Magic in the Machine: Reflections from the First Great Modern Synthesist," *Keyboard* (August 1995): 51–62.

126. Carlos, "Photo Archive," available at http://www.wendycarlos.com/photos.html

127. Carol Wright, personal correspondence, December 18, 2014.

128. Carol Wright, personal correspondence, December 18, 2014.

129. Carol Wright, "Only Human: Touching the Significance," unpublished interview with Wendy Carlos (March 2001), available at http://www.wendycarlos.com/onlyhuman.html.

130. Wright, "Only Human."

131. Wright, "Only Human."

132. Wright, "The Digital Phases of Wendy Carlos."

133. Miller, "Wendy Carlos," 48.

134. Miller, "Wendy Carlos," 48.

135. Carlos, "News," available at http://www.wendycarlos.com/news.html.

136. Carlos, "News."

137. Carlos, "News."

138. Oteri, "Wendy's World," 6.

139. Rob Simonds, personal correspondence, October 30, 2018.

140. Carlos, "Photo Homage: A Farewell to my Father," available at http://www.wendycarlos.com/parents/index.html.

141. Bell, "*Playboy* interview," 96.

142. Carlos, letter to Bob Moog, December 18, 1991.

143. Carlos, "A Farewell to My Father."

144. Carlos, "A Farewell to My Father."

145. Miller, "Wendy Carlos," 47.

146. Miller, "Wendy Carlos," 47.

147. Carlos, "Remastering the Masters (Optimizing versus Remixing)," available at http://www.wendycarlos.com/discnotes.html.

148. Carlos, "Remastering the Masters (Optimizing versus Remixing)."

149. Carlos, "Remastering the Masters (Optimizing versus Remixing)."

150. Miller, "Wendy Carlos," 48.

151. Carlos, "Remastering the Masters (Optimizing versus Remixing)."

152. Carlos, "Lost Filmscores, Rediscovered Music Never Before Available," available at http://www.wendycarlos.com/news.html.

153. Kozinn, unpublished interview with Carlos, 26.

154. Carlos, liner notes to *Rediscovering Lost Scores, Volume 1*, 1.

155. Carlos, liner notes to *Rediscovering Lost Scores, Volume 1*, 2.

156. Holmes, *Electronic and Experimental Music*, 269.

157. "Bob Moog's Comments for SEAMUS 2005 Award," available at http://www.wendycarlos.com/other/moogseamus.html.

158. "Bob Moog's Comments for SEAMUS 2005 Award."

159. Pinch and Trocco, *Analog Days*, 144.

160. "Bob Moog's Comments for SEAMUS 2005 Award."

161. "Bob Moog's Comments for SEAMUS 2005 Award."

162. Wendy Carlos, "Bob Moog—R.I.P.," available at http://www.wendycarlos.com/ moog/index.html.

163. Wendy Carlos, "Bob Moog—R.I.P."

164. Wendy Carlos, "Bob Moog—R.I.P."

165. Wendy Carlos, "Bob Moog—R.I.P."

166. Jake Frankel, "Family Feud Continues Over Moog Archives," *Mountain Xpress* (Asheville, NC) (August 12, 2013), available at https://mountainx.com/news/ community-news/family_feud_continues_over_moog_archives/.

167. "Corrections," *New York Times* (October 8, 2004): A2.

168. Oteri, "Wendy's World," 6.

9

Preserving, Protecting, and Defending
Her Legacy (2006–Present)

In the first decade of the 2000s, CDs were being eclipsed by digital modes of consumption such as MP3 downloads and streaming services. East Side Digital found that operating a licensing-based CD label was no longer viable, and the company let all licenses revert to their owners. The label deleted almost all of its titles in 2009, including the entire Wendy Carlos catalog.[1] This means that all of Carlos's music returned to her ownership. It has been well over a decade since any of her music was released on CD, and she has yet to either reissue her music on physical media or in any digital format. Last updated in 2009, the front page of her website promises to have information about new releases of her music "as soon as possible."[2]

As a result, it is very difficult to listen to Carlos's music online. Anyone who searches for her music on YouTube, Amazon Prime Music, Spotify, iTunes, or other commercial online resources will find very little. She has not released any of her music through any of these new media. Used CDs and LPs of Carlos's music can sell for hundreds of dollars through online retailers like eBay and Amazon. Those who want to buy Carlos's music must rely on finding used copies through online retailers or record shops; many public and university libraries also have copies of some of her albums.

Part of her reluctance to distribute her music through newer channels and formats may have been due to her concerns about audio quality. She far preferred CDs to vinyl, although she has said that a CD that has been mastered "stupidly" could certainly sound far worse than an LP.[3] She was aghast when people told her how great they thought her old analog recordings sounded— she told an interviewer that she couldn't help but wonder if those people had lost their hearing by attending too many rock concerts.[4] She has written that she shuddered in horror the first time she heard *Switched-On Bach* on vinyl in 1968 after having only heard her master tape until that point; the only consolation, she said, was that the groove noises covered up some of the tape hiss.[5] She has expressed strong opposition to MP3s, noting that sound is "thrown away" because the MP3 is a compressed format.[6] She is skeptical of people who ripped their entire music library from CD and now had it only in MP3 format, wondering if those people might cry later when they realized that they no longer had "pure, uncompressed audio versions" of their music any more.[7]

Carlos has also written about the ethics of those who illegally copy and distribute music. By the late 1980s, as CDs were becoming the primary mode of music consumption, she suggested that people should speak up and "get really pissed off" at those who stole music and software programs—instead of accepting those pirated copies.[8] Carlos, like many artists, also had a number of concerns about the financial ramifications of new modes of distribution. She was upset that bootleg CD-R copies of her music for *TRON* and *The Shining* were being passed around in the late 1990s and early 2000s when no such albums had ever been released commercially.[9] To Carlos, when the consumers, the record companies, and the artists couldn't come to a fair agreement about compensation, everyone would lose.[10] At first, she tried to reward those who purchased her music through legitimate means, such as by including bonus items on her audio CDs such as a downloadable synthesizer and lengthy text articles. The 2002 CD release of *Wendy Carlos: By Request* included twelve pages of the "Pompous Circumstances" score.[11] She suggested that other artists should make similar attempts to give people "bang for their buck" when they purchased music.[12]

It seems that Carlos eventually gave up this tactic of trying to reward those who paid for her music through legitimate commercial means. In 2004, she expressed disdain that the advent of MP3s had apparently encouraged everyone to start stealing music.[13] She placed the blame at the feet of those who distributed her music without having paid for it, arguing that what she saw as the "rampant pirating" and "theft" of her music was the equivalent of killing the goose that laid golden eggs: by preventing her and other musicians from being paid for their art, these music thieves were keeping her from making more art because her art now couldn't necessarily guarantee her any kind of financial security.[14] She has suggested that those who pirated music were hitting the artists, and the artists and record companies needed to hit back.[15]

Carlos told an interviewer in 2004 that her lawyer was well aware of the dissemination of "bogus" versions of her music online.[16] Although she didn't mention it in the interview, her lawyer was her partner, Annemarie Franklin. When Carlos said her horrified lawyer came over and showed her the pirated music she had found online, the reader likely envisioned that the lawyer was "coming over" from across town as opposed to another room in their home. Franklin had passed the bar in 1990 and tried to start her own practice, but it seems that one of her major clients was the same person with whom she shared her life.[17]

Franklin had been a tireless advocate for Carlos and her music for decades. She had written a letter to the editor of OPUS magazine in 1985 attempting to correct Allan Kozinn's review of *Digital Moonscapes*.[18] She wrote to *Billboard* magazine to argue that the honor of first classical album to achieve platinum status (more than one million copies sold) belonged to *Switched-On Bach*, not to Luciano Pavarotti's recent *O Holy Night*. In 1986, the magazine responded tersely to Franklin in print: "We must continue to remind Miss Franklin, and others, that platinum can only be awarded to albums released after the plateau was formally recognized by the RIAA in 1976. The Bach album, of course, reached the market many years earlier."[19] Thus, *Switched-On Bach* couldn't be platinum unless the status was awarded retroactively. Franklin likely continued to press the issue, because *Switched-On Bach* was given its platinum status by the RIAA in November 1986.

Once Franklin became licensed to practice law, the two women created Serendip LLC, which then held the ownership of Carlos's music. According to public records on file with the State of New York, Serendip LLC initially filed as a company in December 1999. They had been using the name for many years, though: the 1985 letter to Allan Kozinn, for example, was sent on Serendip letterhead. It seems likely that the company was started in large part as a way to file lawsuits about Carlos's music without making Carlos herself the plaintiff in every case. There are at least three possible personal connections that might have led them to choose "Serendip" as the company's name.

The island of Sri Lanka was once known as known as Ceylon as well as Serendip. The total solar eclipse of June 20, 1955, was, at seven minutes and eight seconds, the longest total solar eclipse since the eleventh century and will not be surpassed in length until the year 2150. One of the best places to have viewed that eclipse was Colombo, the capital city of Sri Lanka. Carlos would only have been fifteen years old at the time, and while she might have known about the eclipse, she would have had no means to travel halfway around the world to experience it.

Serendip was also the setting of the fairy tale *The Three Princes of Serendip*, first recorded in epic poems in the eleventh century. In the tale, three young princes are thrown out of their homeland by their father. Although the princes are well-educated, the king does not think his sons are yet fit to rule. On their journey, the three princes identify a series of clues that lead them to identify characteristics of a camel that they have not actually seen. They are later accused of stealing the same camel, and because they provide such an accurate description of the missing animal—it has one injured leg, is blind in one eye, and is missing a tooth—they are first thought to be guilty. They then explain how they came to identify the camel's features: its tracks had three footprints and a fourth drag mark (so the camel had one injured leg), the grass on one side of the road had been eaten even though it was inferior to the grass on the other side of the road (so the camel must have been unable to see the better grass on the other side of the road), and chunks of grass the size of a camel's tooth were found at regular intervals (so the grass was falling out of the camel's mouth through the gap where a tooth was supposed to be). One of the accusers finds the camel wandering through the desert, and the young princes are cleared of all accusations of wrongdoing.

Carlos might have seen herself as intellectually comparable to the three princes: she had been educated at Brown and Columbia but has said she was effectively left out (she might argue that she was pushed out) of the academic setting because she didn't write serial music. She was exceptionally scrappy, assembling her own synthesizer setup and offering Bob Moog repeated suggestions for improvement of his modules. And despite that fact that her music testified to her intellect and accomplishments, there remained a number of skeptics about her role in the history of electronic music. She has not mentioned this fairy tale in any interviews or writings, but it seems like something that would appeal to her.

There is yet a third possible source for the use of "Serendip" in the LLC. Carlos was a great fan of Arthur C. Clarke, the British science fiction writer. Clarke is perhaps best known as the author of the novel *2001: A Space Odyssey* and the co-author of the screenplay for Stanley Kubrick's film of the same name (the novel and the film were developed concurrently). In 1977, Clarke published a collection of essays called *The View from Serendip*. The title was inspired by his adopted homeland of Sri Lanka, where he had moved in the middle of the 1950s and would remain until his death in 2008. In fact, Carlos and Franklin were such admirers of Clarke that Franklin quoted him in her rebuttal to Allan Kozinn's review of *Digital Moonscapes* that she had sent to the editors of *Opus* magazine in March of 1985. Franklin cautioned the magazine's editors that Kozinn seemed to have misunderstood how groundbreaking Carlos's digital music-making was.[20] She quoted Clarke to make her point that Carlos was clearly ahead of the curve: "It's always wise to cooperate with the inevitable, better yet to exploit it."[21]

Curiously, Carlos and Franklin did not seem to take Clarke's words into consideration when the twenty-first century presented them with options for new modes of music distribution and consumption. They have not yet made Carlos's music catalogue available through online means such as downloading and streaming. None of her music has been released in any digital format since the catalogue reverted to her ownership in 2008 or 2009. Further, Carlos and Franklin, as Serendip LLC, have frequently tried to stop people from trying to share or distribute Carlos's music online through platforms such as YouTube. For more than a decade, they have used legal means against those who post Carlos's music online without permission.

Most of the lawsuits Franklin files on behalf of Serendip are allegations of copyright infringements, usually for videos posted on YouTube that include unlicensed uses of Carlos's music. A typical filing can be found in *Serendip LLC v. Atkin*, filed in December 2016.[22] As Franklin writes in these filings, Carlos's music earns money from the sales of recorded media, from performing rights royalties, and from synchronization and master use licenses. The latter two examples occur when her music is heard on radio, film, television, or in online videos. The synchronization and master use licenses become the primary source of revenue once the music has been available for a few years. According to Franklin in the filing, individual copyright license fees that Serendip LLC requests for synchronization and master use licenses of Carlos's music start at $5,000 and frequently reach as high as $30,000. Each unlicensed use of Carlos's music, the copyright for which is held by Serendip, is treated in lawsuits as the theft of thousands of dollars.

In the filings, Franklin argues that YouTube (founded in 2005) has enabled thousands of unauthorized uses of Carlos's music and therefore has prevented her from earning revenue. Through these lawsuits, Franklin asserts that she and Carlos are protecting their copyrights through provisions of the Digital Millennium Copyright Act (DMCA). When a person posts a video on YouTube that includes unauthorized and unlicensed uses of Carlos's music, Serendip sends a DMCA takedown notice to YouTube. The takedown notice alleges that the copyrighted music heard in the video was not authorized or licensed by Serendip and is therefore in violation of the law. In many cases, this is as far as it goes. The user accepts that their video has been taken down and does not repost it. Some users, though, submit a DMCA counter-notification to YouTube, claiming that YouTube removed the video by mistake. When this happens, Serendip, as the copyright holder, must file a federal court action within ten business days to prevent YouTube from reinstating the video. In many cases, Franklin does file this action on behalf of Serendip.

In these filings, Franklin claims that the defendant has infringed Serendip's exclusive copyrights in terms of exclusive rights of reproduction, preparation of derivative works, and public performance of musical and sound recordings. She writes that such infringement is willful, intentional, and purposeful, and that Serendip is entitled to statutory damages for each copyright infringed. That is, if a person used more than one clip of Carlos's music in a single video, Franklin argues that the person owes statutory damages for each individual piece of music that they used. Further, in many cases, Franklin alleges that the defendants' conduct causes Serendip "great and irreparable injury that cannot be measured or compensated in money." To that end, Franklin requests a permanent injunction to prevent the defendant from ever using music copyrighted by Serendip again, whether on YouTube or on any other website. In addition to the permanent injunction, these suits typically request actual or statutory damages, Serendip's costs and attorneys' fees, and any other relief that the court might deem proper.

In rare instances, if the defendant can make the case that they were using the music as a parody, then copyright is not violated. In the unanimous 1994 U.S. Supreme Court decision in *Campbell v. Acuff-Rose Music, Inc.*, the court ruled that rap group 2 Live Crew did not infringe copyright when they sampled sounds from Roy Orbinson's song "Pretty Woman." Because 2 Live Crew parodied Orbinson's lyrics in their own song, and parodies are considered fair use under the law, then the court ruled that 2 Live Crew did not infringe copyright.[23] In most cases, though, the defendant is using Carlos's music unaltered. The video may be a parody, but unless the music itself is being parodied, then the music is not covered under fair use. For example, Hugh Atkin's 2016 video "A Clockwork Trump vs. A Trumpwork Orange" was a parody of the trailer for Stanley Kubrick's film *A Clockwork Orange*. Carlos's music from the film's trailer was used without modification: only the video was a parody, not the music. Atkin's use of the music was not covered under fair use and was therefore found to be in violation of Serendip's copyright.

These takedown notices from YouTube are often met with vitriol by users. In a 2016 story posted on Torrent Freak about Hugh Atkin's video and the lawsuit from Serendip, commenters on the article were quick to read Carlos, Franklin, and Serendip the riot act, calling them "morons," "idiots," and "ass-backwards retarded."[24] Some of the feedback was gendered female (Carlos is repeatedly called a "cunt" and a "bitch"). Her lawyer is not named or gendered in the article, but a number of commenters assumed the attorney was male and derided "him" as such ("dickhead," "madman"). A few comments were vaguely threatening. Commenter Xim Woem wrote "maybe we should all email the cunt and tell her we all have the copies we can upload. play wack a mole, bitch."

Although Carlos's gender transition was not mentioned in the story, one commenter with the handle YO brought it up in the comments and offered two gendered slurs: "Wendy Carlos is the same bitch/fag that sued that youtuber some time ago." YO then posted a link to a Torrent Freak article about Lewis Bond, another person who had posted a video about *A Clockwork Orange* on YouTube and received a takedown notice from YouTube on behalf of Serendip.

As many users have discovered, sharing Carlos's music on YouTube can be very difficult. Since she has not issued her music in any online streaming formats either, those who want to hear her music need to track down out-of-print hard copies of the music. In the twenty-first century, eBay is a major resource for finding these media. But Franklin, on behalf of Carlos and Serendip LLC, also has disputed particular listings of Carlos's music that have appeared on eBay.

In addition to filing copyright infringement legal claims against YouTube users, Franklin also asks eBay to remove listings that are claimed to be in violation of Serendip's intellectual property rights. This usually done through what eBay calls its Verified Rights Owner (VeRO) program, which allows owners of intellectual property rights to report eBay listings that potentially infringe the holders' rights. Unlike YouTube, eBay does not offer sellers much in the way of recourse if they object to the item's removal. A user can only submit a counter-notice in cases of United States-based copyright reports. In all other cases, they are mostly out of luck. Users are told to contact the rights owner with questions about why their item was removed.

eBay users have the right to auction or sell used copies of Carlos's music, but the way they describe the music seems to be what results in a removal of their listing. In many instances of items that have been removed, the eBay user includes "Walter Carlos," "Walter/Wendy Carlos," or "Walter (Wendy)

Carlos" in the description of the used sound recording that they are selling. Not every album that mentions "Walter Carlos" in the description has
been removed, however. Albums of Carlos's music that were released before
1979—that is, albums that actually say "Walter Carlos" on them—are not reported. (Or, if they are reported, they are not removed.) The only albums on
eBay that include "Walter Carlos" in the item description are LPs that were
released in the 1960s or 1970s using that name on the album. If a Wendy
Carlos album released after 1979, including all of her new albums as well as
East Side Digital CD reissues of her older works, includes the phrase "Walter
Carlos" in the item's description, the user runs the risk of a VeRO report
filed on behalf of Serendip to have the item removed from eBay. A good rule
of thumb for eBay users: if the music is on CD, it should say only "Wendy
Carlos" in the eBay listing.

Some people have reacted with puzzlement when their item was removed.
User Lerias73, in a discussion board on *Film Score Monthly*'s website, asked
a number of questions about why their listing for a used copy of the *TRON*
soundtrack had been removed. When other users explained that it was
likely because Lerias73 had included "Walter Carlos" in the listing, Lerias73
wrote, "I'll let it go and some time in the future I'll relist it without the
word . . . 'Walter.' "[25]

Others have reacted more viciously, often seeking retribution against
Carlos by invoking her gender. In 2008, user Fitz wrote on his blog Firetiki
about receiving a VeRO notification for his eBay listing of *Beauty in the
Beast*.[26] In the eBay listing, Fitz called the artist "Walter Wendy Carlos."
According to Fitz, eBay removed the listing when it received a VeRO complaint from Serendip. When Fitz wrote to Serendip to ask why his listing
was a violation of their property rights, he received this response, quoted
on his blog: "The artist's name is Wendy Carlos, as clearly shown on the LP."
Fitz wasn't satisfied with Serendip's response, despite the fact that a person
named Walter Carlos never released an album called *Beauty in the Beast* and
that name has never appeared on any version of that album.

Fitz claimed that the removal of his listing for *Beauty in the Beast* meant
that his compliance with eBay's PowerSeller requirements was now in danger
of failing. PowerSellers reach bronze, silver, gold, platinum, and titanium
levels based on their positive customer feedback scores, high sales in both
dollar amounts and number of transactions, and adherence to all eBay pol-
icies. PowerSellers receive a prominent seal on all of their listings, and they
receive a discount on certain fees charged by eBay. Fitz wrote that he began

researching Wendy Carlos when his listing was removed, and he learned about her lawsuit against Momus in 1998. He responded to the removal of his eBay listing by posting a copy of the song "Walter Carlos" by Momus on his blog.

Fitz wasn't the only person who invoked Carlos's transition in response to what was perceived as her interference with their own art or commerce. In 2010, a contributor to the website *Eclectic Earwig Reviews* (E.E.R.), calling themselves only "The Editor," wrote that they were removing all reviews of Carlos's music from their site.[27] Prior to 2010, E.E.R. had included favorable reviews of many of Carlos's albums as well as 1980 publicity photo of her taken by Vernon L. Smith in 1980. It seems that The Editor (likely either Jim Brenholts or John W. Patterson, both of whom had written multiple reviews of Carlos's albums for E.E.R.) had used the name "Walter Carlos" in their promotion of their own music compositions and had received a cease-and-desist letter from Serendip. The Editor wrote that they had "tried to reason with Serendip LLC to no avail." As a result, they were removing any positive association with Carlos from their site, including all of these past favorable reviews. The only trace of Carlos left on E.E.R. was this new page explaining why Carlos and her music had been removed. This new page is wallpapered with copies of a publicity photo of Carlos that had been taken before she had transitioned.

Many of these reactions seem at first like sour grapes—recall Aesop's fable in which a fox, unable to reach a bunch of grapes on a high branch, announced that he didn't want them anyways because those grapes probably weren't very good, anyways. Yet these responses often go beyond a simple dismissal of her or her music, frequently turning cruel and vindictive, and almost always bringing up her gender and her transition. Both Fitz and The Editor disagreed with how Carlos, through Serendip, treated them. They not only stopped associating with her but also posted music or photos that they knew had hurt her in the past.

These types of responses are pervasive in websites and postings having to do with Carlos. For example, YouTube user Paige Lestrange complained that YouTube had repeatedly removed her postings of the soundtrack from *A Clockwork Orange*; user Rob Jones, adapting lines from the film, suggested that such actions are "enough to make you ready for a bit of the old ultra-violence."[28] Rob Jones's comment was upvoted by YouTube users more than seven hundred times, and Paige Lestrange wrote that it was "officially my favourite comment" on the post.

Carlos is far from the only woman to receive these kinds of responses online. The advent of social media and unmoderated comment sections have made it easier and easier for people to communicate in every form imaginable. These tools have also enabled the sharing of comments that range from mean-spirited to life-threatening. The dangers that women face online have been documented by, to name just a few, Roxane Gay, Aurelie Nix, and Lindy West. West, for example, was repeatedly harassed online by a man who created a Twitter account using the name and photo of West's recently deceased father in order to tweet cruel things about her.[29] Women who are fat, people of color, disabled, transgender, or otherwise "other" are often particularly singled out for those identities. Kat Blaque has documented the online harassment she has experienced in response to the fact that she is a transgender woman.[30] Julia Serano discontinued the comments section on her blog in 2016 in part because of receiving excessive "angry/insulting/dismissive comments."[31]

Many people have been frustrated with Carlos, Franklin, and Serendip LLC in terms of how they handle copyright claims. These frustrations very quickly turn toward Carlos's gender. Those who once admired her and her music often become angry when she doesn't respond in kind. The responses often include everything from insults to photos to music that is posted with the single intention of injuring her because she is transgender. Further, her gender is what is used to injure her. Nobody tries to seek their revenge by claiming that they now hate her music or that she isn't talented. E.E.R., for example, removed its positive reviews of Carlos's music and replaced them with a photo of her taken before she had transitioned, as opposed to replacing the positive reviews with negative reviews.

A few Carlos defenders have emerged in some of these angry threads, generally people who know her and who try to explain to others why she is so defensive about copyright and distribution of her music. In March 2010, user SynthBaron posted on the forum MuffWiggler, angry that their YouTube video had been removed under a copyright complaint from Serendip LLC. Synthbaron titled the thread, "Dear Wendy Carlos: Go fuck yourself."[32] Synthbaron said they had created their own Moog modular synthesizer renditions of two keyboard inventions by Johann Sebastian Bach and posted them on YouTube. Although the creations were original, SynthBaron had tagged them with "Wendy Carlos," which is what prompted the removal by YouTube on behalf of Serendip.

Other users jumped into SynthBaron's thread to criticize Carlos and to share their own stories of how she (or Serendip) had removed their own YouTube videos or eBay listings because they had used "Walter Carlos" in the descriptions or tags. Many comments included the users' own diagnoses of Carlos's mental health vis-à-vis her gender identity and prescriptions for how they thought Carlos should be acting. User theglyph, for example, suggested that Carlos was insulting "people who switch gender." User BadBadger supplied a link to Carlos's 1979 *Playboy* interview because it had "gory details" about her transition in order "to contribute something to the conversation other than, 'Fuck her!' " BadBadger clarified, however, that they were disgusted by Carlos's legal actions and definitely were not a Carlos apologist, ending their post with the statement, "Fuck her!"

Two different users joined the conversation on Muff Wiggler to defend Carlos, but both users created different usernames exclusively for this thread. They both claimed to be friends of Carlos's and knew she would be furious, humiliated, or both knowing that they were participating in this conversation about her. User forthistopiconly explained that they knew Carlos and that she was "a balanced, wise and decent person with a deep commitment for her art." Forthistopiconly said they felt compelled to speak up (albeit under a different name) because they needed to differentiate Carlos the person from the way that she was being treated in the context of the thread. They were speaking up because they couldn't bear watching the thread unfold because it didn't accord with their knowledge of Carlos. Similarly, user youknowme stated that they had known Carlos for many years. According to youknownme, "I ask you to accept Wendy's flaws in light of her beauty and passion and the legacy she has created that has given you all so much." Youknowme made light of the veracity of their own statement, though, noting, "You can trust me, I'm from the internet."

A similar kind of conversation unfolded on the site Analogue Heaven in 2008.[33] Kenneth Elhardt posted in fury about Serendip's legal actions, calling the company "bullies," "petty," "insane," and "psycho." Matthew Davidson, Carlos's longtime friend and the person who had encouraged her to start her website more than a decade earlier, was a member of the Analogue Heaven forum and weighed in on the discussion. Davidson wrote that Serendip was dedicated not only to pursuing all unlicensed uses of Carlos's music but also all unauthorized uses of her eclipse photography. He said it worked to stop all unlicensed uses of any of Carlos's copyrights, regardless of type or context. Although Elhardt and others might have felt personally blighted or singled out, Davidson said, the action against them wasn't personal. Davidson explained that he personally disagreed with how Serendip went about protecting her copyright but stressed that it was within its legal rights to take the actions that it were taking. As Davidson explained, "It doesn't matter if you feel they should be honored you're exposing new people to Wendy's music, that isn't for you to decide. It is only for the copyright holder to decide, and they've made their position quite clear."

Davidson went on to suggest that those who were angry about copyright law itself should stop complaining about how Carlos and others were using copyright law and instead start seeking changes in copyright law itself. He suggested that those who wanted to subvert what they saw as absurdities in copyright law should create their own art or music and release it via a Creative Commons license. Creative Commons offers artists a variety of copyright license types that enable artists to share their creative work. He also implored readers to contact him directly with further questions instead of posting them on the forum. The thread about Carlos on Analogue Heaven stopped after Davidson's comment.

Even well into the twenty-first century, more than fifty years after Carlos transitioned and more than forty years after she disclosed her transition in the *Playboy* interview, her gender remains the most-discussed aspect of her life and identity for journalists and scholars. For example, a photo of Carlos with her Moog synthesizer was posted on the Reddit thread OldSchoolCool, which is "a pictorial and video celebration of history's coolest kids" where users are told to share photos of "people from the past looking fantastic." The photo is labeled "Pioneering electronic musician Wendy Carlos, 1970s." The most upvoted comment on the photo, made by u/19djafoij02, consists of two words: "Born Walter." Nobody in the thread discusses her music, or the Moog synthesizer itself, or any other aspect of her life and her art. The focal point is her gender.

In many cases, her gender is still treated as a subject for scorn or ridicule. A thread begun April 4, 2005, on the online forum Prog Music Lounge started with user John Gargo asking fellow forum members what they thought about Carlos's music and if her "four 'baroque-gone-space-age LPs" from the 1970s qualified her and her music as progressive rock.[34] The very next comment in the thread, by user Easy Livin, reads, "I don't mean to be picky, but for me, those early albums you mention will always be by Walter Carlos, I still can't get used to the notion of him now being a 'she.' " Nearly every subsequent comment in the thread discusses Carlos's gender identity or body in some way, largely ignoring the initial question posed by John Gargo about her music, despite his repeated attempts to bring the thread back to his question about her music. One user wrote that they were frightened by her because "the whole sex-change thing doesn't sit well with me and I really don't feel comfortable associating myself with it in any way." When pressed, the same user said they would throw away their King Crimson albums if Robert Fripp transitioned to female because "I don't want anyone to have a reason to think I am a pervert." Several users mocked her and made crass suggestions about medical procedures she had undergone, such as one user referring to "the chop" and another suggesting that a person whose "outie became an innie" would be making "regressive" rock, instead of progressive rock. This thread is one example many in which a question or discussion about Carlos's music is almost immediately derailed in favor of a discussion about her gender.

Many online stories about her frame her first as transgender and then as an electronic musician and innovator. A 2016 WFMT article by Stephen Raskauskas is titled, "How Transgender Composer Wendy Carlos Changed Music Forever."[35] In a piece written for *Vice* by Natasha MacDonald-Dupuis, the headline blares, "Meet Wendy Carlos: The Trans Godmother of Electronic Music."[36] MacDonald-Dupuis makes several factual errors in the article (such as claiming that Carlos publicly performed "as a man" during the 1970s), eventually concluding that "no one seemed to give two fucks" about Carlos's gender identity. In contrast, Carlos has said she feels like the media treats her as a talking dog.[37] Her gender, not her music, is prioritized.

In contrast, other scholars and journalists have suggested that Carlos should be left out of certain music histories because of her gender. Musicologist Judy Tsou has argued that Carlos should not have been included in a dictionary of women composers: "How does one explain the inclusion of Wendy Carlos (the surgically altered Walter Carlos)?"[38] Those who do not mention that Carlos is transgender are also criticized. Musicologist Elizabeth Keathley, for example, chided fellow scholar Elizabeth Hinkle-Turner for neglecting to state that Carlos was transgender in her book *Women Composers and Music Technology in the United States*.[39] There seems to be a sense that it is somehow deceptive to not mention that she is transgender.

Other scholars have ignored what little Carlos has said about her gender when analyzing her life and music. Trevor Pinch and Frank Trocco, whom Carlos "awarded" three black leaves on "The Ouch List: A Shortlist of the Cruel," have asserted that Carlos used the Moog synthesizer to "escape the gender identity society had given her" and to "transcend her former body and her former gender identity."[40] Carlos has been clear that her work with the Moog synthesizer was not bound up with her gender identity in the way that Pinch and Trocco suggest. Both she and Elkind, for example, have explained that one reason they didn't want to disclose Carlos's gender transition at the height of the Moog's popularity was because they didn't want people mapping Carlos's gender (and what they feared would be viewed as its freakish nature) on to the Moog's novelty. Both women saw the inevitability of this overly simplistic reading of gender and technology and tried to prevent it.

Although Pinch and Trocco cite Carlos's *Playboy* interview elsewhere in their book, they seem to disregard the part of the interview in which Carlos stated explicitly that her gender had not personally affected her music. In fact, she laughed off the question and asked Bell if he was implying that she should write a work called *The Transsexual Symphony*.[41] Pinch and Trocco also conducted a lengthy interview with Rachel Elkind for the book, during which Elkind said that she and Carlos did not want the music to "get confused" with Carlos's gender.

Carlos didn't use the Moog synthesizer because she was transgender or because she was trying to "escape" or "transcend" her gender identity or her physical body. She had been a workaholic since childhood, and she has said those work habits were responses to fear, depression, and isolation that she experienced. She couldn't disclose her gender identity to anyone out of fear of how they might respond, so she didn't date, had few friends, and threw herself into work. The Moog might have been the recipient of the workaholic energy that resulted from her isolation and depression, but it was not a tool through which she channeled her gender identity to create music.

Pinch and Trocco are not the only scholars who have disregarded Carlos's own words about her gender identity as it relates to her music. Musicologist Judith Peraino has quoted Carlos's quip from the *Playboy* interview about *The Transsexual Symphony* and argued that Carlos was wrong in her own assessment of her own art and life.[42] In fact, Peraino claims, Carlos actually wrote *The Transsexual Symphony* when she created her synthesized rendition of Beethoven's Symphony no. 9 and Bach's Brandenburg Concerto no. 3.[43] Peraino reads those pieces of music as a human body and Carlos's use of the Moog synthesizer as the "radical reassignment surgery," arguing that Carlos has somehow effected a transition between different versions of the same piece of music.[44]

Peraino's assessment is problematic for a number of reasons, first and foremost of which being that it requires her to explicitly and completely disregard Carlos's own words about her music, her identity, her experience, and her perception of her own artistic accomplishments. Further, Peraino's notion of "transition" focuses exclusively on a single surgical procedure, implying inaccurately that a gender transition requires surgery and that only a single surgery is required. This notion leaves out many dimensions of gender transition, including a person's social presentation of their gender that may or may not require any medical treatment or intervention. Peraino also refers to Carlos as "a product of technology," suggesting that a gender transition requires some sort of external intervention and neglecting the social and cultural dimensions of a person's gender presentation.[45]

In a letter she wrote to Arthur Bell a few weeks after the *Playboy* interview was published in 1979, Carlos told Bell that she wasn't upset about what had been printed—after all, she had said all of those things.[46] Instead, she was hurt because of how little he and magazine had printed about what she called the "real" her: her interests, observations, philosophies, humor, and other things that she said made her a "three-dimensional" person.[47] She asked Bell why he couldn't have allowed just a little bit of her "soul" to peek through in the interview instead of focusing "monomaniacally" on her gender and the "medical stuff."[48] She wondered whether he simply found her so boring that he chose to make "90%" of the printed interview about her gender; after all, she pointed out, there were plenty of textbooks he could have quoted about the "medical stuff" if that was what he really wanted to write about.[49]

In the more than four decades since Carlos disclosed her transition, many journalists, scholars, and fans have, like Bell, focused on Carlos's gender instead of (or in far greater proportions than) her music. Even if her gender is not a part of an initial discussion, it is sometimes brought in as a way to hurt her or to make a joke at her expense. If her gender is not mentioned, the writer is accused of being deceptive. The cultural reception of transgender people, particularly with regard to how their careers and accomplishments are framed, has deeply affected how people have written and spoken about Carlos for decades. Her accomplishments and shortcomings are filtered through her gender identity. To Carlos, this focus on her gender has blocked the public from getting to see her soul.[50] In her view, her gender is the least interesting thing about her, and she would far rather talk about just about anything else. As she told Bell, "Just let me live my goddamn life."[51]

Notes

1. Rob Simonds, personal correspondence, October 28, 2018.
2. Carlos, "Wendy Carlos," available at http://www.wendycarlos.com/.
3. Miller, "Wendy Carlos," 48.
4. Miller, "Wendy Carlos," 48.
5. Carlos, liner notes to *SOB2K*, 3.
6. Oteri, "Wendy's World," 6.
7. Oteri, "Wendy's World," 6.
8. Carlos, "The Psychology of Copy Protection," 15.
9. Miller, "Wendy Carlos," 47.
10. Carlos, "The Psychology of Copy Protection," 15.
11. Carlos, "By Request—ESD81962," available at http://www.wendycarlos.com/+br.html.
12. Miller, "Wendy Carlos," 47.
13. Miller, "Wendy Carlos," 47.
14. Miller, "Wendy Carlos," 47.
15. Carlos, "The Psychology of Copy Protection," 15. In this sentence she placed the word "hitting" in italics for emphasis, and in the next sentence insisted that she was not joking.
16. Miller, "Wendy Carlos," 47.
17. In a letter to Bob Moog written in December 1991, Carlos said Franklin was struggling to find clients to get her new practice off the ground.
18. Franklin, letter to *Opus*, March 11, 1985.
19. Unsigned, "Assaying Metal," *Billboard*, February 1, 1986, 62.
20. Franklin, letter to *Opus*, March 11, 1985.
21. Several variations of this statement have appeared in Clarke's writings and talks, including in a transcript of a 1982 lecture he gave at an Institute of Fundamental Studies (IFS) seminar in Sri Lanka.
22. Unless otherwise noted, all information in this section is drawn from Serendip LLC v. Hugh Murray Atkin, 16 CV 08790 (New York, 2016).
23. Joanna Demers, *Steal this Music: How Intellectual Property Law Affects Musical Creativity* (Athens: University of Georgia Press, 2006), 54–59.
24. Andy, "Donald Trump Parody Results in Clockwork Orange Copyright Suit," *Torrent Freak* (November 14, 2016), available at https://torrentfreak.com/donald-trump-parody-results-in-clockwork-orange-copyright-suit-161114/.
25. "General discussion: I have been Tronned at eBay," begun February 4, 2007, by member Lerias73, available at http://www.filmscoremonthly.com/board/posts.cfm?threadID=39790&forumID=1&archive=1.
26. See Fitz, "The Carlos Confusion," Firetiki (blog) (October 14, 2008), available at http://firetiki.blogspot.com/2008/10/carlos-confusion.html.
27. The Editor, "Looking for Walter/Wendy Carlos info?" undated website, available at http://www.eer-music.com/reviews/wendy.html. A capture taken by the Internet

Archive on August 26, 2010, is the first appearance of the new anti-Carlos page. All previous versions of the site captured before this date include the favorable album reviews.

28. See the video and comments on https://www.youtube.com/watch?v=Ceh0-42FXg0.

29. See, for example, Lindy West, "Slaying the Troll" in *Shrill* (New York: Hachette, 2016). Several of West's essays in this collection deal with the online harassment she has experienced.

30. See, for example, many of Blaque's video blog posts at https://www.youtube.com/katblaque.

31. Serano, "I'm Discontinuing Comments On My Blog. Here's Why . . ." (January 7, 2016), available at http://juliaserano.blogspot.com/2016/01/im-discontinuing-comments-on-my-blog.html.

32. SynthBaron, "Dear Wendy Carlos: Go Fuck Yourself," thread on Muff Wiggler begun March 12, 2010. Entire thread available at http://www.muffwiggler.com/forum/viewtopic.php?t=14039&postdays=0&postorder=asc&start=0.

33. "Serendip LLC—Erasing All Traces of Wendy Carlos, Insanity," thread begun January 14, 2008, by user Kenneth Elhardt. Entire thread available at http://analogue-heaven.1065350.n5.nabble.com/Serendip-LLC-Erasing-All-Traces-of-Wendy-Carlos-Insanity-td56830.html.

34. The entire thread is available at http://www.progarchives.com/forum/forum_posts.asp?TID=4868.

35. Stephen Raskauskas, "How Transgender Composer Wendy Carlos Changed Music Forever," WFMT.com (November 17, 2016), available at https://www.wfmt.com/2016/11/17/transgender-composer-wendy-carlos-changed-music-forever/.

36. MacDonald-Dupuis, "Meet Wendy Carlos: The Trans Godmother of Electronic Music" *Vice* (August 11, 2015), available at https://www.vice.com/en_us/article/53agdb/meet-wendy-carlos-the-trans-godmother-of-electronic-music.

37. Carlos, "On Prurient Matters."

38. Judy Tsou, "Review: *The Norton/Grove Dictionary of Women Composers*, edited by Julie Anne Sadie and Rhian Samuel," *Notes* 53, no. 2 (December 1, 1996): 424.

39. Elizabeth L. Keathley, "Review: *Women Composers and Music Technology in the United States: Crossing the Line*, by Elizabeth Hinkle-Turner," *Women & Music* 13 (2009): 101.

40. Pinch and Trocco, *Analog Days*, 138.

41. Bell, *Playboy* interview, 101.

42. Judith Peraino, "Synthesizing Difference: The Queer Circuits of Early Synthpop," in *Rethinking Difference in Music Scholarship*, ed. Olivia Bloechl, Melanie Lowe, and Jeffrey Kallberg (Cambridge: Cambridge University Press, 2015), 300.

43. Peraino, "The Queer Circuits of Early Synthpop," 300–301.

44. Peraino, "The Queer Circuits of Early Synthpop," 300.

45. Peraino, "The Queer Circuits of Early Synthpop," 300.

46. Carlos, letter to Bell, May 1979.

47. Carlos, letter to Bell, May 1979.
48. Carlos, letter to Bell, May 1979.
49. Carlos, letter to Bell, May 1979.
50. Carlos, letter to Bell, May 1979.
51. Bell, "*Playboy* interview," 109.

Glossary

A Note about Terms and Concepts Related
to Transgender Identity

This is a biography about a transgender person, and it has been written with the most current and respectful terminology and conventions that apply to the lived experiences of transgender people. Dated references and terminology are used in context for historical purposes. Understanding of gender is constantly growing and shifting, and new theories and approaches are constantly emerging. Although the nomenclature used here is up-to-date as this book goes to press in 2020, it will certainly continue to grow and become more refined in the future. People of many different gender identities are speaking up and sharing their experiences, constantly shaping and reshaping cultural understanding. This book has benefited greatly from these people who have put into words their experiences.

What follows is a brief introduction to gender identity terminology and concepts. For those interested in gender identity, there are many memoirs, histories, and essays written by transgender people about their own experience. Histories that were indispensable for this book include *How Sex Changed* by Joanne Meyerowitz and *Transgender History* by Susan Stryker. David Valentine's ethnography *Imagining Transgender* is a valuable study about the separation of sexuality and gender identity in American culture during the past couple of decades. Memoirs, editorials, and other first-person writings by Kat Blaque, J. Halberstam, Parker Molloy, Julia Serano, Leslie Steinberg, and Sandy Stone are also valuable resources about transgender people's lived experiences.

The following terms and concepts are used throughout the book. The definitions are drawn primarily from the GLAAD Media Reference Guide Glossary of Terms, the organization's guide for fair and accurate journalistic reporting about transgender people.[1] The Radical Copyeditor (aka Alex Kapitan) has a helpful guide writing about transgender people. Kapitan has regularly updated this guide since first publishing it in August 2017, making additions, deletions, and expansions based on input from transgender people based on their lived experiences.[2] Another resource is Julia Serano's "There is No Perfect Word: A Transgender Glossary of Sorts," in which she defines many terms and concepts while also stressing that none of these meanings are permanent or immutable.[3]

At birth, a person is assigned a **sex**. This sex, which appears on the birth certificate, is usually based on the appearance of the baby's external physical anatomy. Sex itself is a combination of many characteristics, such as (but not limited to) chromosomes, hormones, reproductive organs (internal), and secondary sex characteristics (external).

Gender identity is a person's sense of their own gender. Some people have a gender identity of either "female" or "male." A **transgender person** has a gender identity that does not match the sex they were assigned at birth. Some people are also nonbinary, meaning that they do not identify their gender as either male or female. **Gender expression** refers to how a person manifests their gender, such as their name, their pronouns (he, she, or they, for example), their clothing, their hairstyle, and their behaviors.

In many cases, transgender people align their gender expression with their gender identity and not with the sex assigned to them at birth. This alignment process is called **transitioning**. A person's transition can take months or years. It may or may not involve medical procedures such as hormones or surgeries. It may or may not involve legal procedures such as name and sex designation changes. Many people who transition use a different name and pronouns than those they were given at birth, and they may also begin to change their gender expression in ways that are consistent with that gender identity. These expressions may include clothing, hairstyles, and body language—changing one's "social presentation."[4] Each transgender person is different in how they choose to express their gender.

Over the past several decades, terms that were once considered appropriate and respectful have become problematic, particularly the concepts of "sex-change operation," "pre-operative," and "post-operative." Although they were once the accepted parlance—these were often the terms that doctors and journalists used to refer to Wendy Carlos and others—they are overly simplistic. In particular, the idea that one must undergo surgery in order to transition is inaccurate, and referring to a person's gender solely in the context of a surgery is misrepresentative. If a person does undergo surgical interventions, then those are called **gender confirmation surgeries**. For many people who choose this route, more than one surgery may be required, so again, the idea of a single "sex-change operation" is usually inaccurate.

The term **transsexual** (also spelled **transexual** with a single s) has undergone some changes in meaning over the past several decades. This term originated in one of the first English-language books published on the subject of transgender identity, written by Dr. Harry Benjamin. This was the preferred nomenclature in the 1960s and 1970s. In the twenty-first century, some transgender people find the term outdated and even offensive, but others prefer the term "transsexual."[5] Carlos herself said she preferred the term "transgender" for her identity, so that is the term used to describe her throughout the text. [6] The term "transsexual" is primarily used in an historical context when referring to books, interviews, or other documents from the twentieth century.

Although not a part of Carlos's story, **gender nonconformity** and **nonbinary** or **genderqueer identities** are also gaining visibility in the twenty-first century. These identities are not synonymous with transgender identity. For example, a gender-nonconforming person's gender expression is different from conventional notions of masculinity or femininity, but a gender nonconforming identity does not necessarily mean a person is transgender. Further, people whose gender identity is beyond or between the male/female binary often identify as nonbinary or genderqueer. People who identify as nonbinary sometimes use gender-neutral pronouns such as "they" or "ze" instead of "he" or "she." Despite some initial resistance against using "they" in the singular form, most journalism outlets and style guides have now accepted the use of "they" in their reporting.[7]

Finally, terms such as "transvestite," "drag queen," and "cross-dresser" do not refer to transgender people. They are frequently conflated with transgender identity by scholars and journalists alike. Each of those terms has its own complicated history and culture, and those are beyond the scope of this current book and not relevant to the subject at hand.

All of the terms and concepts presented here deal only with gender and sex. None of them refers to sexual orientation or to sexual behavior. Gender identity and sexual orientation are frequently conflated, which is erroneous. A woman who is attracted only to men is heterosexual, regardless of whether either person is cisgender or transgender. Further, gender identity and sexual orientation are also both often conflated with sexual behavior, and particularly with criminal sexual behavior. For example, government bills that would require a person to use the public restroom or locker room that matches the sex they were assigned at birth (the so-called bathroom bills) have been defended as a means of protecting women and children from sexual predators, falsely assuming that transgender women who use a women's restroom are also likely to be sexual predators.[8] Even in the twenty-first century, fear and ignorance of transgender identity and lived experience often result in dangerous misunderstandings about the relationship between a person's gender identity and their sexual orientation and behavior.

For decades, beginning in the 1950s, if a person underwent a gender transition, they were encouraged (sometimes even forced) to leave their previous identity behind and never look back. Following a transition, people were encouraged to move away and start new lives where no one ever might have known them by another name or gender. Being transgender was shameful, dangerous, and not a topic to be discussed. Now, some transgender people are able to be more open about their identities and transitions if they choose to disclose that information. In 2015, Caitlyn Jenner disclosed her transition by posing on the cover of *Vanity Fair* magazine, and Chaz Bono and Jazz Jennings have shared aspects of their transitions through film and television documentaries. Decades ago, this kind of openness was unthinkable for anyone.

But life in the twenty-first century isn't easy for a person who is openly transgender. Bathroom bills have been proposed in several states, including Colorado, Florida, Massachusetts, and Texas. In 2018, U.S. Secretary of Defense James Mattis and President Donald Trump proposed a policy that would disqualify transgender people who had transitioned from serving in the U.S. military and also require those who had not transitioned to serve under their sex assigned at birth; the U.S. Supreme Court voted in 2019 to uphold this ban while cases challenging it are making their way to the court.[9] Even more drastically, the Trump administration announced that it was considering defining gender as biological and immutable, defined by the appearance of an infant's genitals at birth and unable to be changed.[10] According to these strictures, a person's sex as listed on their birth certificate is definitive proof of their gender unless genetic testing can demonstrate otherwise.

Notes

1. GLAAD, "GLAAD Media Reference Guide—Glossary of Terms—Transgender," available at https://www.glaad.org/reference/transgender.
2. Alex Kapitan, "The Radical Copyeditor's Style Guide for Writing about Transgender People," available at https://radicalcopyeditor.com/2017/08/31/transgender-style-guide/.

3. Julia Serano, "There is No Perfect Word: A Transgender Glossary of Sorts," available at http://www.juliaserano.com/terminology.html.

4. My many thanks to Dana Baitz for use of the phrase "social presentation." She introduced it in a paper given November 2, 2018, at the national meeting of the American Musicological Society.

5. I am very grateful to Stephan Pennington for bringing this important distinction to my attention, and this is a reminder about the importance of listening to an individual person's lived experience.

6. Bell, "*Playboy* interview," 82.

7. See, for example, Geoff Nunberg, "Everyone Uses Singular 'They,' Whether They Realize It or Not," *Fresh Air* (National Public Radio) (January 13, 2016), available at https://www.npr.org/2016/01/13/462906419/everyone-uses-singular-they-whether-they-realize-it-or-not.

8. See, for example, Alia E. Dastagir, "The Imaginary Predator in America's Transgender Bathroom War," *USA Today* (April 28, 2016), available at https://www.usatoday.com/story/news/nation/2016/04/28/transgender-bathroom-bills-discrimination/32594395/.

9. See, for example, Adam Liptak, "Supreme Court Revives Transgender Ban for Military Service," *New York Times* (January 22, 2019), available at https://www.nytimes.com/2019/01/22/us/politics/transgender-ban-military-supreme-court.html.

10. See, for example, Erica L. Green, Katie Benner, and Robert Pear, "'Transgender' Could Be Defined out of Existence under Trump Administration," *New York Times* (October 21, 2018), available at https://www.nytimes.com/2018/10/21/us/politics/transgender-trump-administration-sex-definition.html.

Bibliography

Print Sources

Aikin, Jim. "Wendy Carlos: A Visionary Composer Wrestles Her Computers into Submission." *Music and Computers* (November/December 1997): 51–59.

Andy. "Donald Trump Parody Results in Clockwork Orange Copyright Suit." *Torrent Freak*. November 14, 2016. Available at https://torrentfreak.com/donald-trump-parody-results-in-clockwork-orange-copyright-suit-161114/.

Aston, Martin. "A Song for You." *Times* (London) (August 28, 1999): 14.

Baker, Alan. "An Interview with Wendy Carlos." *American Public Media* (January 2003). Available at http://musicmavericks.publicradio.org/features/interview_carlos.html.

Barrett, Michael S. "An Electronic Studio in a Box." *Washington Post* (October 8, 1972): L6.

Bell, Arthur. "Wendy/Walter Carlos: A Candid Conversation with the 'Switched-On Bach' Composer who, for the First Time, Reveals Her Sex-Change Operation and Her Secret Life as a Woman." *Playboy* 26, no. 5 (May 1979): 75–109.

Blinx, Andy. "Wendy Carlos: From Bach to the Future." *Grand Royal* 3 (1994): 60–61.

Bond, Jeff. "A Clockwork Composer: Wendy Carlos Switches Back on Soundtracks and Revisits Her Premiere Score." *Film Score Monthly* (March 1999): 18–23.

Bozung, Justin. "Interview: The Shining and A Clockwork Orange Co-Composer Rachel Elkind Talks about Stanley Kubrick." *TV Store Online* (September 2, 2017). Available at http://blog.tvstoreonline.com/2014/09/interview-shining-and-clockwork-orange.html.

Campbell, Mary. "Record Review: Recording Surf is Slippery Job." *Associated Press* (August 1972).

Carlos, Wendy. "Errors in Wendy Carlos Article." *Computer Music Journal* 11, no. 4 (Winter 1987): 10–11.

Carlos, Wendy. "Moog Soundings" (letter to the editor). *Billboard* (August 5, 1972): 6, 10, 86.

Carlos, Wendy. "On Synthesizers" (letter to the editor). *Last Whole Earth Catalog* 1160 (June 1971): 330–331.

Carlos, Wendy. "Prelude." Foreword to Scott R. Wilkinson, *Tuning In: Microtonality in Electronic Music*. Milwaukee, WI: Hal Leonard, 1988.

Carlos, Wendy. "The Psychology of Copy Protection" (guest editorial). *Keyboard* (January 1988): 12.

Carlos, Wendy. "Tuning: At the Crossroads." *Computer Music Journal* 11, no. 1 (Spring 1987): 29.

Carlos, Wendy. "A Variable Speed Tape Drive." *Electronic Music Review* 7 (July 1968): 18–20.

"Wasted Tools" (guest editorial), *Keyboard* (October 1990): 12.

Carlos, Wendy and Benjamin Folkman. "Multi-Track Recording in Electronic Music." *Electronic Music Review* 6 (April 1968): 20–25.

Carlos, Wendy and Benjamin Folkman. "The Quality Race: A Survey of the Big Three." *Electronic Music Review* 6 (April 1968): 14–17.

Cary, Tristram. *Illustrated Compendium of Musical Technology*. London: Faber and Faber Ltd., 1992.

Contemporary Keyboard editors. "Simple Gifts: Twelve Variations." *Contemporary Keyboard* (November 1980): 15–36.

Crockett, Jim. "From the Publisher." *Contemporary Keyboard* (December 1980): 3, 78.

Demers, Joanna. *Steal this Music: How Intellectual Property Law Affects Musical Creativity*. Athens: University of Georgia Press, 2006.

DeRosa, John. "Interview with Momus [Nick Currie] Backstage at Fez." Silbermedia. com (October 17, 1998). Available at http://www.silbermedia.com/qrd/thieves/momus.htm.

DiCrescenzo, Brent. "Review: Momus, *Stars Forever*." *Pitchfork* (August 24, 1999). Available at https://pitchfork.com/reviews/albums/5383-stars-forever/.

Diliberto, John K. "An Interview with Wendy Carlos." *Polyphony* (June 1984): 10–13.

DiMartino, Dave. "Wendy Carlos Invents New Sounds." *Billboard* 99, no. 8 (February 21, 1987): 23.

Doerschuk, Robert L. "Wendy Carlos: The Magic in the Machine: Reflections from the First Great Modern Synthesist." *Keyboard* (August 1995): 51–62.

Estrada, George. "Synthesizer Pioneer Wants to Go Further." *Oakland Tribune* (January 10, 1984): D1, D3.

Fraser, Jamie. "Bob Moog: Scientific Method Man." *Grand Royal* 3 (1994): 54–57.

Freff [Connor Freff Cochran]. "Tuning in to Wendy Carlos." *Electronic Musician* 2, no. 11 (November 1986): 20–37. Available at http://www.wendycarlos.com/cochran.html.

Gengaro, Christine Lee. "'It Was Lovely Music that Came to My Aid': Music's Contribution to the Narrative of the Novel, Film, and Play, *A Clockwork Orange*." PhD dissertation, University of Southern California, 2005.

Gould, Glenn. "The Record of the Decade," *Saturday Night* (December 1968). Reprinted in *The Glenn Gould Reader*, pp. 429–434. Edited by Tim Page. New York: Alfred A. Knopf, 1984.

Hansen, Liane. "Listener Responses." *Weekend All Things Considered*. National Public Radio (August 23, 1992).

Henahan, Donal. "Mark II is Dead: Long Live the Moog!" *New York Times* (December 11, 1968): 56.

Hansen, Liane. "'Switched-On Bach' Back after 25 Years." *Weekend All Things Considered*. National Public Radio (August 9, 1992).

Henahan, Donal. "Switching on to Mock Bach." *New York Times* (November 3, 1969): 146.

Henahan, Donal. "A Tale of a Man and a Moog." *New York Times* (October 5, 1969): HF1.

Heroux, Gerard. "Wendy Carlos: Music Maker, Dreamer of Dreams." Rhode Island Music Hall of Fame Historical Archive. Available at http://www.ripopmusic.org/musical-artists/musicians/wendy-carlos/.

Hess, Nick. "Copyright Like Clockwork." Medium.com (March 1, 2016). Available at https://medium.com/@thehessmachine/copyright-like-clockwork-8a0f61ddaff1#.ax0ec2lu1.

Hilburn, Robert. "Many Discs Suited as Time Killers." *Los Angeles Times* (October 19, 1969): U36.

Hinkle-Turner, Elizabeth. *Women Composers and Music Technology in the United States*. Burlington, VT: Ashgate, 2006.

Hollingworth, Roy. "The Walter Carlos Sonic Boom." *Melody Maker* (September 23, 1972): 42.

Holmes, Thom. *Electronic and Experimental Music: Technology, Music, and Culture.* 5th ed. New York: Routledge, 2016.

Houtkin, Andrea. "Review: *Digital Moonscapes* by Wendy Carlos." *Computer Music Journal* 10, no. 1 (Spring 1986): 103–104.

Hugill, Andrew. *The Digital Musician.* 2nd ed. New York and London: Routledge, 2012.

Jarrett, Michael. *Sound Tracks: A Musical ABC.* Philadelphia: Temple University Press, 1998.

Kjar, David. "Wanda, Gould, and Sting: Sounding, Othering, and Hearing in Early Music." PhD dissertation. Boston University, 2015.

Klady, Leonard. "Review: *Woundings.*" *Variety* (November 1, 1998). Available at https://variety.com/1998/film/reviews/woundings-1200456089/.

Kobel, Peter. "Wendy Carlos synthesizes the sciences and humanities." *Chicago Tribune* (April 5, 1987): K16.

Kozinn, Allan. "Carlos: *Cosmological Impressions; Moonscapes*" (review). *Opus: The Magazine of Recorded Classics* 1, no. 3 (April 1985): 24–25.

Kozinn, Allan. "The *Fugue* Interview: Wendy Carlos." *Fugue* (May 1980): 25–32.

"'Switched-On Bach' Creator Returns." *New York Times* (February 17, 1980): D22.

Larson, Randall D. "The Sound of *TRON.*" *CinemaScore* 11 & 12 (1983).

Lees, Gene. "The Electronic Bach: Johann Sebastian in a Wild, Wild Breakthrough." *High Fidelity* (December 1968): 3.

MacDonald-Dupuis, Natasha. "Meet Wendy Carlos: The Trans Godmother of Electronic Music." *Vice* (August 11, 2015). Available at https://www.vice.com/en_us/article/53agdb/meet-wendy-carlos-the-trans-godmother-of-electronic-music.

Meyerowitz, Joanne. *How Sex Changed: A History of Transsexuality in the United States.* Cambridge, MA: Harvard University Press, 2002.

Milano, Dominic. "Rachel Elkind." *Contemporary Keyboard* (December 1979): 36–37.

Milano, Dominic. "Wendy Carlos." *Contemporary Keyboard* (December 1979): 32–76.

Milano, Dominic. "Wendy Carlos: Defying Conventions, Discovering New Worlds." *Keyboard* (November 1986): 50–55, 61, 70–82.

"Wendy Carlos and the LSI Philharmonic Orchestra; Excerpts from 'Ganymede' and 'Io.'" *Keyboard* (December 1984): 26–30.

Miller, Chuck. "Wendy Carlos: In the Moog." *Goldmine* 613 (January 24, 2004): 47–48.

Molloy, Parker Marie. "Can Media Please Stop Focusing on Trans People's Bodies?" *Advocate* (January 9, 2014). Available at https://www.advocate.com/commentary/2014/01/09/op-ed-can-media-please-stop-focusing-trans-peoples-bodies.

Moog, Robert. "The Columbia-Princeton Electronic Music Center: Thirty Years of Explorations in Sound." *Contemporary Keyboard* (May 1981). Reprinted June 7, 2016. Available at https://www.keyboardmag.com/miscellaneous/the-columbia-princeton-electronic-music-center-thirty-years-of-explorations-in-sound.

Moog, Robert. "On Synthesizers: Vocal Sounds Part II: Vocoders." *Contemporary Keyboard* (May 1978): 54.

Moog, Robert. "On Synthesizers: Wendy Carlos on Computers." *Keyboard* (December 1982): 64.

Moog, Robert. "On Synthesizers: Wendy Carlos on Control Devices." *Contemporary Keyboard* (January 1980): 67.

Moog, Robert. "On Synthesizers: What Is a Synthesizer?" *Contemporary Keyboard* (September–October 1975): 45.

Moog, Robert. "On Synthesizers: Why They Don't." *Keyboard* (April 1983): 58.

Moog, Robert. "Wendy Carlos and Michael Fremer Reveal the Secrets behind the Soundtrack of *TRON.*" *Keyboard* (November 1982): 53–57.

Moog, Robert. "Wendy Carlos: New Directions for a Synthesizer Pioneer." *Keyboard* (November 1982): 52, 58–63.

Morris, Chris. "Wendy Carlos Takes Her Moog Music to East Side Digital." *Billboard* (October 3, 1998): 69.

Moser, Margaret. "Review: Wendy Carlos, *Switched-On Boxed Set* (East Side Digital)." *Austin (TX) Chronicle* (December 17, 1999). Available at https://www.austinchronicle. com/music/1999-12-17/75124/.

No author. "New Pop Albums." *Melody Maker* (November 8, 1969): 34.

No author. "Wendy Carlos: *Switched-On Bach 2000.*" *Quarter Notes: The Telarc International Newsletter* 6, no. 1 (Spring/Summer 1992): 1, 11.

No author. "What's the Strangest Artistic Collaboration You Can Think Of?" *Keyboard* (January 1989): 58–64.

Nunziata, Susan. "Wendy Carlos Goes 'Bach' and Forward All at Once with New Reading of Old Set." *Billboard* (August 15, 1992): 67.

Oestreich, James R. "Play it Jazzy, Switched On or Straight, It's Bach." *New York Times* (April 2, 1997): C9.

Oteri, Frank J. "Wendy's World: Wendy Carlos in Conversation with Frank J. Oteri." *NewMusicBox* (January 18, 2007). Available at http://www.newmusicbox.org/articles/ wendys-world/.

P. H. "The Switched-On Bach Bit." *Washington Post* (February 9, 1969): 171.

Peraino, Judith. "Synthesizing Difference: The Queer Circuits of Early Synthpop." In *Rethinking Difference in Music Scholarship*. Edited by Olivia Bloechl, Melanie Lowe, and Jeffrey Kallberg. Cambridge: Cambridge University Press, 2015.

Pinch, Trevor, and Frank Trocco. *Analog Days: The Invention and Impact of the Moog Synthesizer* (Cambridge, MA: Harvard University Press, 2002).

Raskauskas, Stephen. "How Transgender Composer Wendy Carlos Changed Music Forever," WFMT.com (November 17, 2016). Available at https://www.wfmt.com/2016/ 11/17/transgender-composer-wendy-carlos-changed-music-forever/.

Raymond, Janice. *The Transsexual Empire: The Making of the She-Male*. Boston: Beacon Press, 1979.

Reed, Susan. "After a Sex Change and Several Eclipses, Wendy Carlos Treads a New Digital Moonscape." *People* 24, no. 1 (July 1, 1985).

Reighley, Kurt B. "Vocoder Questions" (interview with Wendy Carlos). Available at http:// www.wendycarlos.com/vocoders.html

Schonberg, Harold C. "A Merry Time with the Moog?" *New York Times* (February 16, 1969): D17.

Schoonhoven, Sarah Marie. "Gender, Timbre, and Metaphor in the Music of Wendy Carlos." Master's thesis, University of Texas at Austin. May 2017.

Serano, Julia. "Laura Jane Grace and coming out as trans in the public eye." *Whipping Girl* (blog), May 2012. Available at http://juliaserano.blogspot.com/2012/05/ laura-jane-grace-and-coming-out-as.html.

Serano, Julia. *Whipping Girl: A Transsexual Woman on Sexism and the Scapegoating of Femininity*. Berkeley, CA: Seal Press, 2007.

Slonimsky, Nicolas. "Carlos, Wendy (née Walter)." In *The Concise Edition of Baker's Biographical Dictionary of Musicians*. 8th ed. Edited and revised by Nicolas Slonimsky (New York: Schirmer, 1994).

Sprauge, David. "Rockbeat: Three Minutes of Fame." *Village Voice* (June 29, 1999): 138.

Stone, Sandy. "The 'Empire' Strikes Back: A Posttranssexual Manifesto." *Camera Obscura* (Spring 1994).

Stryker, Susan. *Transgender History*. Berkeley, CA: Seal Press, 2008.

Tucker, Marilyn. "A Heady Experience at the Berkeley Symphony." *San Francisco Chronicle* (January 13, 1984): 64.

Twomey, Chris. "Wendy Carlos: Still Switched On." *Exclaim!* (December 1998/January 1999).

Vail, Mark. *The Synthesizer: A Comprehensive Guide to Understanding, Programming, Playing, and Recording the Ultimate Electronic Music Instrument*. New York: Oxford University Press, 2014.

Vowell, Sarah. "Toccata and Fugue in Me, A Minor." *This American Life* (June 5, 1990). Transcript available at http://www.thisamericanlife.org/radio-archives/episode/104/transcript.

Wilkinson, Scott R. *Tuning In: Microtonality in Electronic Music*. Milwaukee: Hal Leonard, 1988.

Willis, Thomas. "Tribune Interviews Music Meteor Solti." *Chicago Tribune* (December 22, 1968): A1.

Wolk, Douglas. "Bizarre Publicity Stunt Alert." *Spin* 15, no. 3 (April 1, 1999): 57.

Wren, Christopher. "Moog is More Than a Vogue." *Look* 34, no. 7 (April 7, 1970): 24–26.

Wright, Carol. "The Digital Phases of Wendy Carlos." Unpublished interview (December 2, 2000). Available at http://www.wendycarlos.com/intvw01.html

Wright, Carol. "Only Human: Touching the Significance." Unpublished interview with Wendy Carlos (March 2001). Available at http://www.wendycarlos.com/onlyhuman.html.

Wright, Carol. "Wendy Carlos: Something Old, Something New: The Definitive Switched-On." *New Age Voice* (November 1999).

Young, Taylor. "Review: *By Request*," *Contemporary Keyboard* (January 1977): 4.

Zuckerman, Gabrielle, "An Interview with Milton Babbitt." *American Public Media* (July 2002). Available at http://musicmavericks.publicradio.org/features/interview_babbitt.html.

Archival and Special Collections

Allan Kozinn, personal collection.

Arthur Bell papers, Billy Rose Theatre Division, New York Public Library.

Berkeley Symphony Orchestra archives.

Columbia-Princeton Electronic Music Center Archives, Rare Book & Manuscript Library, Columbia University Libraries.

Harry Benjamin papers. Kinsey Institute and Library, Indiana University.

Leonard Bernstein Collection. Library of Congress, Music Division.

Lucy Kroll Client File 1916–1998, Library of Congress.

Robert Moog papers, #8629. Division of Rare and Manuscript Collections, Cornell University Library.

Trevor Pinch, personal collection.

Discography and Videography

Bernstein, Leonard. *Young People's Concerts: Bach Transmogrified*. Original CBS air date April 27, 1969. Reissue Kultur International Films Ltd. 862170555, disc 8, 2013. DVD.

Carlos, Wendy. *Beauty in the Beast*. Audion SYNCD 200, CD 1986. Reissue East Side Digital ESD 81552, 2000, CD.

Carlos, Wendy. *Digital Moonscapes: An Evolutionary Synthesizer Tour de Force*. CBS M 39340, 1984, LP and CD. Reissue East Side Digital ESD 81542, 2000, CD.

Carlos, Wendy. *Moog 900 Series—Electronic Music Systems* (demo record). R. A. Moog Company Inc. RDM 100, 1967, LP.

Carlos, Wendy. *Rediscovering Lost Scores—Volume 1*. East Side Digital ESD 81752, 2005, CD.

Carlos, Wendy. *Rediscovering Lost Scores—Volume 2*. East Side Digital ESD 81762, 2005, CD.

Carlos, Wendy. *Secrets of Synthesis*. CBS FM 42333, 1987, LP. Reissue East Side Digital ESD 81202, 2003, CD.

Carlos, Wendy. *Sonic Seasonings*. Columbia Records PG 31234, 1972, LP. Reissue East Side Digital ESD 81372, 1998, CD.

Carlos, Wendy. *Switched-On Bach*. Columbia Records MS 7194, 1968, LP. Reissue East Side Digital ESD 81602, 2001, CD.

Carlos, Wendy. *Switched-On Bach II*. Columbia Records KM 32659, 1973, LP. Reissue East Side Digital ESD 81622, 2002, CD.

Carlos, Wendy. *Switched-On Bach 2000*. Telarc CD-80323, 1992, CD. Reissue East Side Digital ESD 91732, 2004, CD.

Carlos, Wendy. *Switched-On Boxed Set*. East Side Digital ESD 81244, 1999, CD.

Carlos, Wendy. *Switched-On Brandenburgs*. CBS 79227, 1980, LP. Reissue East Side Digital ESD 81632, 2001, CD.

Carlos, Wendy. *Tales of Heaven and Hell*. East Side Digital ESD 81352, 1998, CD.

Carlos, Wendy. *TRON (Original Motion Picture Soundtrack)*. CBS SM 37782, 1982, LP and cassette. Reissue Walt Disney Records 60748-7, 2001, CD.

Carlos, Wendy. *The Well-Tempered Synthesizer*. Columbia Records MS 7286, 1969, LP. Reissue East Side Digital ESD 81612, 1999, CD.

Carlos, Wendy. *Wendy Carlos: By Request*. Columbia Records M 32088, 1975, LP. Reissue East Side Digital ESD 81692, 2003, CD.

Carlos, Wendy. *Wendy Carlos' A Clockwork Orange*. Columbia Records KC 31480, 1972, LP. Reissue East Side Digital ESD 91362, 2000, CD.

Carlos, Wendy and "Weird Al" Yankovic. *Peter & the Wolf/Carnival of the Animals—Part II*. CBS FM 44567, 1988, LP and CD.

Cliburn, Van. *Tchaikovsky: Concerto no. 1*. RCA Victor LSC 2252, 1958, LP.

Gould, Glenn. *The Goldberg Variations*. Columbia Records ML 5060, 1956, LP.

Lishon, Charles, and Hans Wurman. *The Moog Strikes Bach... (To Say Nothing of Chopin, Mozart, Rachmaninoff, Paganini and Prokofieff)*. RCA Victor SRA 2642, 1969, LP.

Marks, J., and Shipen Lebzelter. *Rock and Other Four Letter Words*. Columbia Records MS 7193, 1968, LP.

The Moog Machine. *Switched-On Rock*. Columbia CS 9921, 1969, LP.

Musilli, John, producer and director. "An Examination of Kubrick's 'A Clockwork Orange.'" *Camera 3*, Creative Arts Television, 1972.

Rifkin, Joshua. *The Baroque Beatles Book*. Elektra EKL-306, 1965, LP.

Riley, Terry. *In C*. Columbia Records MS 7178, 1968, LP.

Subotnick, Morton. *Silver Apples of the Moon*. Nonesuch H-71174, 1967, LP.

The Swingle Singers. *Jazz Sébastien Bach (Bach's Greatest Hits)*. Philips PHS 600-097, 1963, LP.

Various composers. *Stanley Kubrick's A Clockwork Orange (Music from the Soundtrack)*. Warner Bros. Records K 46127, 1971, LP. Reissue Warner Bros. Records FM 21440, 2001, CD.

Index

Note: *For the benefit of digital users, indexed terms that span two pages (e.g., 52–53) may, on occasion, appear on only one of those pages.*
Figures are indicated by *f* following the page number